A TRAILS BOOKS GUIDE

PADDLING KANSAS

Dave Murphy

Trails Books
Madison, Wisconsin

A Note of Caution

The reader is advised that paddling sports can be dangerous. This guidebook is not a substitute for proper training, experience, and common sense. The users of this guidebook assume full responsibility for their own safety. Weather, water conditions, and individual abilities must be considered before undertaking any of the trips in this guide.

Library of Congress Control Number: 2008921777
ISBN: 978-1-934553-10-7

Editor: Mark Knickelbine
Designer: Colin Harrington
Cover Photo: Nicoya Helm
Maps by Magellan Mapping Co.

Printed in the United States of America.
13 12 11 10 09 08   6 5 4 3 2 1

Trails Books, a division of Big Earth Publishing
923 Williamson Street • Madison, WI 53703
(800) 258-5830 • www.trailsbooks.com

DEDICATION

To Jo Anne, the current that carries me;
T.J. Hittle, for his inspiration and knowledge of rivers;
Suzanne Murphy, first for believing, then for editing;
and the Kansas Environmental Leadership Program, for the grant that jump-started this project.

CONTENTS

FOREWORD

by T.J. Hittle

Over recent years in Kansas, whenever one attended a public meeting or a hearing on a bill in the Kansas Legislature that could impact waterways in Kansas, you would find Dave Murphy both in attendance and speaking as an advocate. With his confidence and ability to see things clearly, he has been a great voice for outdoor enthusiasts in Kansas. Dave is truly a consummate keeper of the rivers. His knowledge and passion for Kansas streams are without equal.

My association with Dave began nearly 15 years ago, when he was President of the Kansas City Whitewater Club. We became great paddling friends, running rivers all over the United States and Central America. From 1997 to 1998, Dave guided the Kansas Canoe & Kayak Association (KCKA) as president. In 2005, KCKA presented Dave with its Distinguished Service Award. His longtime associations with the Friends of the Kaw and the Kansas Natural Resources Council have served to complement his breadth of knowledge.

Given the limited number of public waterways in Kansas and the lack of information available, a guide-book like this is unquestionably long overdue. As one of Kansas' long-time paddlers, I welcome this publication and encourage all visitors to tour Kansas and experience the wonder of our great prairie waterways.

ACKNOWLEDGMENTS

I thank the staff of the Kansas Environmental Leadership Program (KELP) for their inspiration and for the start-up money they contributed. Brian Loving, Julie MacLachlan, and Mary Lou Ponder were on my KELP team in 2003. Brian Loving, with the U.S. Geological Survey (USGS), supplied me with many of the baseline maps that I used to record the raw information for the finished maps you see in this book. Julie MacLachlan helped with initial design and funding ideas. Thanks go to the Kansas Department of Wildlife and Parks, the U.S. Geological Survey, the Kansas Geological Survey, the Kansas Department of Transportation, and the U.S. Army Corps of Engineers for all of their cooperation.

I relied heavily on donations of time, knowledge, and experience gathered and shared by many people. Among those who contributed are Scott Barlow, Jeff Bender, John Breyfogle, Kevin Burke, Chris Collins, Michael Farmer, Nolan Fisher, Kurt Grimm, Nicoya Helm, T.J. Hittle, DeEtte Huffman, James Hulbert, Dave Irvin, Jim Johnson, Jim Jones, Karl Karrow, Brent Konen, Dennis Knuth, Susan Kysela, Doug Lauxman, Cliff Long, Rick Martin, Stan McDaniel, Brian Meiwes, Tim Menard, Julie Mueller, Jill Murphy, Suzanne Murphy, Greg Nichols, Doyle Niemeyer, Pat O'Connell, Jason Pankraz, Don Patton, Darin Porter, Brad Rueschhoff, Keith Salmans, Craig Thompson, Shawn Tolivar, Bob Sinnett, Bruce Waters, and David Yeamans. While some of you contributed substantially and others gave in smaller ways, I thank everyone who contributed in any way and appreciate the help and time you gave so freely. If you contributed but I forgot to include your name, I apologize.

The trees still drip from last night's dew as your canoe slides off the sandy shore. You drift into a thin veneer of fog that swirls just above the cool water. Reading the patterns in the stream and sensing the movement under the thin shell of your boat, the feel of the river comes back to you. Now quietly gliding, you pass unnoticed through the forest, your senses alive. Discovery and adventure at every turn, there is something about a river that takes you to a place that you cannot get to in any other way.

Unlike waterways in neighboring states, Kansas rivers and streams are not crowded. Most of them have excellent fishing and plenty of wildlife. Best of all, they are right here. Local river recreation provides for regional quality of life, teaches respect for our land and natural heritage, builds local economic prosperity and—it is fun! Paddling and exploring Kansas rivers and streams with our children will remind us, and teach them, to enjoy and appreciate our rivers and streams as something worth preserving.

This is not the first attempt to create a paddler's guide to the rivers of Kansas. In 1976, Don Charvat authored a small booklet titled *Kansas Canoe Trails*. His booklet was produced in the days when most paddlers thought all Kansas streams were open to the public. That work was soon out of print and has become a collector's item. More recently, T.J. Hittle has published maps and descriptions of some of his favorite rivers and streams on his "Kansas Paddler" Web page, at www.kansas.net/~tjhittle.

CAUTION

Outdoor recreational activities are, by their nature, hazardous. Participants in the activities suggested in this book must assume the responsibility for their own actions and safety. This guide and the information it contains, does not disclose all hazards and risks that may be associated with river-related activities and cannot replace personal good judgment. For a safer and more enjoyable experience, learn as much as you can about outdoor activities; improve your outdoor skills; boat, hike, and camp with experienced paddlers; learn self-rescue skills; be alert; be prepared; and expect the unexpected.

Except for the western parts of the Arkansas River that were too dry these last few years, I have paddled all of the rivers in this book at least once, but I have not paddled all of them at all water levels. Although I have paddled most of the rivers, some of them were either very low or very high when I saw them. Thus, my experience with each river may be different than the experience that you will have at a different water level or during a different season. Rivers, streams, roads, road names, and their surroundings can and do change frequently. Thus, you may

find errors in the mapping, descriptions, shuttle directions, and distances. I know these discrepancies will crop up and I apologize for them. If you would like to correct me or suggest changes, please contact me, Dave Murphy, at kansasriversandstreams@yahoo.com. Your comments, suggestions, and photos will be appreciated.

The Elk River

This guide is not intended to be a comprehensive guide to all of the rivers and streams of Kansas. Although there are other good river and stream segments, I picked the longest and/or the most scenic segments for this first edition. Only "public" rivers and stream segments that pass through public property are covered.

USE OF THIS GUIDE

The rivers in this guide are arranged by major river watersheds. In addition to the state map at the front of the book and the maps provided with each river segment, the Appendix contains lake maps that will help orient you to the arms of lakes above which most of the public river segments in this state are found.

Knowing everything about a stream before you start is like knowing the end of a book before you read it. Exploration and discovery make each river more enjoyable. This guide was written from an expert paddler's perspective, in a style that preserves the sense of adventure and discovery in every run. Thus, it is not a stroke-by-stroke, hand-holding river guide. To the contrary, my intent is to provide you with just enough information to help you form a mental image of the river and to help you find a place to get on and off. When paddling, you should keep your brain tuned to the river, not this book.

For each river and stream in this book, I have provided a general description of the river segment, a brief narrative of the river, a difficulty rating, an estimate of the float time, minimum recommended flow, gradient, gauging stations, access points, and local contact numbers where appropriate.

Most of the trips can be done in a single day. Some can be either shortened or lengthened by use of alternate put-ins and take-outs. Some river segments, or combination of segments, are so long that more than one day is required to complete them. Most paddlers can estimate their paddling speed at 1.5–3 miles per hour. Added to the speed of the river, that average can be used to estimate the amount of time it will take to complete a trip. Other factors that can affect your speed of travel include wind, weather, type of boat, navigation and river reading, physical conditioning, and dawdling time. Although I have provided float-time estimates for most segments in this guide, you should make your own estimates based upon your own averages and experience or add a 20 percent safety margin to my estimates.

Since Internet addresses are subject to frequent change, I have not provided the exact USGS Web address for each river. Instead, I have included only the name of the gauging station. Once you bookmark the USGS Real-Time Data for Kansas Web site (http://waterdata.usgs.gov/ks/nwis/rt) on your computer, you will become accustomed to using that site more effectively. Additional useful Web sites for lake levels, weather, and local contacts are included in the Appendix.

I hope you enjoy this book and use it to discover the beautiful rivers and streams of Kansas. I also hope you send your comments and suggestions to kansasriversandstreams@yahoo.com so that I can make the next edition even better.

KANSAS PROPERTY RIGHTS

Kansas property owners own the riverbanks and the riverbed, not the water itself. The Kansas Supreme Court decided in 1990 (Meek v. Hays, 246 Kan., 99) that if you paddle across private land without permission, even though you do not touch the riverbed, you may be considered a trespasser by Kansas law. There are three "public" rivers in the state: the Kansas River, the Arkansas River, and the Missouri River. Only those three public rivers, plus various river and stream segments that cross public property, are considered open for your use without the permission of the landowners.

According to the high court's decision, on those three "public" rivers, the riverbed and banks, up to the usual high-water mark, are public property. The "usual high-water mark" includes the land up to the line along the top of the riverbank above where the largest trees (if any) regularly grow, the upper line below which the signs of the river's erosion are visible, and the line below which river debris has been deposited ("trash line") along the banks and in the trees and brush within the river channel.

All of the river and stream segments in this guide are publicly accessible by virtue of public ownership of their riverbeds.

MAPS

Great effort was made to create maps that are accurate and useable, yet simple and concise. Each river map contains the river, major tributaries, large islands, bridges, power and gas lines, shuttle and access roads, access points, mile markers, railroads, rapids, towns, campsites and campgrounds, state parks, and bicycle routes where appropriate. A key on each map identifies the symbols used. If you are not familiar with the river, you should carry a compass to help you identify your location based upon landmarks and the river's direction of travel. Others may prefer a GPS.

Many of the distances, elevations, and gradients have been estimated using GPS software. After 9/11, all counties were required to move away from using rural route numbers and to name or number all roads and put up road signs. That process was only partially completed as of this writing, and most counties were unable to provide me with accurate maps. To overcome the inaccuracies inherent in the existing maps, I drove over 15,000 miles to gather the most current road names. Even then, many roads still had no signs and even local residents tell me that the road they live on has no name and that they still use rural route numbers to get their mail.

General highway navigation to the vicinity of rivers will require a current state road map, but anyone who drives the back roads of Kansas should own a current copy of the *Kansas Atlas & Gazetteer* by Delorme. The *Gazetteer* is a full set of topographic maps for the whole state. The book has 80 large pages and the list price is $19.95. If you prefer more detail, you can buy more detailed topographic maps. For ordering information, contact the USGS at http:/ask.usgs.gov/to_order.html, or call (888) ASK-USGS (275-8747).

The lake maps in the Appendix are intended to orient you to the geographic area and to help you find campgrounds near the rivers where you paddle. They are not intended or suitable for general navigation.

OVERVIEW OF KANSAS

Kansas is a widely diverse landscape of flatlands and rolling hills. Vegetation progresses from west to east from sagebrush to shortgrass prairie, to tallgrass prairie, and to upland forest. The rainfall that shapes our rivers and landscape varies from an average of only 18 inches per year at the western edge of the state to 40 inches per year along the eastern edge.

THE STATE OF ACCESS AND PADDLING IN KANSAS

Only in recent years have local paddlers, birders, anglers, campers, and nature lovers begun networking effectively with local volunteer organizations, businesses, municipalities, counties, and the Kansas Department of Wildlife and Parks to gain better access to public rivers and streams. People and their communities are organizing to open and promote river recreation opportunities in or near their home towns. The state is finally aware of the need, but individuals and communities are still required to promote and move the process forward.

There are several paddling clubs in the state: the Kansas Canoe & Kayak Association, the Kansas Whitewater Association, and the Kansas City Whitewater Club and Friends of the Kaw. XE Contact numbers for these organizations are in the Appendix.

Although I slip once in a while, I have attempted to be consistent in my terminology. If I use the term "boat ramp" to describe an access point, you can be fairly sure that you won't have to scramble through too much poison ivy to get to the river. If I refer to it as only an access, then it could be a nice gravel road down to the edge of the river or it could be an overgrown, poison ivy-covered, steep-banked, muddy drop-off, with no off-road parking at all. In most cases, I have left the worst known "accesses" off my maps. In other cases, I have indicated the condition of the accesses. In reality, if a road crosses a river on public ground, any access is what you make of it. That being said, if you only stick to those streams that have concrete boat ramps, you will miss some of the best paddling in the state.

RIVER SAFETY

Before venturing out on the water, you should consider a class in boater and river safety. Such classes are available from paddling clubs in the state. From other skilled paddlers, you can learn proper stroke techniques and how to negotiate obstacles and rapids safely. The basic guidelines below are no substitute for good paddling skills and complete training in river safety and first aid.

Basics.
- Don't boat alone.
- Let another responsible person know where you are going and when to expect you back.
- Know your limitations and do not exceed them.
- Match your choice of rivers, conditions, and weather to your skill level.
- Be a competent swimmer.
- Wear a well-fitting personal flotation device (PFD) (aka life jacket).

- Know the river.
- Beware of cold- and hot-weather conditions.
- Beware of high winds, especially on wide rivers.
- Have the right clothing and gear for the weather and boating conditions.
- Stay well hydrated.
- Stow gear low in the boat for stability.
- If in doubt, portage.
- Stay clear of fallen trees and obstructions.
- Be sure everyone can identify the take-out.
- Know how long your trip will take and be prepared for double that time.
- Know local laws and regulations.
- Be prepared to deal with the worst that could happen.

Water Levels. Every river in this book is dangerous at high water. It is important to know how the water level affects paddling safety. Rivers are often high in the spring and early summer, but they can also rise quickly after a hard thunderstorm, especially if the ground is already saturated. When a river is extremely high, the current picks up speed and carries tree branches and other debris. The hydraulics and objects floating in a river at flood can be lethal, and the water quality can approach conditions you would expect in a dirty toilet. It may be tempting to challenge yourself under flood or near-flood conditions, but it is not smart. At the other extreme, scraping down a river when the water level is too low is not much fun and is hard on good equipment. Kansas is a dry state and finding enough water to float your boat can be a challenge.

A team effort on the Smoky Hill River above Kanopolis Lake

River conditions can change rapidly, and gauging stations can be wrong. If you are in doubt about the accuracy of any information, make some phone calls before taking a long drive. Local contacts can provide useful information. Even after you head out the door, a storm upstream or a dam release can change water levels within minutes. If you think a river looks too high or too low, you are probably right. Don't chance it. In the end, the decision about whether or not to run a river belongs to you.

The descriptions and narratives used in this guide apply to optimum flows. For the purpose of this guide, an optimum water level is 20 to 50 percent higher than the minimum flows that I recommended for each river segment.

For each river in this book, I have included a Web site where you can find current streamflow data. The U.S. Geological Survey has a great Web site (http://waterdata.usgs.gov/ks/nwis/rt). When you go to that site, a color-coded map similar to the map shown below will show you at a glance where to find good boating conditions. The colored dots depict streamflow conditions as a percentile of their average flow as computed from the period of record for this day of the year compared with current conditions.

This Web site shows you, at a glance, where you can find enough, too little, or too much water for paddling. As you pass your mouse over each site, a box appears on your screen that provides the name of the river and the location of the gauging station, the flow in cubic feet per second, the gauge height in feet, the flood stage in feet, and the date and time of the last reading.

If you click on any of the dots, another screen opens that shows you graphs of recent flow, gauge heights, and precipitation. A few of the gauging stations can provide water-quality information such as temperature, turbidity, and bacterial counts. This real-time data is typically recorded at 15- to 60-minute intervals, stored onsite, and then transmitted to USGS offices every one to four hours. Recording and transmission times may be more frequent during critical events. Data from real-time sites are relayed to USGS offices via satellite, telephone, and/or radio and are available for viewing within minutes of arrival.

The U.S. Army Corps of Engineers maintains a Web site (http://corpslakes.usace.army.mil/visitors/states.cfm?state=KS) that is very useful for gathering information about the lakes that it owns or manages in Kansas.

Minimum Recommended Flow. Each trip description includes a minimum recommended flow. My estimates, by intent, are at the extreme end of what is possible yet still fun. This, at best, is an educated guess, based upon my experience, the experiences of others, the size and contour of the riverbed, and the gradient. It is not a guarantee that your trip will be safe or enjoyable. You may find my estimates too low for your use. The variance may be due to a bad estimate on my part or because of the kind of boat you are using, how it is loaded, your skill level, and what kind of water conditions you consider fun.

Estimate Float Time. Most of the river segments have an estimate of how long it takes to paddle that section. Those numbers may vary dramatically. Factors that

you must apply to calculate your float-time estimate include flows, wind and weather, type of boat, loading, skill, strength, and dawdling time.

Dams, Low-Head Dams, Weirs, and Other Man-Made Structures. Low-head dams, weirs, pipes, diversions, bridge pilings, and dredges are also among the most dangerous obstacles on rivers. Approach such man-made structures with great caution.

A man-made dam is a structure that blockades the river and discharges water over a defined spillway or through tubes below the structure. The natural dams in Kansas are not dangerous. The most dangerous obstacle you will find on a river in Kansas is a low-head dam. A low-head dam is typically only one to five feet high and may not look very dangerous from upstream. Sometimes all you see is a horizon line. The water that flows over low-head dams forms recirculating holes (called hydraulics) immediately below the dam and usually all the way across the river. The holes are uniform in shape and extend across the width of the channel. At the right water levels, these are drowning machines and must be avoided. Bridge pilings, piers, large pipes, dredges, and other manmade structures, because they are usually uniform in shape and sharp edged, can be very dangerous compared with natural features that tend to be nonuniform in shape.

Strainers. A strainer is the most common and often the most dangerous obstacle in a river. Strainers are usually caused by trees or large tree branches that have fallen or are leaning into the water. As the water approaches a strainer, it is forced downward, carrying whatever (and whoever) is in the water with it. The branches strain the water that flows through them, catching and trapping boats and people. Strainers can also be caused by bridge pilings, pipes, fences, and rocks. Avoid strainers if possible. If you find yourself out of your boat and floating into a strainer, swim sideways to the current and away from the strainer. As a last resort, if you cannot avoid being carried into a strainer while swimming, try to get on top of the brush pile to avoid being dragged under.

Logjams. Logjams and beaver dams are common to small streams. They may look innocuous, but treat them like strainers if there is any sign of current.

Rapids and Riffles. Very few of the rivers and streams in this book have significant rapids. Typically a riffle is a segment of the river where the current is faster but there is little or no obstruction in the channel. The faster current can be caused by a constriction in the channel or an increase in the river's gradient. A rapid is typically faster and may have obstructions, holes, ledges, or standing waves. If you are unsure about a rapids or your ability to run it safely, get out and scout it. If still in doubt, portage it.

Swimming and Capsizing. It isn't so much a matter of whether you will swim, so much as a matter of when. There are only two kinds of boaters, says my friend Bob Harris—the ones who have flipped and the ones who are going to flip. Taking a swim once in a while is no big deal. Just learn to do it safely. If you have the kind of kayak in which you sit inside, learn to do a wet exit in a lake or swimming pool so that you know how to get out of your boat quickly and safely. If you take a swim in fast-moving water, stay upstream of your boat to avoid being pinned between it and any obstacles. Swim with your feet pointed downstream and your toes up and out of the water. This will allow you to kick off from any obstructions and will prevent your feet from being entrapped below the surface under a rock or in the crotch of a submerged tree. Once free of the rapids, stroke for shore as quickly as you can. If you are swimming a rapid and approaching a strainer, swim for safety as hard and fast as you can.

Scout. If in doubt, scout. Do not run a rapid unless you are sure you can negotiate it safely. Scouting is a good way to learn how to read a river and protect yourself.

Float Participants and Trip Coordinators. If you're participating in a group trip, do not expect those who are planning your trip to think for you. Trip participants are responsible for their own choices and they cannot delegate those choices for any reason. Every member of a group is responsible for his or her own safety and cannot transfer that responsibility to other participants or trip coordinators. Participants should understand that the trip coordinator's only unique responsibility is to provide the participants with the information they need to get to the agreed-upon place at the agreed-upon time.

Medical Conditions and Physical Limitations. If you have a medical condition, let others know in advance.

Wind. Kansas is windy much of the time, so the chances of getting caught on the river under windy conditions are high. A short, low-profile kayak is the boat of choice in windy conditions. On open water, a sea kayak or touring kayak with a rudder is preferred. A low-profile canoe is preferred to one with a lot of rocker (upturned ends). In a tandem boat, a strong paddler in the bow is a

big help. If you are caught in the wind in a solo canoe, weighting your boat down with rocks and balancing it from end to end will add stability and reduce your exposure to the wind. Avoid paddling in low-water conditions—it is hard to get a good purchase on the water if you can't get the blade of your paddle in the water. In higher water the current can help overcome the force of a headwind.

The Kansas River from Scenic Drive between Lawrence and Topeka (photo by Craig Thompson)

THINGS TO TAKE

Minimum requirements—Boat, paddle(s)/oars, and PFD. Add a helmet for whitewater and a skirt for some kayaks. If you are using a motor, take enough fuel.

Basic equipment—Spare paddle, throw rope, flotation bags, bailing bucket or sponge, drinking water and/or filter, appropriate dry clothes (in a waterproof container), map and compass, river shoes, and rain jacket and pants. If you're in a motorized boat, have tools and spare parts as you are likely to need and know how to use them.

Emergency—First-aid kit, knife, whistle, waterproof matches/lighter, and duct tape.

Miscellaneous—Sunglasses with strap, hat, sunblock and lip balm, insect repellent, fishing tackle and license, food, trash bags, camera, extra set(s) of keys for the shuttle vehicle(s), binoculars, and personal medications.

Camping—Tent, ground cloth, sleeping bag, and kitchen stuff.

Other—Cell phones are nice in an emergency, but rarely work on the river. If you take one, it is helpful to know where along your route you can get reception.

Drinking Water. Most novice paddlers fail to bring and drink enough water while paddling. Drink all day. Carry all you will need or invest in a water purification system.

Hypothermia. Hypothermia is a decrease in body temperature that can cause the brain and body to fail. Few paddlers die of hypothermia, but it is very often a contributing factor in drowning. As the body cools, there is a significant loss of strength, coordination, alertness, and the ability to make sound decisions. Cold water robs body heat 25 to 30 times faster than cold air and can kill an ill-prepared boater. In swift 50° water with other typical river hazards, a person without adequate protection may survive only a few minutes.

Hypothermia does not always occur in cold weather. A sudden storm may soak an unprepared boater and wind can steal heat rapidly. A long swim or multiple swims in cool water or on a cool overcast day may make rewarming difficult. An injured person may experience hypothermia very quickly as shock sets in.

- Learn the symptoms and treatment for hypothermia.
- Be smart: prevention is the best treatment.
- Dress appropriately for sudden immersion in the water.
- Carry a dry bag with extra clothes and fire starter.
- Be skilled in self-rescue and know how to rescue others.
- Avoid conditions that put you at unreasonable risk.
- Be aware of weather and river conditions.
- Do not paddle alone and be aware of other paddlers.
- Eat and drink often to maintain your energy reserve.
- Know and do not exceed your skill limits.
- Avoid alcohol and substances that may impair good judgment or reactions.
- Use good judgment.

PFD. A personal flotation device is what some people call a life jacket. When on the water, always wear a properly fitted and properly secured, Coast Guard-approved PFD of type III or V.

GRADIENT AND CURRENT SPEED

Gradient is the river's rate of descent. Gradient is figured by calculating the elevation change (stated in feet) from the top of a river segment to the bottom of the river segment and then stating that number in terms of the length of the river segment (stated in miles). Thus, the gradient is stated as so many feet per mile. For example, the average gradient on the Grand Canyon segment of the Colorado River is 16 feet per mile and the average gradient on the Kansas River is 2 feet per mile.

Generally, the higher the gradient, the faster the water moves. Gradient is one indicator to help you judge the difficulty of a run, the speed of the current, and the time it will take to paddle a given distance, but gradient alone does not provide enough information to judge either difficulty or speed. A river segment may have a high average gradient, but that average may include one

or more significant drops, with mostly flat water in between. Such is the case on the Arkansas River through the middle of Wichita. On that urban segment of the Ark, the average gradient is about 3.5 feet per mile. Looking at gradient alone, you would expect the river to move right along. But it doesn't. There are several mandatory-portage, low-head dams that account for most of the 3.5-foot-per-mile gradient in that river segment. So rather than moving along at a good clip, this section is a series of long, slow-moving pools that are interrupted by dangerous drops.

Another factor that affects the speed of the current is the shape of the river's channel. The Missouri River between St. Cloud and Kaw Point has en elevation change of 98 feet over a distance, by river, of 122 miles. The gradient is less than one foot per mile. You would expect the current to be very slow, but it is not. The Missouri River's channel has been straightened and cleared of obstructions. The result is a very fast, 3 to 6 miles per hour.

A river's stage also affects current speed and difficulty. In general terms, stage is the elevation of the river's surface above the elevation of the riverbed. When a river's stage is high, it flows faster than when it is low. This is because the obstructions in the channel, including the contour of the riverbed, present less relative resistance to the larger volume of water. This is one of the reasons why it can be dangerous to paddle on rivers and streams that are in flood.

There are only a few publicly accessible rivers in Kansas with anything greater than a riffle. A few natural rapids can be found on segments on the Elk, Fall, Wakarusa, and Marais des Cygnes Rivers, and on Grouse, Otter, Rock, Mill, and Dragoon Creeks. Manmade structures such as strategically placed boulders, weirs, and broken dams have created rapids on the Big Blue, Kansas, Arkansas, and other rivers and streams across the state. All significant rapids are noted with their respective river segments in this guide.

DIFFICULTY RATING

This guide uses the International Scale of River Difficulty, a rating system that is used throughout the world to compare the difficulty of rivers. This system is not exact. Rivers do not always fit easily into one category and regional or individual interpretations may cause misunderstandings. Therefore, this guide is no substitute for accurate, firsthand knowledge of a stream and of your own personal skill level.

Paddlers attempting difficult runs on an unfamiliar stream should act cautiously until they get a feel for the way the scale is interpreted and how their skills match the water conditions. River difficulty may change rapidly due to fluctuations in water level, downed trees, recent floods, geological disturbances, or weather conditions. Stay alert for unexpected problems!

As river difficulty increases, the danger to boaters and swimmers becomes greater. As rapids become longer and more continuous, the challenge increases. There is a difference between running an occasional Class III rapid and dealing with an entire river classed in this category. Allow an extra margin of safety if you do not know the river, when the water or weather is cold, or if the river is remote and inaccessible.

The ratings given to most of the rivers and streams in this book were assigned on the basis of minimal to normal, recreationally acceptable flows when I paddled them. Regardless of a river's difficulty rating, paddlers are advised that these ratings may not apply at all flows. Further, any stream at high flows can be much more difficult and dangerous than my ratings indicate.

THE SIX DIFFICULTY CLASSES:

Class I: Easy. Fast-moving water with riffles and small waves. Few obstructions, all obvious and easily avoided with little training. Risk to swimmers is slight; self-rescue is easy.

Class II: Novice. Straightforward rapids with wide, clear channels that are evident without scouting. Occasional maneuvering may be required, but rocks and medium-sized waves are easily missed by trained paddlers. Swimmers are seldom injured and group assistance, while helpful, is seldom needed. Rapids that are at the upper end of this difficulty range are designated "Class II+."

Class III: Intermediate. Rapids with moderate, irregular waves that may be difficult to avoid and that can swamp an open canoe. Complex maneuvers in fast current and good boat control in tight passages or around ledges are often required. Large waves or strainers may be present but are easily avoided by skilled boaters. Strong eddies and powerful current effects can be found, particularly on large-volume rivers. Scouting is advisable for inexperienced parties. Injuries while swimming are rare; self-rescue is usually easy, but group assistance may be required to avoid long swims. Rapids that are at the lower or upper end of this difficulty range are designated "Class III-" or "Class III+," respectively.

Class IV: Advanced. Intense, powerful, but predictable rapids requiring precise boat handling in turbulent water. Depending on the character of the river, it may feature large, unavoidable waves and holes or constricted passages demanding fast maneuvers under pressure. A fast, reliable eddy turn may be needed to initiate maneuvers, scout rapids, or rest. Rapids may require "must" moves above dangerous hazards. Scouting may be necessary the first time down. Risk of injury to swimmers is moderate to high, and water conditions may make self-rescue difficult. Group assistance for rescue is often essential but requires practiced skills. A strong Eskimo roll is highly recommended for kayakers. Rapids that are at the lower or upper end of this difficulty range are designated "Class IV-" or "Class IV+," respectively.

Class V: Expert. Extremely long, obstructed, or very violent rapids that expose a paddler to added risk. Drops may contain large, unavoidable waves and holes or steep, congested chutes with complex, demanding routes. Rapids may continue for long distances between pools, demanding a high level of fitness. What eddies exist may be small, turbulent, or difficult to reach. At the high end of the scale, several of these factors may be combined. Scouting is recommended but may be difficult. Swims are dangerous and rescue is often difficult even for experts. A very reliable Eskimo roll, proper equipment, extensive experience, and practiced rescue skills are essential. Because of the large range of difficulty that exists beyond Class IV, Class V is an open-ended, multiple-level scale designated 5.0, 5.1, 5.2, etc. Each of these levels is an order of magnitude more difficult than the last. Example: increasing difficulty from Class V to Class 5.1 is a similar order of magnitude as increasing from Class IV to Class V.

Class VI: Extreme and Exploratory. These runs have often never been attempted and typically exemplify the extremes of difficulty, unpredictability, and danger. The consequences of errors are very severe and rescue may be impossible. For teams of experts only, at favorable water levels, after close personal inspection, and taking all precautions. After a Class VI rapid has been run many times, its rating may be changed to an appropriate Class V rating.

TERMINOLOGY AND OTHER INFORMATION

River running has its own terminology with which you should be familiar. This allows a basis of understanding between boaters and makes it quicker and easier to communicate information, including the information in this guide.

Access. For simplicity, I will refer to only two types of river access in this publication:
Boat Ramp—A developed access that has a paved or maintained gravel boat ramp. Such accesses generally have all-weather parking areas, but not always.
Access—A river access that does not have a boat ramp.

An access is merely a point at which it is possible to get a boat in or out of a river or stream. For some of these, a rope can be handy to help lower and raise you and/or your boat in and out of the water. A good throw rope should be a part of every river paddler's safety gear. I have attempted to let the reader know if an access has serious deficiencies, but these things can change rapidly.

Backwater. This is the stream water that is blocked by a lake's surface elevation. When a lake is high, the backwater reaches farther upstream, sometimes for great distances. Backwater has little if any perceptible current. The normal riparian vegetation is often absent or in poor condition due to long periods of immersion. Without healthy vegetation to stabilize them, the banks quickly erode, spilling soil into the stream. In this way, an otherwise beautiful, free-flowing stream can become a steep-sided, muddy backwater. Due to heavy silt loads and erosion in their watersheds, some rivers have formed large alluvial fans in the upper reaches of lakes. These alluvial deltas can become impassable at low flows and low lake levels.

The ideal situation is when the lake is low and the river is flowing fast. This maximizes the effects of the river and minimizes the effects of the lake. A less desirable situation is when the lake is high, blocking the river's flow. It's even less desirable when the river is low and the lake is low. When a low-flow river meets the alluvial fan at the head of a low-level lake, you can find yourself stuck in the middle of a muddy delta, unable to get to shore.

If you do not have personal knowledge of the river and lake levels, you may want to contact the authorities who control the lake level (usually the Army Corps of Engineers or the local wildlife area manager) to at least be sure the delta area is floatable.

CFS—cubic feet per second. This is a measure of how many cubic feet of water pass a given point along the riverbank in one second. To determine the significance of the CFS measurement, you have to know a little bit about the size of the river channel. For instance, a 20,000-CFS flow on the Missouri River at Kansas City would be an extremely low flow, but 20,000-CFS on a small stream, such as Mill Creek in Johnson County, would cause significant flooding. Check the USGS or Army Corps of Engineers Web addresses shown for each river or go to http://waterdata.usgs.gov/ks/nwis/rt to find the river and gauging station of your choice. Compare the flows indicated with the flows that I have recommended for each river segment as a loose guideline, not a rule.

Holes and Hydraulics. A hole (also called a hydraulic) develops where fast-moving water flows over an object and then curls back on itself. As the water drops over the object, it first moves toward the bottom of the river and then is deflected back toward the surface and recirculates back upstream, behind the object. This depression and recirculating water are very dangerous if the hole is wide and regular in shape, because whatever falls into the hole tends to stay there, being recirculated over and over. A swimmer stuck in a recirculating hole, often called a "keeper," is at the mercy of the river. The level of danger that a hole presents is relative to its size, depth, and shape. Avoid deep, large, regularly shaped (straight across) holes. Holes made by low-head dams are straight across and have no weak points from which to escape. Skilled boaters learn to how to read holes and to surf the safe ones.

River Right or River Left. As you go downstream, "river right" is on your right and "river left" is on your left. If you turn around and look upstream, "river right" is now your left and "river left" is on your right.

BOAT RENTALS

It can be difficult to find rental boats in Kansas. I have provided rental information where it is available but, like any contact information, it can become dated very quickly. The most current rental guide and retail information is on the Kansas Paddler Web page at www.kansas.net/~tjhittle/, maintained by T.J. Hittle.

RIVER ETIQUETTE
• Be responsible for your own safety.
• Help others when they need it, but only when you can do so without endangering yourself.
• Abstain from alcohol and drugs.
• Be quiet so you do not disturb the peace of the local landowners and your fellow paddlers. If you must have a radio, wear headphones so that the rest of us can hear the wilderness.
• Leave things made of glass at home.
• Respect private property.
• If you build a fire, build it below the high-water mark so that the next rain will wash the ashes away. Keep it small and put it out.
• Whether hiking, camping, or boating, leave nothing behind but footprints and take nothing but pictures and memories. Leave no trace of your passing, except to clean up where others have failed.

WATER QUALITY AND QUANTITY

Water quality has improved since the 1970s as cities have installed wastewater-treatment plants. Yet as those improvements have been made, our cities have grown. This growth has produced more streets, more roofs, and more parking lots and thus more runoff and more pollution. While runoff from municipalities has an increasing impact on the quality of the surface water, by far the worst contributions to water pollution in the state come from disease organisms, sediment, fertilizers, and pesticides that run off from poorly managed farm fields and improperly located and managed feedlots (2000 Kansas Water Quality Assessment [305(b) Report] and 1998 Kansas Water-Quality Limited Segments [303(D) List]).

According to the U.S. Geological Survey, 89% of water usage in Kansas is for agricultural irrigation, 87% for irrigation, 2% for livestock. Most of this irrigation is done in the most arid regions of the state. To that end, wells have been over-pumped along our rivers and streams to the point where much (and sometimes all) of the rain and snowmelt that gets to the streams quickly drain into the dry sand and gravel and disappears from the surface. Thus, not only have we lost the sustainable flow of our streams, we are losing many of the streams themselves. At this writing, Kansas is attempting to buy back some of the irrigation rights along the Arkansas River to improve flows and to extend the life of the Ogallala Aquifer. Kansans must do more to protect our rivers, streams, and groundwater from this plight—not for the sake of recreation, but for the sake of our local economies and our quality of life throughout the state.

The Arkansas River once required ferries and large bridges to span its watercourse in the western part of the state. The western half of the river is now mostly a dry riverbed. Colorado has diverted and pumped it, leaving nothing but a trickle or a dry scar most of the time. A similar problem exists on nearly all of the rivers in the western two-thirds of the state. For this, we have no one to blame and no one to fix it but ourselves.

It is important that we all do our part to protect rivers and streams. For without them we lose not just our rivers and streams, but the diversity of wildlife that go with them. If you see a pollution problem caused by someone else, report it as quickly and with as much detail as possi-

ble to the Kansas Department of Health and Environment at (785) 296-5500. Don't turn your back on Kansas.

Hygiene. The bacterial pollution load in our streams has wide swings. After a heavy rain, the bacteria can be hundreds of times the concentration recommended for human contact. A week or two later, the concentration of bacteria often drops within a range that is suitable for wading, fishing, and boating. With a little care, you can minimize your risk.

• Consider your personal health. Individuals with immune system deficiencies or weakened medical conditions should reduce or avoid exposure to the water.

• Rivers and streams are at their worst within the first few days of rain or snowmelt. The first rise of water in a stream is called the "first flush." It well describes what

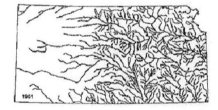 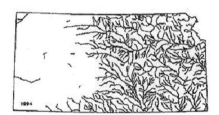

The major perennial streams of Kansas, 1961 vs. 1994. The left illustration is adapted from the U.S. Geological Survey map complied in 1961. The right illustration summarizes streamflow observations made by the Kansas Department of Health and Environment from October 1989 through January 1994.

is happening. If you are concerned about possible negative effects on your health, avoid paddling in that first flush if you can help it.

• If you think the water is polluted, keep your boat upright. Avoid activities that increase the chances of getting contaminated water in your mouth.

• You may also want to avoid windy conditions that can make paddling difficult and cover you with spray. Consider paddling early in the morning or the evening, when winds are generally lighter.

• Wash your hands frequently and before eating or smoking. Alcohol-based hand sanitizers seem to work well. Use them liberally.

• Clothing and equipment used on polluted water should be washed thoroughly or stored in a secure location, away from children.

I have been asked why I promote river recreation on polluted rivers. Are Kansas rivers unnecessarily polluted? Yes! Does this present a health risk to those who use them? Yes! Should we stop enjoying our rivers and streams until they are cleaned up? No! Every activity has its associated risks. Knowing and managing the risks is the best any of us can do. This problem is not unique to Kansas; to one extent or another, it applies to every river and stream throughout the nation and the world. So why do I promote river recreation? Because the sooner we learn to love our rivers, the more pressure there will be to clean them up. In the meantime, I enjoy this sport so much that I like to share it with as many friends as possible. We can retreat from the things we love, giving way to pollution, or we can teach our children to appreciate and enjoy these wild and beautiful places and to take care of our rivers for themselves and for all of the generations to come.

The beautiful Arkansas River through the Kaw Wildlife Area

WILDLIFE AND WILDLIFE MANAGEMENT AREAS

River and stream corridors provide wildlife a place to travel and find food, shelter, and water. The diversity and number of animals present along the river can vary dramatically at any given time, depending on the migratory season, hunting pressure, the condition of the habitat, the food supply, and the seasonal needs of the animals.

While on the river, you may see many species that are both common and uncommon to the area. Do not feed, pet, or harass any wildlife. Do not leave behind scraps of food, fish bait, bait containers, hooks, cigarette butts, wrappers, or other things that could interfere with the health, safety, or appearance of these wild areas and animals. Do not hunt or fish without the appropriate licenses and permits required by law.

The rivers and streams immediately upstream of most lakes are designated as Federal or State Wildlife

Management Areas. Some of these areas do not allow public access during critical migratory or nesting periods. I provided some current information on such closings but, if in doubt, please call local wildlife area managers at the numbers that I have provided.

SPECIAL PADDLING TIPS FOR SANDY-BOTTOMED RIVERS

Not withstanding normal river safety practices, the rivers of Kansas, for the most part, require no special skills or daring to navigate. That being said, there is one river skill that paddlers from other states may not have acquired that could be very useful in Kansas. This somewhat unique skill is the art of following the main channel on a shallow, sandy-bottomed river.

On rivers such as the Kansas, Saline, Smoky Hill, and Arkansas Rivers, shifting sand that forms most of the riverbed creates unique challenges for paddlers. New islands, sandbars, deep holes, and flats are formed, moved, and reformed, sometimes very quickly. These rivers are typically very broad, but also very shallow. As long as the river stage is fairly high, most of these changes to the riverbed's contour have little impact on your ability to navigate above the contours of the riverbed. As the flows subside, the main channel may be the only part of the river where you can find enough water to clear a plethora of sandbars. During low flows, your ability to find and stay in the main channel can be an important skill and an enjoyable pastime.

If you paddle sandy rivers at low flow, you *will* find yourself stranded on a sandbar from time to time. Even the best of us do. Have patience with the river but, more important, have patience with yourself. When you find yourself lodged on a sandbar, look for the clues that you might have missed; then learn from them.

All rivers and streams carry sediment downstream. The transported material is called the *bedload*. On a sandy river, the bedload is mostly sand, but can include gravel and usually some fines (fine sediments), such as clay and other small soil particles. During periods of high water, the fines are carried long distances downstream while the heavier materials float and roll just inches above the riverbed. The river deposits the coarse materials wherever the current slows down—the heaviest materials such as gravel settle first, then the coarsest sand particles, then the finer sand. Your understanding of this information will help you understand how, why, and where sandbars are formed and will give you clues on how to find and maintain the main channel.

A sandbar may or may not be visible above water

and may or may not have vegetation on it. An island is more permanent than a sandbar and is vegetated with more permanent growth than sandbars. A *run*, for the purpose of this discussion, is where the main channel is moving in somewhat of a straight line and maintains enough water for navigation even during fairly low flows. A *flat* is a broad transition area where the river is migrating across a shallow area from one channel to another.

Guideposts. You should learn and practice using the following generalities as guideposts for finding and following the main channel on sandy-bottomed rivers.

On any river, you can almost always find the deepest and fastest water at the **outside of a bend.** When the water enters a bend, centrifugal force pushes it to the outside of the curve. Forced into the narrower channel along the outer edge of the turn, the water accelerates and exerts greater force on the riverbank and riverbed. The bedload and any new sediment that was scoured from the outside of the curve and riverbed are quickly transported downstream by the fast-moving water. The tighter the bend, the deeper and faster the river will cut into the sandy riverbank and channel.

Rivers also try to take the shortest route to where they are going, unless something blocks their path. On a sandy-bottomed river, the "something" that blocks their path is usually a shallow sandbar that is only a few inches higher than the main channel and can be difficult to spot. Yet, if you know what you are looking for, you can read the river to find and stay in main channel.

As the faster-moving water slingshots out of the curve, it is still carrying its speed and heavy bedload. If the next river bend is nearby, the current will slow down only slightly as it cuts straight for the outside of the next turn. Since the current doesn't have much time to slow down, it doesn't drop much of its bedload and the channel stays fairly clear. Therefore, as you paddle out of the first bend, you should stay in the water that is moving toward the outside of the next bend. In this case, staying in the main channel is simple and easy.

When bends in the river are far apart, the main channel can be more elusive. This is where river-reading skills can provide you with a best-guess route that you will need to adjust as you proceed. Remember: the following tips are guides, not rules. They should be used in combination at all times. As you will discover, no single tip or combination of tips will keep your boat afloat all the time.

CHANNEL GUIDES

1. Look for where the river is up against the steepest shoreline. The shoreline probably became steep because the faster, deeper current eroded it. Therefore, look for deep water where the bank is the steepest and watch for shallows where the riverbank is low and gradual.

2. As you leave the river bend, look first to see if you can see where the current is headed, both near and far. What side of the river will you need to be on farther downstream? The speed of floating leaves and bubbles is a good indicator, but leaves and bubbles are not always there. The most common channel markers will be from logs and even small sticks that protrude from the water's surface. Each of these will have a wake. The size and angle of the wake can help indicate the speed and direction of the current. Watch all such signs to find the best route.

3. Very small waves or ripples on the water can mean two things: either the moving water is very shallow or wind is hitting the water's surface. Where water is moving over a shallow, sandy riverbed, small ripples will form on the water's surface that correspond to the tiny ripples on the riverbed. Experience will teach you to identify and use these tiny ripples to follow the main channel when other indicators are hard to find.

4. Where long distances separate meanders, the main channel, instead of crossing directly from one side of the river to the other, just bleeds its water over shallow sandbars until there is nothing left in the original channel.

Especially on the broader rivers of the Kansas River and parts of the Arkansas River, you will sometimes look ahead and, at first, see no clear channel. These are the *flats*. In the flats you will first need to determine, by looking ahead at the next turn, which side of the river you will need to end up on. Then the challenge becomes how to find the best water to get there. Notwithstanding a short route into a dead pool, and using the guidelines above and below, the best route is usually the first one that presents itself. There are three reasons. First, your original channel is bleeding water over into the next channel. If you stay in the original channel very long, it won't have enough water to carry you anywhere. Second, water tends to take the shortest route. Therefore, it will usually get there using the first and shortest possible route. Third, if you have picked the correct channel, once you are in the new channel, water will continue to build into it as the old channel bleeds over.

5. When a sandy-bottomed river is very low, you will sometimes see a line of small ripples in front of you that extends all the way across your channel. You know the ripples indicate where the fast-moving water is flowing over a shallow sandbar, but since the ripples extend all the way across the channel, you can deduce that the sandbar ahead extends across the entire channel. In such a case, try to

cross the shallows where the water is deepest. The deepest water, if there is any, will be where the ripples are slightly larger than the surrounding ripples.

6. Experienced boaters are familiar with the terms "downstream V" and "upstream V." A *downstream V* is a V-shaped wave that is formed as current converges. As the name implies, a downstream V points downstream. The force of the current is focused at the center of the V so, unless there is some obstruction, that part of the channel is usually the deepest. The *upstream V,* on the other hand, is caused by an obstacle at or below the water's surface. An upstream V will point exactly upstream and can show you the direction of the current at that exact spot.

It's easy to learn these clues, yet your degree of mastery will depend on your powers of observation and deduction. On a slow-moving, sandy-bottomed river, the tiniest twig or blade of grass can help show you the way.

Watch your step. Submerged sandbars are usually very steep on their downstream side. When walking your boat over a shallow sandbar, always watch your step as you approach the downstream side or you may find yourself stepping into a pool six feet deep.

SHUTTLES

Each trip in this book includes a map and a description of how to get to and from the various access points along your paddling route. I have often been asked how, after paddling downstream, a paddler can get back upstream to his or her car. Creating a convenient shuttle depends on several factors, but the following tips will get you started.

Shuttle from the top. If you are boating with a group that has more than one car, meet at the put-in, and unload your boats and gear. Then all vehicles are driven to the take-out. Then one shuttle vehicle returns all drivers to the put-in. After the float trip, one of the drivers will take the shuttle vehicle driver back to the put-in to get his or her car.

Shuttle from the bottom. Meet at the take-out first. Leave a shuttle vehicle at the take-out and take all of the other vehicles to the put-in. The rest of the shuttle process is the same as before. This method may require transferring gear and boats back and forth between vehicles but, under the right circumstances, it can save time and fuel.

Shuttle Buddy System. Have a buddy who is not paddling with you drop you at the put-in and then, at an appointed time, pick you up at the take-out.

Bicycle. Leave a bicycle at the take-out, well hidden or chained to something solid. When you arrive at the take-out, hide or chain up your boat and ride your bike back to the put-in. Then drive your vehicle to the take-out to get your boat.

Alternate Accesses. If not everyone is taking out at the same spot, just leave a vehicle at each access that will be used.

Keys. When running a shuttle, take two sets of your vehicle keys. Keep them in separate containers that float.

Dry Clothes. It is usually a good idea for everyone to leave some dry clothes in a vehicle at the take-out.

CAMPING IN KANSAS

Camping facilities are often available either on the river or within a reasonable distance. With only a few exceptions, the only rivers that you can camp along are the Missouri, the Kansas, and the Arkansas Rivers. Most other river segments in this book pass through public lands that are managed by the Kansas Department of Wildlife and Parks (KDWP) or the Army Corps of Engineers. Neither KDWP nor the Corps allows camping on any of the land they manage, except in designated campsites. These state parks, though conveniently located for the general public, are generally located around the edge of lakes and only rarely along the rivers themselves. I have noted those exceptions within this guide.

In addition to the state park contact list, the Appendix at the back of this book includes lake maps showing both state and federal campgrounds. For rivers in this guide other than the three public rivers, the narrative includes a list of nearby campgrounds and their phone numbers.

A daily or annual motor vehicle permit is required

Preparing a raft expedition on the Republican River (photo by Suzanne Murphy)

for all vehicles entering a Kansas state park. All daily vehicle permits expire at noon the day following purchase, except on Sundays, Memorial, Independence, and Labor Days, when they expire at 2 P.M.

Temporary permits, which must be exchanged for permanent permits, are now available online at www.kdwp.state.ks.us/news/state_parks/park_fees. To exchange a temporary permit or purchase a permanent permit, visit a Kansas Department of Wildlife and Parks office or a licensed agent. If you are purchasing a second vehicle permit, you must provide vehicle registration at the time of purchase and it must be in the same name as the first vehicle.

When camping, choose a site that is high enough that a dam release or an upstream storm will not inundate your camp in the middle of the night. Always tie your boat to something that won't float away overnight.

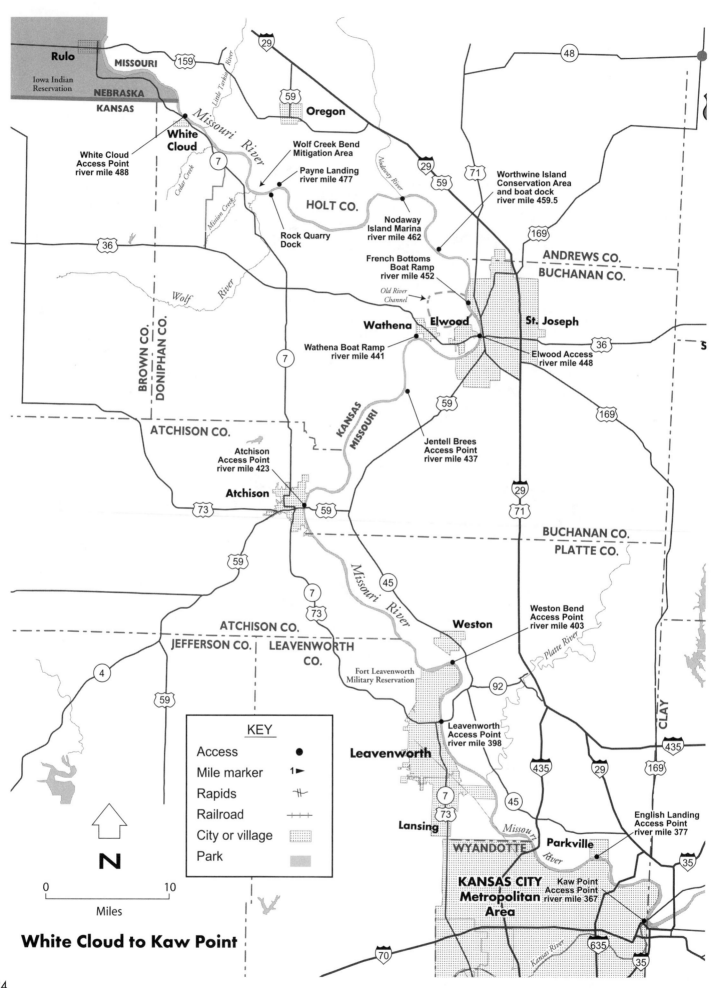

Rulo

Iowa Indian
Reservation

MISSOURI

NEBRASKA

KANSAS

White Cloud
Access Point
river mile 488

White
Cloud

159

Little Tarkio River

Missouri River

Cedar Creek

Mission Creek

7

Wolf Creek Bend
Mitigation Area

Payne Landing
river mile 477

Rock Quarry
Dock

HOLT CO.

Oregon

59

29

Nodaway River

Worthwine Island
Conservation Area
and boat dock
river mile 459.5

59

71

48

Nodaway
Island Marina
river mile 462

169

ANDREWS CO.

BUCHANAN CO.

36

Wolf River

French Bottoms
Boat Ramp
river mile 452

Old River
Channel

Elwood

Wathena

Wathena Boat Ramp
river mile 441

St. Joseph

36

Elwood Access
river mile 448

BROWN CO.

DONIPHAN CO.

7

59

KANSAS

MISSOURI

Jentell Brees
Access Point
river mile 437

ATCHISON CO.

Atchison
Access Point
river mile 423

Atchison

73

59

45

Missouri River

BUCHANAN CO.

PLATTE CO.

29

71

169

59

7

73

ATCHISON CO.

JEFFERSON CO.

LEAVENWORTH
CO.

4

59

Weston

Weston Bend
Access Point
river mile 403

Platte River

Fort Leavenworth
Military Reservation

92

CLAY

435

KEY

Access ●

Mile marker 1►

Rapids

Railroad

City or village

Park

Leavenworth
Access Point
river mile 398

Leavenworth

435

45

29

169

35

N

0   10

Miles

7

73

Lansing

WYANDOTTE

Missouri River

KANSAS CITY
Metropolitan
Area

Parkville

English Landing
Access Point
river mile 377

Kaw Point
Access Point
river mile 367

35

70

Kansas River

635

35

White Cloud to Kaw Point

MISSOURI RIVER AND WATERSHED

121 miles, Class I-II difficulty

Born from a small spring in the Rocky Mountains of Montana, dammed and controlled through South Dakota, and then confined between rock-lined banks from Nebraska to St. Louis, the "Mighty Mo" has lost most of its natural wild manner but has added new dimensions of danger.

For convenience, I have divided the 121 miles of the Missouri River that flow past Kansas into five single-day floats that can easily be combined for a multi-day adventure. All of those segments share similar dangers, challenges, history, and wildlife, so I have provided an overview of the river here. For detailed information on each of those segments, please refer to the segment descriptions to follow. Additional safety and navigation information is available from a booklet titled *Rules of the Road*, which can be downloaded at http://www.navcen.uscg.gov/mwv/navrules/ navrules.htm.

The entire watershed of the Missouri extends over 420,000 square miles. Through the Kansas portion of the river, your view will largely consist of forested rolling hills and bluffs. Cottonwood, sycamore, maples, willows, and elms dominate the riparian forest. On higher ground you will find walnut, hickory, green ash, and many other native and nonnative trees. Beavers, otters, muskrats, foxes, white-tailed deer, coyotes, and many bird species are common to these areas. The **average gradient** is only .9 feet per mile, but the current runs very fast and wide.

Although the Missouri River technically only rates a Class II difficulty, it is not suitable for novice paddlers because of the difficulties associated with the width of the channel, the speed of the current, the complications of barge traffic, the dangers related to channel markers, wing dams and the consequences of a swim. Once you're on the river, the countryside will pass by quickly. Wing dams, built along the edge of the river, focus the flow of the river toward the main channel. This keeps the channel deep and moving at an average of four to five miles per hour. At those speeds, there is a lot of turbulence and obstacles come at you fast—or rather, you come at them fast. This is no place for timid strokes or indecision. A paddler must make strong moves, fast and early. A swim in the Missouri is never a good experience. The speed, width, and turbulence of the river can make getting to shore very difficult. Follow all safety rules; especially, never paddle alone, always wear a PFD, and tell someone responsible where you are going.

The Missouri River is not a typical Kansas float stream. In addition to the current being fast, the banks are far apart. The wake from barges and speedboats can be four feet high. Keep your distance from any barge. If you encounter a large wake, it is best to turn into the wave rather than to take it broadside. After the wake passes, check to be sure the reaction wave off the shore does not get you.

Navigation buoys are used to mark the center of the channel. They float at normal to low river levels, but at higher stream flows the current can push them under. When they explode to the surface, they have enough force to break a canoe in half.

You want to stay in the main channel to avoid the hazards along the banks, but avoid the center of the channel. To stay in the main channel, keep the black, cylindrical can buoys on your right going downriver and on your left going upriver. The opposite is true for red, conical *nun* buoys.

Landing your boat can be hazardous with a strong current pushing you. Turn your boat upstream and then "ferry" (paddle laterally across the current) into the landing, approaching it from below rather than risk being pushed into or under it.

Since the river never gets too low to float, there is no minimum recommended flow, but it can get too high. Whenever the river is high or is rising, it will carry a lot of tree limbs. Most of the limbs will float, but some will bounce along the bottom. If a large piece of driftwood is rolled by the current, it can explode to the surface with great force. Stay off the river if you see a lot of big logs and trees floating by.

Dikes can be a threat to paddlers. The dikes can extend far out into the channel and are most dangerous when the current is just barely flowing over them. They can be nearly invisible from upstream. Your first clue may be a ripping or roaring sound. The rocks, hydraulics, turbulence, and strong currents associated with these dikes can be extremely dangerous and should be avoided.

Wind can be an important factor on any big river. A 20- to 25-mile-per-hour breeze can pin a canoe against the shore. So the paddle craft of choice on the

Missouri River is a kayak or a low-profile canoe with flotation and a pair of strong paddlers. In a canoe, a strong bow paddler can make a big difference on a windy day. If you are in an open boat, caught in the wind, and having moderate difficulty, try loading some weight into your boat. I have seen desperate paddlers rope a five-gallon bucket to the bow of their boat to act as a "sea anchor." The effect is that the bucket, caught by the current, will pull the boat downstream. The danger is that the boat will be much less maneuverable and, worse, that a snagged bucket or rope can result in a sudden and catastrophic accident.

With the speed of the current, other obstacles, and inclement weather, the Mighty Mo can sometimes be more than you want to deal with. Yet on a good day, the bald eagles, good fishing, and interesting destina-

tions make the Missouri River a great weekend destination. To some people, the attraction is the challenge of the size, speed, and sense of adventure. To others, it is the fishing or the feeling that destinations downstream are almost unlimited. Still others find that paddling this river provides a sense of connection to the past. The journey of Lewis and Clark and the men of their Corps of Discovery is documented by historic markers that you will find along the river.

Many boaters find the interesting towns along the river's edge enough reason to explore the Mo. Throw a clean shirt into a dry bag, so you won't look like a complete river hobo when you stop to enjoy the unmatched hospitality, casinos, eateries, shops, breweries, wineries, city markets, B&Bs, and historic river towns like White Cloud, St. Joseph, Atchison, Weston (MO), Leaven-

Yacht on Missouri River by John Breyfagle.

worth, Parkville (MO), and Kansas City. When campsites are hard to find, try a bed-and-breakfast or the city, county, and state parks along the river.

The best times to find large, clean sandbars for camping is whenever the Army Corps of Engineers is not releasing water for barge traffic. These releases change from season to season and year to year, but generally late fall through early spring is the best time to find large sandbars. These seasons conveniently correspond with the migratory flyway for all manner of waterfowl, as well as bald eagles and osprey that fish the open water on their way north and south.

Detailed Missouri River navigation charts can be downloaded from the Army Corps of Engineers' Web site at http://www.nwk.usace.army.mil/rivercharts/. Open the section between White Cloud and Kansas City and then click on the individual map segments that you want. The maps load very slowly, but the detail that they provide is worth the wait.

You can also **check current and forecast flows** at www.nwd-mr.usace.army.mil/rcc/reports/resf cast.html. Click on "Forecast Information" and then on "Missouri River Station Flows." You will get today's readings and an eight-day forecast with flows stated in terms of thousands of feet per second (KCFS). Thus "24" is 24 KCFS or 24,000 CFS. Station MSJF is at St. Joseph and station MKCF is at Kansas City. To check current and recent flows, check the USGS **gauging stations** (see Web site above) on the Missouri River at Rulo, Nebraska, and on the Missouri River at St. Joseph, Missouri.

The State of Missouri has good river accesses and conservation land at short intervals along the river, especially between White Cloud and St. Joseph. Each site has good signage that helps you find the accesses and know where the conservation land starts and stops. These conservation areas along the river are open for public access, including hiking, camping, and hunting (during the appropriate seasons). In these areas, you can camp and hike above the "normal high water mark." Combined with the access points along the Kansas side, you can float any part of the river in one-day or multi-day segments.

Water quality has improved somewhat in recent years, but it is never suitable for swimming. Bacterial contamination comes from feedlots and towns along the river and up in the watershed, so practice good river hygiene.

The Missouri, though not the river it once was, is still home to great fishing. Bluegill, crappie, sunfish, largemouth bass, walleye, sauger, drum, and carp are abundant, as well as channel, flathead, and blue catfish.

During low-water conditions, channel catfish are found in deep water along main channel borders or along the upstream faces of rock wing dams. At night, they feed in shallow sandbar habitat. During high-water conditions, look for them in the backwaters and tributary streams. During cold weather, channel catfish move to deep holes at the ends of wing dams and in tributary streams. Flathead catfish sometimes exceed 50 pounds and are prized for their flavor. The best time of the day to catch large flathead catfish is after sundown, when they begin feeding. Fish in deep water, off the end of wing dam, and along the main channel borders. Flathead catfish prefer live bait.

Blue catfish can weigh over 60 pounds. Specimens over 150 pounds or more were caught in the 19th century. They prefer the swift current of the main channel and main channel borders.

Bullhead catfish feed on a variety of items, ranging from insects to smaller fish. Earthworms are a common bait, but liver, crayfish, and frogs are also good. When it is too hot for other fish to be interested, bullheads keep biting.

A few special safety rules must be followed on the Missouri River. Just as you would stay on the far right side of the road when driving your car, you are expected to stay to your far right (starboard) side when traveling either upstream or downstream. If you cross the channel, you must give way to power-driven vessels coming from either upstream or downstream. If you are moving upstream in a powered vessel, you must give way to those moving downstream.

The only **canoe rentals available** are at A-1 Rentals, 14891 East U.S. Highway 40, Kansas City, MO, (816) 373-0234. The nearest full-service boat dealer is Kansas City Paddler, 21911 Branic Drive, Peculiar, MO, (816) 779-1195.

MISSOURI RIVER: WHITE CLOUD TO NODAWAY ISLAND

25.9 miles, intermediate access available, Class I-II difficulty
White Cloud at river mile 488 to the Nodaway Island Boat Ramp at river mile 462.1

In 1804, the Lewis and Clark expedition rested at the spot now called White Cloud. Long before the white men came to the area, the Iowa tribe lived here. In the mid-1800s, the chief of the Prairie Sioux (Iowas), Ma-Hush-Kah, lived near the Missouri River at a place called Iowa Point. In 1856, only two years after the Kansas-Nebraska Act opened the territories to white settlement, Enoch Spaulding and John H. Utt laid out the plans for the town and named it for Ma-Hush-Kah, using the English version of his name, James White Cloud.

The town of White Cloud was one of the earliest and grandest in the new Kansas Territory. The port town was a regular stop for the big steamboats that carried supplies bound for the frontier. In its heyday, the town boasted a population of over 2,000. By the 1860s, supplies began to travel via the rails and most of the jobs and people began to leave. Today's population of about 200 maintains the traditions of a friendly river community.

This is the most remote part of the Missouri River as it passes between the states of Kansas and Missouri. The **Four-State Overlook**, located at the top of the hill and north of town, is a great place to take your camera and a good pair of binoculars. The city park, only about three blocks from the river, is available for camping. The American Legion Hall serves good meals Friday, Saturday, and Sunday evenings.

Put in at the **White Cloud Boat Ramp**. The boat ramp is located on Kansas Highway 7, a little bit north of where White Cloud's Main Street meets the river. If you plan to leave your vehicles overnight in White Cloud, move them to a lighted area in the downtown area. The 110-mile **round-trip shuttle** route, from White Cloud to the Nodaway Island Marina Boat Ramp and back, goes northwest on K-7. Once you get to Nebraska the road name changes several times, but continue north to Rulo and then turn east on U.S. Highway 159. Continue on U.S. Highway 159 to I-29 and then turn south on I-29. Take Exit 60 and go south on Missouri Highway K into Amazonia. From Amazonia, go west on Missouri Highway T roughly 3.5 miles

to the Nodaway Island Boat Ramp.

This is the only Kansas side access between White Cloud and Elwood (just downstream of St. Joseph). The current will quickly accelerate you and your belongings downstream. The temptation is to stay near the banks for safety, but don't. Stay in the main channel and follow the rules outlined in the section above. Mid-channel will seem easy and relaxing, but trouble comes at you fast, so don't become complacent. Stay alert, watch downstream, make your moves early, and follow the guidelines in the prior section.

The **Bob Brown Conservation Area** begins on river left at river mile 486.3 at the confluence of the Little Tarkio River and extends downstream to Cannon Creek at river mile 482.8. The Bob Brown Conservation Area, in Holt County, Missouri, offers waterfowl hunters wade-and-shoot hunting. Wade-and-shoot hunting requires hunters to wade or boat out into the marsh with the equipment necessary needed to hide and hunt comfortably. This means there are no duck blinds on this area. The Bob Brown area can be waded and small boats can be used in three of the four wetland pools. Hunting access is determined by a lottery. The area closes to waterfowl hunting at 1:00 P.M. each day.

Cedar Creek enters on river right near river mile 485. It is about 30 feet wide at the mouth. From river mile 480 to 477, the river left side of Wolf Creek Bend is under development to mitigate the impacts of river channelization. Indian Creek and Wolf Creek enter on river right near river mile 479. The **Payne Landing Access** is at river mile 477 on river left. Mosquito Creek enters from river right at river mile 471.5. There is a dock for a rock quarry at river mile 469. The **Jim and Olivia Hare Wildlife Area**, river mile 466-464 on river left, is yet to be developed and has no access at this time. At river mile 463 on river left, the **Tom Brown Access** is immediately upstream of the confluence with the Nodaway River. This is a poor access for canoes or kayaks, so **take out** just downstream of the Nodaway River confluence at the **Nodaway Island Marina**.

Four Corners Overlook at White Cloud overlooks Kansas, Nebraska, Iowa, and Missouri

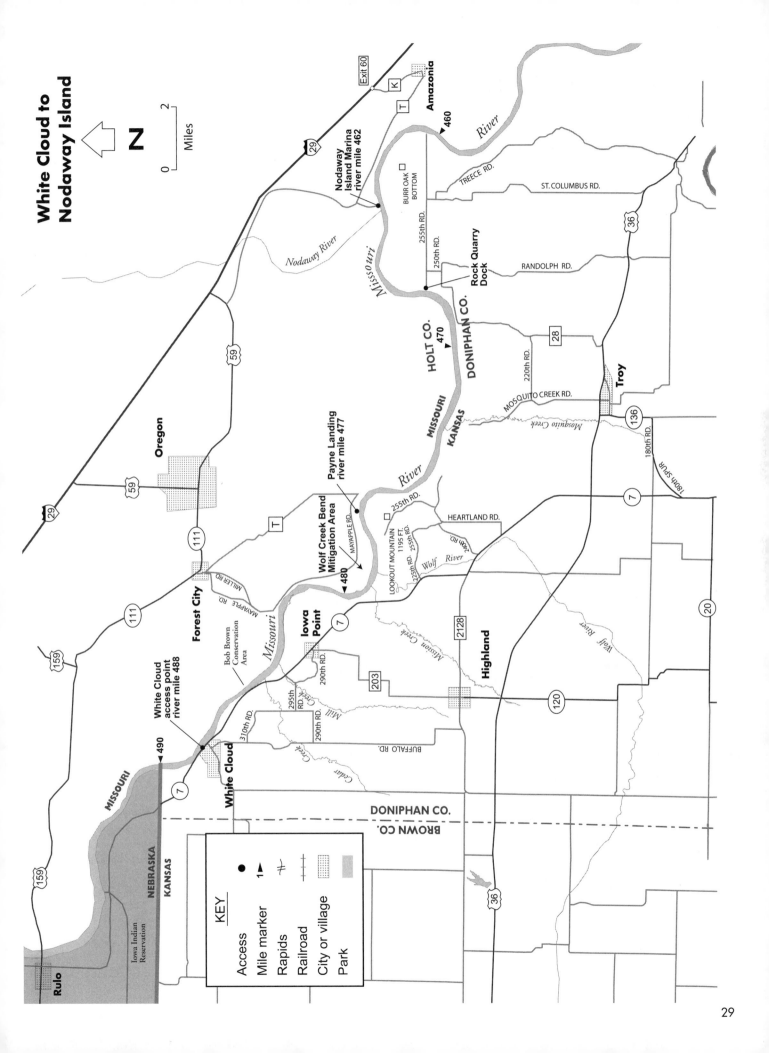

White Cloud to Nodaway Island

N

0 — 2 Miles

Amazonia

Exit 60

K

T

▼ 460

Nodaway Island Marina
river mile 462

River

TREECE RD.

ST. COLUMBUS RD.

BURR OAK
BOTTOM

36

29

255th RD.

250th RD.

Rock Quarry
Dock

RANDOLPH RD.

Nodaway River

HOLT CO.

DONIPHAN CO.

470 ▲

28

220th RD.

MISSOURI

KANSAS

Troy

59

Mosquito Creek

MOSQUITO CREEK RD.

136

180th RD.

180th SPUR

River

Payne Landing
river mile 477

255th RD.

HEARTLAND RD.

7

Oregon

Wolf Creek Bend
Mitigation Area

LOOKOUT MOUNTAIN
1195 FT.

225th RD.

255th RD.

Wolf River

Wolf River

59

T

480 ▼

MAYAPPLE RD.

59

290th RD.

20

111

Bob Brown
Conservation
Area

Forest City

MAYAPPLE RD.

MILLER RD.

Iowa
Point

7

290th RD.

Mission Creek

2128

203

Highland

159

White Cloud
access point
river mile 488

Missouri

295th
CREEK RD.

120

111

310th RD.

290th RD.

Mill Creek

BUFFALO RD.

490 ▼

7

White Cloud

Cedar Creek

MISSOURI

DONIPHAN CO.

NEBRASKA

KANSAS

BROWN CO.

KEY

● Access

1▲ Mile marker

≠ Rapids

╫ Railroad

City or village

Park

159

Iowa Indian
Reservation

Rulo

36

29

MISSOURI RIVER: NODAWAY ISLAND TO ST. JOSEPH
10 miles, Class I-II difficulty
Nodaway Island Boat Ramp at river mile 462.1 to French Bottoms in St. Joseph at river mile 452

To get to the Nodaway Island Boat Ramp from Amazonia, Missouri, go west on State Highway T roughly 3.5 miles. The 36-mile **round-trip shuttle** route, from Nodaway Island to the French Bottoms Boat Ramp in St. Joseph and back, goes east on Missouri Highway T to Amazonia, north on Missouri Highway K to I-29, and then south on I-29 to I-229 south into St. Joseph. Take Exit 7 onto Highland Avenue. Turn west and follow the signs to St. Jo Frontier Casino at the junction of McArthur Drive and Waterworks Road. The boat ramp is right next to the casino parking lot.

Put in at the **Nodaway Island Boat Ramp.** The Lewis and Clark expedition camped at the mouth of the Nodaway River on July 8, 1804. A carpenter named Joshua James George lived on Nodaway Island until the flood of 1880 washed the island away. From this access it is about 10 miles and 2.5 hours to the French Bottoms Access in St. Joseph. As soon as you launch, you will notice a series of private boat ramps on river left. If you are looking for a close campground, make your way across the river as quickly as you can to use the large sandbar downstream just across the river from the access.

The private boat ramps end at river mile 459.5, where you will find a public access just above the

At once, beautiful, graceful, bountiful, and powerful, the Missouri River is all of this and more (photo by John Breyfogle).

Worthwine Island Conservation Area. This is southwest of Amazonia; visitors can reach the area from I-229 by taking the exit for Amazonia and Missouri Highway K, traveling north on Highway K nearly two miles and then west 3 miles on gravel County Road 392, which crosses County Road 395 and becomes County Road 396.

The Worthwine Island Conservation Area, which extends from river mile 460 to 456, is not an island. The area was an island before the Corps of Engineers channelized the Missouri River. The Army Corps of Engineers acquired this area and has proposed cutting a chute through the existing dike and making the area into a wetland to mitigate the environmental impacts of river channelization. Journal entries from the Lewis and Clark Expedition mentioned an abundance of wildlife along the broad marshlands of the heavy bottomland timber near the Missouri River. The area was purchased from the Indians by the U.S. government in 1836 as part of the Platte Purchase. Now the area is managed for game and nongame wildlife species and is available to the public for camping, hunting, fishing, frogging, and hiking.

Smith Creek enters on river right at river mile 457.5.

The **Sunbridge Hills Conservation Area** begins on river left at river mile 453.3 and extends to river mile 452.3. This area is undeveloped except for a gravel parking lot and a trail through 190 acres of fields and forested areas of redbuds, maples and oaks. The Lewis and Clark expedition passed here on July 8, 1804, and again on September 11, 1806, to hunt and camp.

Near river mile 453, on river right, where the river is heading almost due east, you'll find a high sandbar that makes a good campsite with plenty of driftwood for those cool autumn evenings. This spot is at the 3.5-mile mark on the air traffic approach to the Rosencrans Memorial Airport, but it is also the best camp spot between there and St. Joseph. **Take out** at the **French Bottoms Boat Ramp** on river left at river mile 452. You can't see it from the river, but if you walk up the boat ramp you will see the St. Jo Frontier Casino.

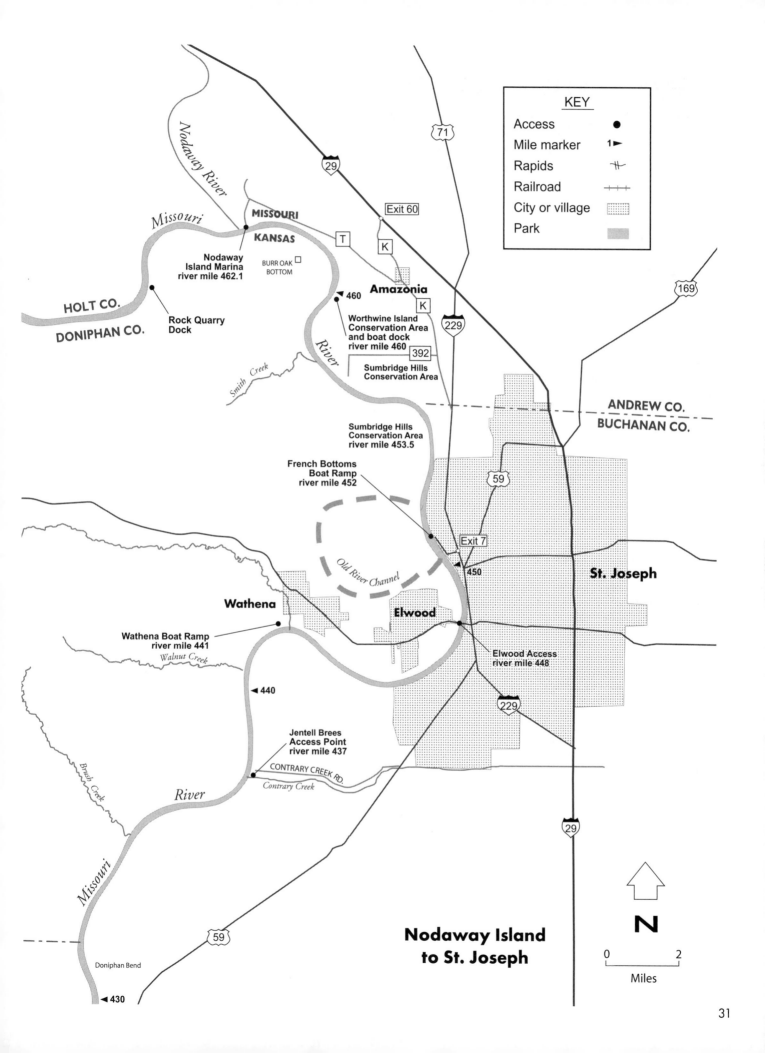

KEY

Access	●
Mile marker	1▶
Rapids	⊬
Railroad	+++
City or village	
Park	

Nodaway River

Missouri River

HOLT CO.

DONIPHAN CO.

MISSOURI
KANSAS

Nodaway Island Marina
river mile 462.1

Rock Quarry Dock

BURR OAK BOTTOM

Smith Creek

River

460

Amazonia

Worthwine Island Conservation Area and boat dock
river mile 460

392

Sumbridge Hills Conservation Area

Sumbridge Hills Conservation Area
river mile 453.5

French Bottoms Boat Ramp
river mile 452

Old River Channel

ANDREW CO.
BUCHANAN CO.

Exit 60

T

K

K

71

29

229

169

59

Exit 7

450

St. Joseph

Wathena

Elwood

Wathena Boat Ramp
river mile 441

Walnut Creek

440

Elwood Access
river mile 448

Brush Creek

River

Jentell Brees Access Point
river mile 437

CONTRARY CREEK RD.

Contrary Creek

229

Missouri

59

Doniphan Bend

430

29

Nodaway Island
to St. Joseph

N

0   2
Miles

MISSOURI RIVER:
ST. JOSEPH TO ATCHISON

29 miles, intermediate access available, Class I-II difficulty
French Bottoms in St. Joseph at river mile 452 to Atchison at river mile 423

The Pony Express route, which carried mail 2,000 miles to Sacramento, California, in 10 days, started in St. Joseph. Their posters and handbills read, "Wanted: Young skinny wiry fellows, not over 18. Orphans preferred. Wages $25 per week. Apply Central Overland Express." Although this add is thought, by some historians, to be a phony, it may not have been far from the truth. Little wonder that the Pony Express operated for only two years, from 1860 to 1861 and the company employed only 120 riders.

Directly across the river is Elwood, Kansas. It was established in 1856 and first called Roseport. Emigrants were dropped off at this once-bustling town and outfitted for their long march to Oregon and California. In 1859, after Abraham Lincoln made a speech in Elwood, he remarked, "If I went west, I think I would go to Kansas."

Also in 1859, construction of the first railway west of the Missouri was started here. The first locomotive, the Albany, was brought across on a ferry and pulled up the banks by hand in 1860. Also that year, Elwood was the first station of the Pony Express and laid the first paved road in Kansas. In 1866, the ferry across the river ran about every 15 minutes and cost 25 cents. Elwood's future was dashed as the river undermined the banks and washed away most of the town.

Put in at the **French Bottoms Boat Ramp**. This access is upstream of the St. Joseph downtown area and about one mile from I-229. Take exit 7 from I-229 onto Highland Avenue. Turn west and follow the signs to the St. Jo Frontier Casino. The boat ramp is right next to the casino parking lot, so you won't have far to walk for a good meal or, if you like, to win or lose a few greenbacks. The 70-mile **round-trip shuttle** route, from St. Jo to Atchison and back, returns to I-229, then goes south about 2 miles to the exit for U.S. Highway 36, west on U.S. Highway 36 across the Missouri River and about 18 miles to U.S. Highway 7, south on U.S. Highway 7 to Main Street in Atchison, and then east to the river. Follow the river (River Road) north to Independence Park and the boat ramp.

After you put in, move your vehicle to a good parking area around the edge of the lot. At river mile 449, on river left, the Spirit of St. Joseph Show Boat has a landing that is more suitable for motorboats than canoes and kayaks, but it is possible to scramble up the rip-rap banks if you really want to.

Near river mile 448 you will pass under a railroad bridge and then under the US 36 Bridge.

The **Elwood access** at river mile 448 is across the river from St. Joseph and just downstream of the southwest side of the **Pony Express Bridge** on State Highway 36. Elwood has a boat ramp and maintains a portable toilet for us river folk. On river left, the south bank, you will pass by numerous commercial docks between river mile 447.5 and 445.5. Downstream of river mile 445, the **Flathead Fishing Club** maintains a boat ramp and the **St. Joseph Outboard Motor and Yacht Club** has another small

ramp at river mile 444. Once out of town, opportunities for camping are more common. If you are looking for a campsite, areas near tributaries, such as Peters Creek near river mile 444 on river right, are worth checking out. The **Wathena Boat Ramp** is at river mile 441 on river right. There is a decent sandbar on river right, just across the river from the Jentell Brees Access.

Jentell Brees Access is at river mile 437.2. South of St. Joseph, off U.S. Highway 59, exit on Contrary Creek Road, and then follow this west (right) to the access. On the morning of July 6, 1804, Sergeant Floyd, a member of Lewis and Clark's Corps of Discovery, made note of a "Jentell Brees from the southwest." This is the approximate location of that July 6, 1804, campsite.

At river mile 433, the Cloverdale Drain enters on river left.

The **Benedictine Bottoms Wildlife Area** extends from river mile 428 to 424, along river right. The 2,112-acre wildlife area is entirely within the floodplain of the river and is managed to promote hunting and wildlife. The habitats include 550 acres of native grasses and 450 acres of wetlands, plus new plantings of timber. The area is only open to the public from April 1 through September 30. From October 1 to March 31, a special access/hunting permit is required. These permits are drawn by a KDWP lottery. Applications are available in June and need to be submitted by early July. Except along the river, camping is not permitted within the wildlife area.

From about river miles 427 to 425, numerous wing dams present opportunities for fishing and camping along the inside of the bend. Near river mile 424, Independence Creek enters on river right. As you approach Atchison, watch for the access about a half mile above the bridges.

You will find numerous docks on river right as you enter the **Atchison** area. **Take out** at the **Atchison Parks Boat Ramp and Dock** at river mile 423, a half mile upstream of the U.S. 59/Highway-7 bridge. Near the ramp and docks, you can enjoy a picnic area, drinking fountains, and a public shower house. The downtown area and restaurants are a short walk to the south.

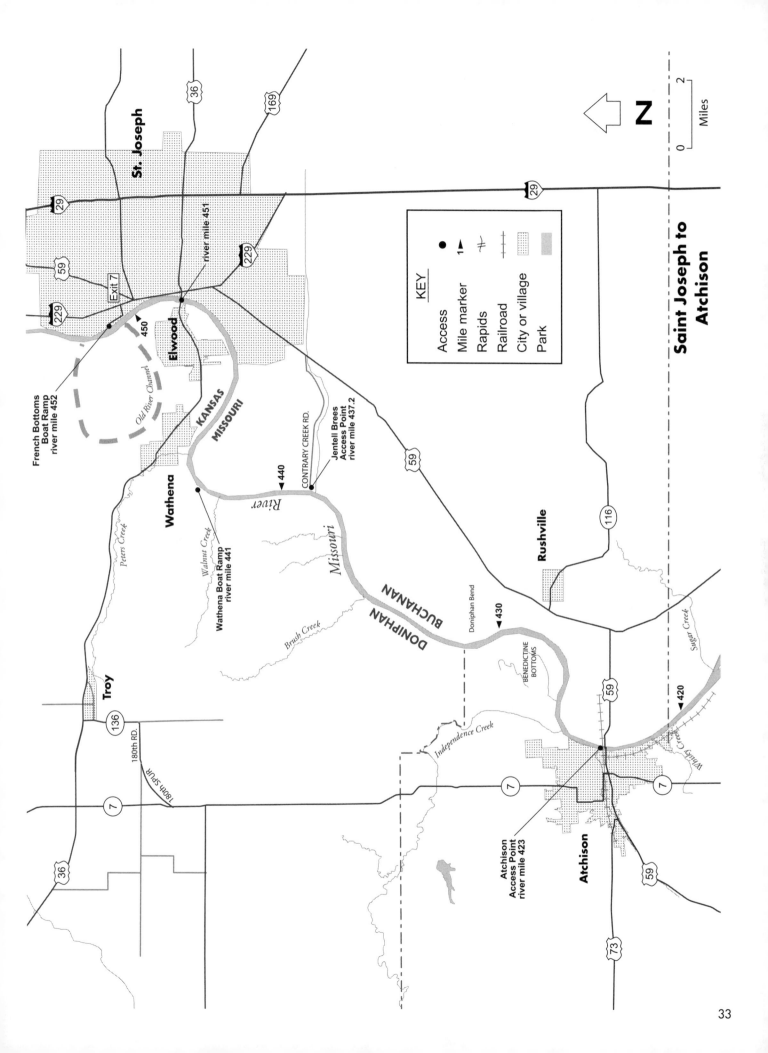

St. Joseph

river mile 451

Exit 7

French Bottoms
Boat Ramp
river mile 452

450

Old River Channel

Elwood

KANSAS
MISSOURI

Wathena

CONTRARY CREEK RD.

Jentell Brees
Access Point
river mile 437.2

440

Peters Creek

Walnut Creek

Wathena Boat Ramp
river mile 441

Missouri

River

Brush Creek

DONIPHAN
BUCHANAN

Doniphan Bend

430

Rushville

BENEDICTINE
BOTTOMS

Troy

180th RD.

180th SPUR

Independence Creek

Atchison
Access Point
river mile 423

Atchison

Whisky Creek

420

Sugar Creek

KEY

● Access
▲ Mile marker
╫ Rapids
┼┼ Railroad
▓ City or village
█ Park

Saint Joseph to
Atchison

N

0   2
Miles

MISSOURI RIVER: ATCHISON TO LEAVENWORTH
25 miles, intermediate access available, Class I-II difficulty
Atchison at river mile 423 to Leavenworth at river mile 398

The boat ramp is close to fine restaurants and within walking distance of the historic downtown area, good shopping, and museums. The location of the town, founded in 1854, was picked by Missouri Senator David R. Atchison, with the intent of making it a gateway for proslavery forces to take control of the new Kansas Territories.

Put in is at the **Atchison Parks Boat Ramp and Dock**. To drive there, take State Highway 7 to Main Street, then go east to the river. Follow the river (River Road) north to Independence Park and the boat ramp. The 50-mile **round-trip shuttle route**, from Atchison to Leavenworth, takes you south on U.S. Highway 73 (Highway 7). In Leavenworth, U.S. 73/K-7 becomes Metropolitan and then turns right at North 4th Street. Three blocks south on 4th Street, turn left to take Dakota Street east to the river, where you will find the **Leavenworth Boat Ramp** in **Riverfront Park**.

Just north of the **put-in** at **Independence Park** are water, restrooms, outdoor showers (in the stone building), and picnic tables. Camping is not allowed.

The Missouri River looking south from Weston Bend State Park (photo courtesy of the Weston Chamber of Commerce and Pimento Creative Partners)

As you leave town, Whiskey Creek enters on river right near river mile 421. Sugar Creek enters on river left near river mile 418. Walnut Creek enters on river right at river mile 417. Short Creek, the drainage from Bean Lake, enters on river left near river mile 415. Power lines mark river mile 410.5. Near river mile 407, 407.5, and 406, large sandbars at the inside of the meanders make good campsites. Salt Creek enters from river right near river mile 406. The last of these good sandbars is at river mile 403, directly across from Bear Creek and Weston Bend State Park.

Weston Bend State Park is at river mile 403. This is a very good place to stretch your legs and then some. The **access** is at Bear Creek in Weston Bend State Park. There are no boat ramps or facilities at the river, but historic 1837 Weston is worth the stop. Hike about 200 yards to the top of the bluff, cross the tracks, and follow Bluff Road north a mile or so into town. You will have your choice of over 60 shops, seven restaurants, a real winery, an underground pub at a real brewery, eight B&Bs, and a renovated 1846 hotel. Weston is one of Missouri's finest little tourist towns. Weston Bend State Park has hiking trails with great views of the river. There are secluded picnic sites, a playground, and an open shelter ([816] 640-5443). The park's campground features basic and electric campsites, modern restrooms, hot showers, and laundry facilities.

From Weston, the run down to **Leavenworth** is short, but very beautiful. The first good campsite is directly across the river from Weston. Then there is a series of very large sandbars on the inside of the bend near river mile 402. Between river miles 403 and 402, the Army Corps of Engineers owns a 12-acre tract of land along river left that will someday be developed into a shallow-water habitat area to mitigate the impacts of river channelization. Bee Creek enters near mile 401 on river left.

Take out at the **Leavenworth Boat Ramp**, on river right, immediately downstream of the State Highway 92 bridge, at river mile 397.5. The boat ramp is located on Dakota Street, 0.3 mile east of Highway 7. The park includes a full-service campground ([913] 682-6398). You can take out there, camp, or just clean up and then walk a few blocks into the downtown area.

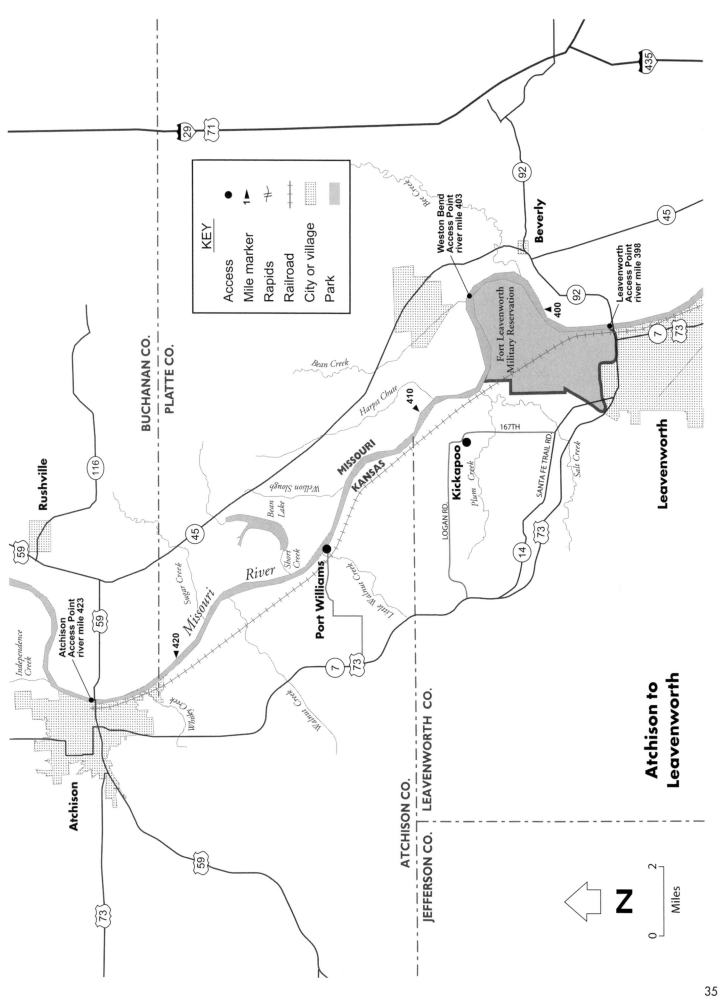

KEY

- ● Access
- 1▲ Mile marker
- ≠ Rapids
- ┼┼┼ Railroad
- ▦ City or village
- ▨ Park

Weston Bend Access Point river mile 403

Leavenworth Access Point river mile 398

Beverly

Fort Leavenworth Military Reservation

▲ 400

Bee Creek

Bean Creek

Harpst Chute

▲ 410

167TH

Kickapoo

Plum Creek

LOGAN RD.

SANTA FE TRAIL RD.

Salt Creek

Leavenworth

BUCHANAN CO.

PLATTE CO.

Rushville

MISSOURI

KANSAS

Wilson Slough

Bean Lake

Sugar Creek

Short Creek

Port Williams

Little Walnut Creek

River

Missouri

▲ 420

Whiskey Creek

Walnut Creek

Atchison Access Point river mile 423

Independence Creek

Atchison

ATCHISON CO.

LEAVENWORTH CO.

JEFFERSON CO.

LEAVENWORTH CO.

Atchison to Leavenworth

N

0 — 2 Miles

MISSOURI RIVER: LEAVENWORTH TO KAW POINT

31 miles, intermediate access available, Class I-II difficulty
Leavenworth at river mile 398 to Kaw Point in Kansas City, Kansas, at river mile 367

The **put-in** is at the **Leavenworth Boat Ramp** in **Riverfront Park**. It is located 0.3 mile east of State Highway 7, on Dakota Street. The 63-mile **round-trip shuttle** route, from Leavenworth to Kaw Point and back, goes south on Highway 7 about 16 miles to I-70, then east on I-70 to Exit 423. Follow the signs to Fairfax Trafficway. As you come to the bottom of the bridge, turn east (right) into the first parking lot and follow the signs to the access.

The put-in at Riverfront Park has a full-service campground ([913] 682-6398). This river town was named after Fort Leavenworth. During the territorial days, Leavenworth surpassed all other Kansas cities in trade. Walking the nearby downtown area provides an enjoyable glance into the past and/or a lot of good food. While you are there, stop by the U.S. Coast Guard Facilities. They are located about a half mile south of the boat ramp at 50 Dakota Street ([913]-758-0254).

Parkville, Missouri, is only about five miles downstream, river left, but if you are looking for a good spot to camp, you'll find plenty of medium-sized sandbars for the first five miles along the inside of the bends. The confluence of the Platte River (aka Little Platte River) is near river mile 391.5 on river left. If you are looking for some respite from the wind, try paddling up the Platte. Near river mile 386.6 you will see the first of three commercial barge docks on river right and another one on river left, near river mile 385 at the confluence with Ellis Branch. Power lines mark river mile 384 and the I-435 bridge comes shortly afterward, at river mile 383.5. Conner Creek and Brush Creek enter on river right and left respectively at river mile 383.

At river mile 377, river left, **Parkville** is a very good place to visit. The downtown area, with all of its amenities, is next to the river. You can pull in at **English Landing Park** (open from 5:00 A.M. to midnight). The Parkville **boat ramp** is at English Landing Park, located one block south of historic downtown Parkville. This beautifully rustic downtown area is well known for its excellent restaurants, shops, and city market. Your choice for sandbar camping is slim along this section. Barge docks begin near river mile 376 as you begin to enter the Kansas City area. The first bridge, I-635, is at river mile 374. A mile and a half downstream is the U.S. Highway 69/169 bridge. Further downstream, on river right, is the Argosy Casino. Line Creek enters from river left at river mile 372. As the river makes its turn to the southwest, move to river right. Even though you will want to watch airplanes coming and going from Kansas City Downtown Airport, you must **watch for the confluence with the Kansas River** entering river right.

You must turn upstream on the Kansas River to get to **Kaw Point**. **Take out** on river right, as you paddle up the Kansas River. It is approximately 200 yards up the Kansas River, river right.

Kaw Point is in Kansas City, Kansas, at river mile 367. Kaw Point is the historic campsite of the Lewis and Clark expedition. From here, the entire Kansas City area is at your fingertips.

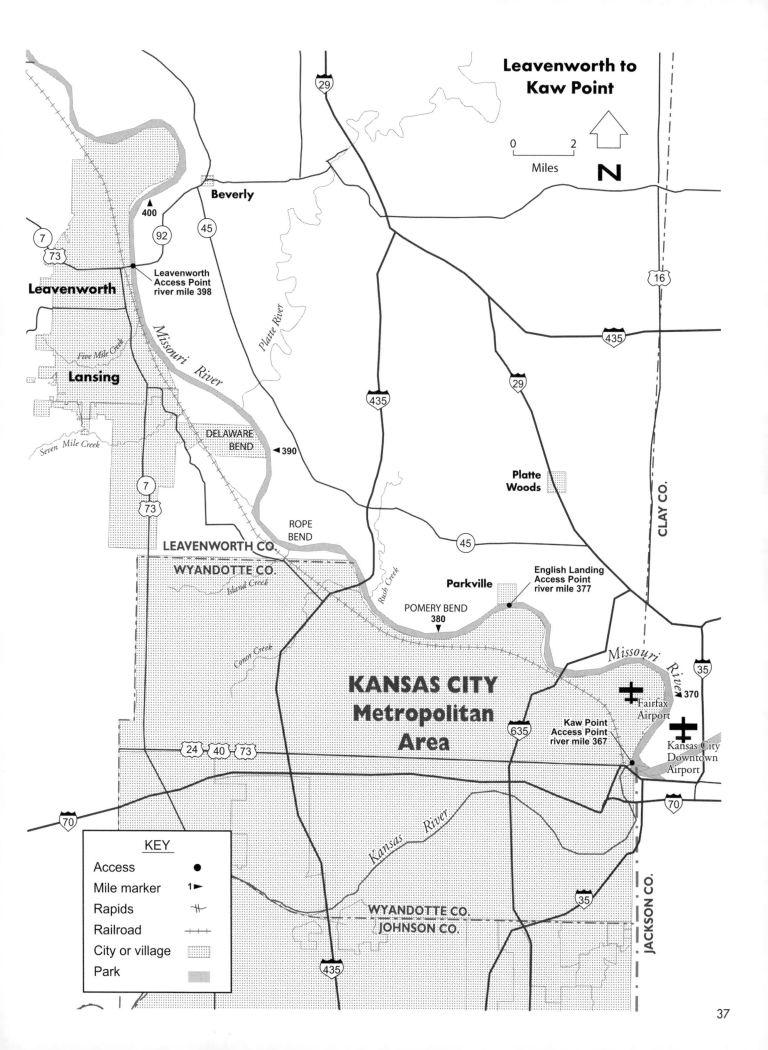

0   2
Miles
N

Beverly

▲ 400

92

45

7

73

Leavenworth

Leavenworth
Access Point
river mile 398

Missouri River

Five Mile Creek

Lansing

Seven Mile Creek

Platte River

29

16

435

29

**DELAWARE
BEND**

◄ 390

**Platte
Woods**

7

73

ROPE
BEND

45

LEAVENWORTH CO.

WYANDOTTE CO.

Island Creek

Rush Creek

Parkville

English Landing
Access Point
river mile 377

POMERY BEND
380
▼

Conor Creek

**KANSAS CITY
Metropolitan
Area**

Missouri River

◄ 370

**Fairfax
Airport**

35

24 40 73

635

Kaw Point
Access Point
river mile 367

**Kansas City
Downtown
Airport**

70

CLAY CO.

70

Kansas River

35

435

WYANDOTTE CO.
JOHNSON CO.

JACKSON CO.

KEY

Access	●
Mile marker	1▶
Rapids	╫
Railroad	+++
City or village	▒
Park	▓

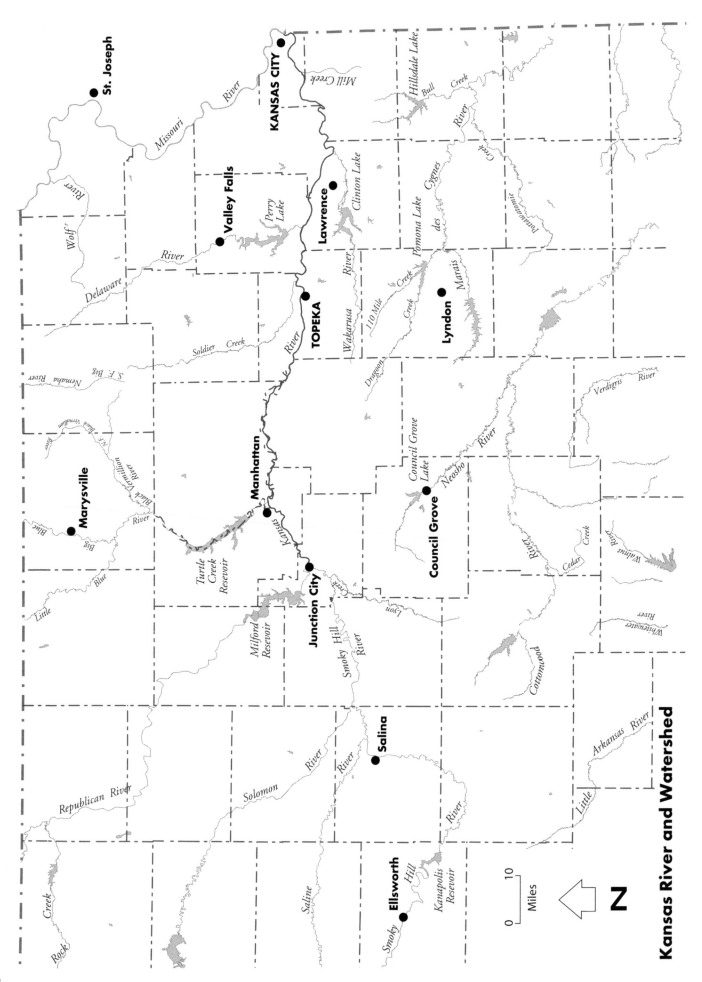

Kansas River and Watershed

N

Miles
0 10

St. Joseph

KANSAS CITY

Missouri River

Mill Creek

Hillsdale Lake

Bull Creek

Valley Falls

Lawrence

Clinton Lake

Cygnes River

des

Pomona Lake

Perry Lake

Wolf River

River

Delaware

TOPEKA

Soldier Creek

Wakarusa River

110 Mile Creek

Dragoon Creek

Marais

Lyndon

Pottawatomie

River

S. F. Big Nemaha River

Nemaha River

Verdigris River

Manhattan

N.F. Black Vermillion River

Black Vermillion River

Council Grove Lake

Council Grove

Neosho River

Marysville

Big Blue River

Turtle Creek Resevoir

Kansas River

River

Cedar Creek

Walnut River

Milford Resevoir

Junction City

Creek

Lyon Creek

Cottonwood

Blue

Little

Republican River

River

River

Smoky Hill River

Salina

Whitewater River

Arkansas River

Solomon River

Saline River

Little

Ellsworth

Smoky Hill River

Kanapolis Resevoir

Rock Creek

38

KANSAS RIVER AND WATERSHED

Fed by the headwaters of western Kansas, eastern Colorado, and southern Nebraska, the Kansas River is formed at the confluence of the Republican and Smoky Hill Rivers in Junction City. Other rivers that drain into the Kansas River (aka "The Kaw") include the Solomon, Saline, Delaware, Blue, and Wakarusa. In all, the Kaw drains over 60,000 square miles and carries an average of 4.75 million acre-feet of water per year. The Kansas River's land area makes up roughly a seventh of the Missouri River's entire watershed. Including its longest tributary, the Smoky Hill River, the Kansas River is 710 miles long and ranks as the 75th-longest river in the world. On its 170.5-mile journey to the Missouri River, the Kaw has a gradient of almost two feet per mile as it meanders past the majestic Flint Hills, across wide plains, and then into the limestone hills of eastern Kansas.

French mapmakers named the river "Konza" after some of the indigenous people who lived here. Historic references suggest that the Native American word "Konza" meant "wind," "wind people," or "people of the south wind." Over the years, it has had many spellings and pronunciations. One derivation is the name "Kansas," after which the river and then the state were named. The French shortened "Konza" to "Kaw," a name that is still used by locals in reference to the river and the valley.

The entire river is rated as Class I difficulty. Those who paddle the Kaw for the first time are surprised by the paradox of its size, wild beauty, and gentle nature. The Kaw is shallow, sandy-bottomed, and blessed with big sandbars and islands that make this unique river a delight for paddlers, campers, and beachcombers delight. Though gentle and only mildly turbid most of the time, the Kaw can rise and increase in speed and turbidity very quickly after a hard rain upstream.

In a state where water is rare, it is no accident that most of the state's major cities, including Junction City, Manhattan, Topeka, Lawrence, and Kansas City, and roughly half of the state's population sit on the banks of the Kansas River.

Depending on the flow, the river speed ranges from near zero to about three miles per hour. At low flows, you will need all of your river-reading skills to stay in the main channel. At higher flows, the river becomes one large channel and you can just "go with the flow."

If you wanted to "get away from it all," this is where you would go. Since the entire length of the Kansas River and its banks are held in trust for the people, you can camp and hike anywhere below the normal high-water mark. Sandbars and islands make great spots for lunch, fishing, and overnight camps. Fossil and artifact hunting is good. Bison bones are common along the entire river and, between Lawrence and Kansas City, mastodon bones are still found in the sand and imbedded in the riverbanks. Overall, you will see less of man's mark than you might imagine.

There are two low-head dams in the Topeka area and one in Kansas City. Do not attempt to run these dams—the hydraulic formed at the bottom can be fatal.

Because the river is so wide, wind can be an important factor. A 20- to 25-mile-per-hour breeze can push you upstream or pin you against the shore. (See "Wind" under the section on "River Safety" in this book to learn about paddling strategies in windy conditions.) The upper reaches of the river are more protected from the winds than the wider reaches farther downstream. When choosing the kind of boat to take on the river, consider a kayak or low-profile canoe with a strong paddling partner in the bow.

THE KANSAS RIVER WATERSHED WITHIN CENTRAL AND EASTERN KANSAS

Wildlife is plentiful in and along the water. The river is home to many native bird species and is on the migratory flyway for many others, including the bald eagle. The endangered least tern is native to the larger and higher sandbars and islands. It nests on open beach areas that are devoid of vegetation in late May through June. Please avoid hiking and camping on these high, bare, sandy areas during the nesting season.

While on the river, the paddler's immediate view is dominated by a riparian forest of cottonwood, sycamore, maples, willows, and elms. On higher ground, you will find walnut, hickory, and green ash. It is easy to spot bald eagles, osprey, owls, mergansers, beavers, otters, bobcats, foxes, white-tailed deer, coyotes, and many other animals.

Well known for its big channel cats and flatheads, the Kaw is home to at least 60 species of fish. Drop your line in the deep holes next to the bank for the big cats or go for other sport fish by casting toward overhanging banks and old logs.

The Kaw has an interesting but short geological history that dates back only to the last ice age. The Kansan Glacier piled up rock and soil along its edge as it pushed south. When the glacier began to melt, temporary lakes formed. When the dam broke, the flood cut a deep valley along the southern edge of the glacier and the river settled into its present location.

The distant views along the upper part of the river are dominated by flat to gently rolling prairie landscapes, changing to hillier country as you approach the Flint Hills near Manhattan, then back to flat to gently rolling prairie, and finally to hills and limestone bluffs and hardwood forests approaching Kansas City.

The artifacts of human history can be seen throughout the valley, but are rarely visible from the river. Native Americans fished and hunted here. The Spanish claimed the area but, in 1803, they sold it with the Louisiana Purchase. By the 1830s, the Native Americans were being forcibly displaced. The four oldest settlements in the state—Wyandotte (now Kansas City), Lawrence, Lecompton, and Topeka—are all along the banks of the Kaw. Once European settlers moved in, they began plowing under the native prairie, often to the very edge of the streams, resulting in the pollution of many clear prairie streams. By the end of the 1960s, 90 percent of the watershed had been dammed to control flooding and to provide more water for irrigation, indus-

try, municipalities—even to support commercial navigation on the Missouri River.

Between 1854 and 1866, as many as 34 steamboats paddled up the Kaw; one made it all the way to Fort Riley. But shallow water and sandbars eventually made riverboat traffic unprofitable.

In the early 1990s, local citizens organized a group called "Friends of the Kaw" (FOK) to oppose the dredging of a previously undredged reach of the Kansas between Lecompton and Lawrence. Since that time, they have organized to protect the entire watershed and to promote recreational use of the river. In 2003, FOK teamed up with the city of St. George, the Green Team from Westar Energy, and KDWP to build the first new river access on the river in many years. Since then, realizing the values of having a 170-mile recreational corridor in their own backyards, many communities have teamed up with FOK and state and federal agencies to construct new boat ramps along the river.

NARRATIVE ON THE KANSAS RIVER

Due to the length and the similarities of adjacent river segments, for the sake of economy of space, most of the color and editorial comments are written into the description of the watershed rather than into each river segment.

Kansas River looking upstream towards the confluence with the Delaware (photo by Craig Thompson)

Surfing the Kansas River at Kaw Point. Top to bottom: Dave Irwin, Kate O' Connel and Steve Matthys, Monty McCain and James Smith (photos by Pat O'Connel)

KANSAS RIVER: JUNCTION CITY TO OGDEN
7 miles, Class I difficulty
Junction City at river mile 170.5 to the Ogden Access at river mile 163.5

The upper reach of the Kaw is magnificent. The Flint Hills begin to rise along the southern horizon, while the northern prairies lay out in the distance. The river is comparatively narrow and more intimate.

This is an easy, half-day float. Your struggle doesn't start until you try to get off the river below the Ogden Bridge. For that reason, paddlers often prefer to combine this section with the Ogden to Manhattan section to make either a long, high-water float or a comfortable two-day trip. The best levels are around 1,500 CFS and the **minimum recommended flow** for a good time is 1,100. The best **gauging station** for the Kansas River is at Fort Riley, KS. The average **gradient** for this segment is 2.7 feet per mile

Canoe rentals are available at Tuttle Creek State Park, located a few miles north of Manhattan below Tuttle Creek Lake Dam ([785] 539-7941). You will have to pay a park fee to enter the park prior to picking up your boats. Kansas State University in Manhattan ([785] 532-6980 or [785] 532-6894) rents canoes to students and faculty who have an ID. The Fort Riley Outdoor Recreation Center, on Fort Riley Military Reservation, in Building 9011 ([785] 239-6368 or [785] 239-2364), rents to people with a military ID.

Put in at **Junction City** at the east end of Grant Avenue Park at river mile 170. From I-70, take exit 296 onto Washington Street and go 2.5 miles north on Washington to Grant Avenue. Go two miles east on Grant Avenue to the small park in the median between the two sides of Grant Avenue, just before it crosses the Republican River and you get to the gates at Fort Riley. If you plan to leave your car overnight, you might want to move it to an area that has better security. The 27-mile **round-trip shuttle** route takes you back to I-70, then east to State Highway 18, and then northeast about 3 miles to the southeast edge of where Highway 18 crosses over the river. Construction is underway to upgrade Highway 18 to a four-lane road. A new boat ramp is planned for this site when the new bridge is completed. For now, this access is steep (take a rope), overgrown, and peppered with poison ivy.

The put-in at Junction City is on the Republican River, about 100 yards upstream from the confluence with the Smoky Hill River. The joining of these two rivers forms the Kansas River ("The Kaw"). A new boat ramp is in the work for this site within the next year or two; for now just carry your boats down between the two bridges.

The spillway for Milford Lake is less than 10 miles upstream on the Republican River. A release from the lake can raise or lower the river very quickly. At all but higher levels, the river is a series of sandbars and small islands. Although the entire river channel may be 300 feet wide, water does not usually occupy more than a fraction of this sandy channel. If the river is a little bit low and if you have trouble following the main channel as it migrates from one side of the river to another, you might want to reread the special tips for sandy rivers in the introduction of this guide. At river mile 169 you will cross under Henry Road. When the river is high, an island forms upstream of the bridge. The Well House sandbar near mile 166 makes an excellent camp.

Take out downstream of the **Highway 18 bridge**. This is a very difficult access. The best place to try to scramble up the steep banks is about 100 feet or so downstream of the bridge. Get out wherever you can get a foothold on the steep banks on river right (south side), then bushwhack through the poison ivy and other brush to your vehicle. The surrounding area is private property, so please stay on the highway right-of-way.

The author's family launched below Milford Lake on the Republican River, then floated past Junction City and on to the Kaw for a family-reunion weekend.

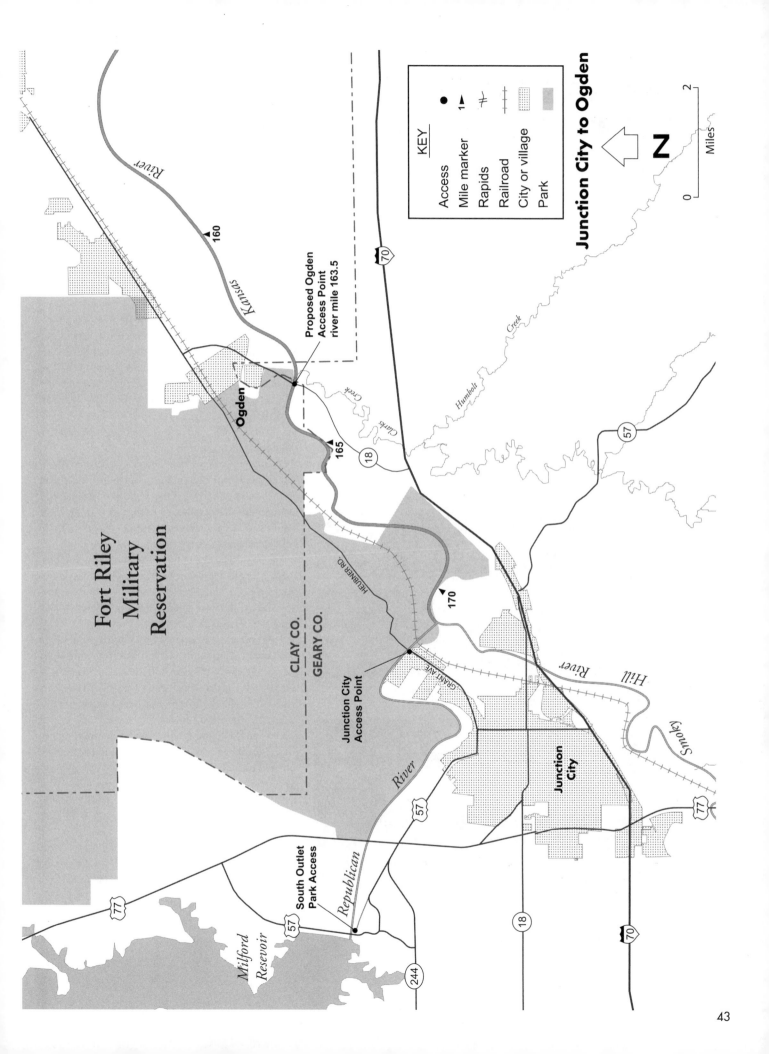

KEY

Access
Mile marker
Rapids
Railroad
City or village
Park

Junction City to Ogden

N

Miles
0   2

160

Proposed Ogden
Access Point
river mile 163.5

70

Creek

Ogden

165

Humbolt

18

Clarks Creek

57

Fort Riley
Military
Reservation

CLAY CO.
GEARY CO.

170

HUEBNER RD.

Junction City
Access Point

GRANT AVE.

Kansas

River

Smoky

Hill River

River

Republican

57

Junction
City

18

77

South Outlet
Park Access

Milford
Resevoir

77

57

244

70

KANSAS RIVER: OGDEN TO MANHATTAN

14.2 miles, Class I difficulty
Ogden Access at river mile 163.5 to Manhattan Boat Ramp at river mile 149.3

The town of Ogden was named in honor of Major E.A. Ogden, who was commissioned to select a site and oversee the construction of a military post (Fort Riley) in the geographic center of the United States in 1853.

It is slightly easier to put in at the Ogden Access than to take out, but the steep terrain and poison ivy convince many paddlers either to wear long pants to avoid the rash or to launch in Junction City and either have a very long day on the river or make it an overnighter.

Canoe rentals are available at Tuttle Creek State Park, located below Tuttle Creek Lake Dam, ([785] 539-7941). The best levels are around 1,500 CFS and the **minimum recommended flow** for a good time is 1,100. The best **gauging station** for the Kansas River is at Fort Riley, Kansas. The average **gradient** for this river segment is 1.5 feet per mile.

Put in at **Ogden** at the southeast edge of where State Highway 18 crosses over the river. This is anoth-

Ariel and Sophia Moore with mom, taking it easy on the Kansas River near Ogden.

The Flint Hills from the Kansas River (photo by Craig Thompson)

er steep and overgrown access that is slated to receive a new boat ramp when the highway upgrade is completed. The 24-mile **round-trip shuttle** route, from Ogden to Manhattan and back, goes east 11.5 miles on Highway 18 to State Highway 177, then south about 400 yards on Highway 177 and across the Kansas River Bridge, and then right (west) at the first turn, onto McDowell Creek Road. Take the next right turn at the Kansas River Access sign to drive under the bridge. The boat ramp and parking area are under the bridge. If you intend to be on the river overnight, it is best to leave vehicles in the lighted mall parking lot across the river. Vehicles left at the Ogden Access should be parked on the small dirt road southeast of the bridge (not on the shoulder of the highway).

This 13.2-mile segment between Ogden and Manhattan is especially beautiful, with the Flint Hills rising on the southeast horizon. One of the most remote segments of the Kaw, it moves far enough away from cities, big roads, and the almost ever-present railroad tracks to feel like wilderness. Large sandbars and good campsites are the norm. The first of these is at the Odgen Sandbar, about 1.5 miles into your float at the river's first meander. In general, look for the best places to camp at the river bends. Another good one is the Eureka Lake Sandbar, near river mile 156.

As you come around that bend at river mile 156 and start heading southeast, you will be getting your first good view of the **Konza Prairie**. The Konza is a research area that is a small part of the Flint Hills, the largest contiguous native prairie in the country. This is a particularly beautiful sight in the evening as the sun sets on the Kansas prairie. Your next campground is the Moehlman Sandbar, near river mile 153.5. The remaining sandbars between there and Manhattan are very small and too low to make safe camps, unless you are willing to risk a fast retreat in the middle of the night. There is a sand plant at river mile 152 that could be used in an emergency since the banks are high, but it isn't camper-friendly. Wildcat Creek enters near river mile 150.5 on river left. **Take out** at the **Manhattan Boat Ramp**, under the Highway 177 bridge on river right.

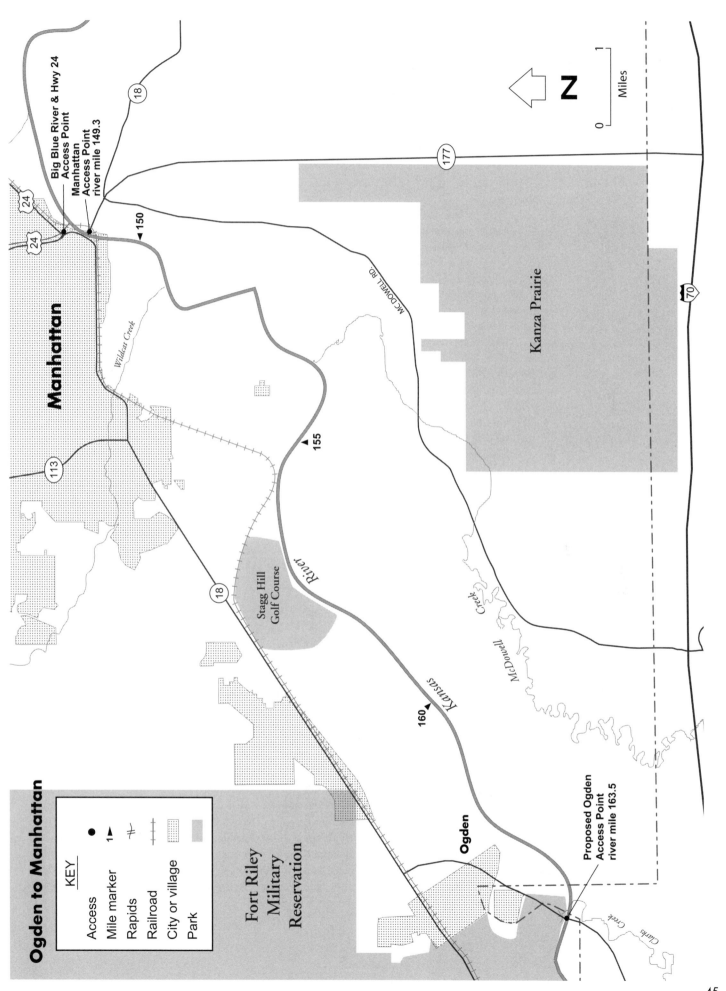

Ogden to Manhattan

KEY

- ● Access
- ▲1 Mile marker
- ≠ Rapids
- ┼┼┼┼ Railroad
- City or village
- Park

Big Blue River & Hwy 24 Access Point

Manhattan Access Point river mile 149.3

Manhattan

Wildcat Creek

Fort Riley Military Reservation

Stagg Hill Golf Course

Kanza Prairie

McDowell Creek

McDowell Rd.

Kansas River

Ogden

Proposed Ogden Access Point river mile 163.5

Clarks Creek

N

0   1

Miles

45

KANSAS RIVER: MANHATTAN TO ST. GEORGE

12 miles, one intermediate access available, Class I difficulty
Manhattan Boat Ramp at river mile 149.3 to St. George at river mile 137.3

Manhattan is home to Kansas State University. The old downtown area and Aggie Ville have interesting shops and good restaurants. A walking and biking trail parallels the Kansas River along the south side of town. In the woods south and west of this access, local mountain bikes have built an interesting course. You will launch on the Blue River, paddle downstream about a half mile, and then turn left at the Kansas River. Due to its proximity to Manhattan and its ideal length for a one-day float, this is one of the most popular runs on the river. As the river continues through the northern edge of the Flint Hills, the near scenery is that of a mostly wild and unmarked river, with a background of beautiful, rolling tallgrass prairie hills.

The float from Manhattan (river mile 149.3) to St. George (river mile 137.3) is sometimes combined with the 10.3-mile float from St. George to Wamego. The combined distance can be done in a single day, but most paddlers will prefer to do these segments as two separate day floats or as an overnighter. The recommended **minimum flow below Manhattan is 1,100 CFS**. You can get by with a little less if you are good at following the main channel. Use the USGS **gauging station** on the Kansas River at Fort Riley to check the flow at the put-in. Also check the gauging station at Wamego. The difference between these readings is, roughly, the amount of water that is coming down the Big Blue River from Tuttle Creek Reservoir. If the Kansas River is very low, you may prefer to launch on the Big Blue (see below) to get the additional water. The average **gradient** for this segment is 1.2 feet per mile.

Canoes and kayaks can be rented at Tuttle Creek State Park, located below Tuttle Creek Lake Dam ([785] 539-7941). Kansas State University also rents canoes, but a student or faculty ID is required ([785] 532-6980).

The **put-in** for this section of the river is at the **Manhattan Boat Ramp**, located under the south side of the State Highway 177 Bridge in Manhattan. There is plenty of room for parking, but if you leave a vehicle overnight, it is best to park in the lighted mall parking lot on the other side of the river. The 18-mile **round-trip shuttle** route, from Manhattan to St. George, runs north across the Kansas River Bridge and then right about a quarter mile to U.S. Highway 24 east. Go four miles east on U.S. 24 to Military Road. Turn right on Military Road and follow it four miles into St. George. Watch for the River Access sign on the right side of the road just before you enter the downtown area. The take-out is at the end of this road at Bogg's Landing.

From the put-in, it is only a 2-mile run down to the Big Blue River (river mile 147.5). The Big Blue drains Tuttle Creek and is controlled by the Corps of Engineers. Even during dry conditions, the Corps sometimes releases huge volumes of water to help float barges on the Missouri River. Expect to see a boost in flow and a widening of the channel below the confluence of these rivers.

Only 0.8 miles up the Big Blue is a nice boat ramp and a parking lot just downstream of the U.S. 24 bridge on the southwest side. The Big Blue/U.S. 24 access makes a good alternate put-in if the river above the confluence is too low. It also makes a good alternate take-out if the Big Blue is not running too fast. Check the release from Tuttle Creek ahead of time at the USGS gauging station on the Big Blue River near Manhattan.

Just below the mouth of the Big Blue River, there is a large sandbar that becomes an island at moderate flows. Over the next eight miles, the river rapidly transitions from one bend to another. As the river cuts its deep channels along the outside of these bends, it deposits giant sandbars on the inside of each curve. This close series of meanders makes the main channel easy to follow. Giant sandbars and perfect campsites are at every bend for the next 8 miles. The best two of these start at river miles 144 and 143 and are located on river left and river right, respectively. The former is a larger sandbar, but the latter may provide more evening shade. The boost in flow from the Big Blue River and the distinct channel make these miles go by very easily and the long views to the south show the Flint Hills as they continue to rise, though not quite so high as before.

As the river comes out of the last bend, near river mile 139, it passes Plum Creek and begins heading almost due east toward St. George. The **take-out** is at **Bogg's Landing**, just downstream of Black Jack Creek, at river mile 137.3. A sandbar sometimes blocks access to the ramp, so you may have to carry your boat a short distance to the ramp. This city park has picnic tables, good parking, a nice outhouse, and a boat ramp.

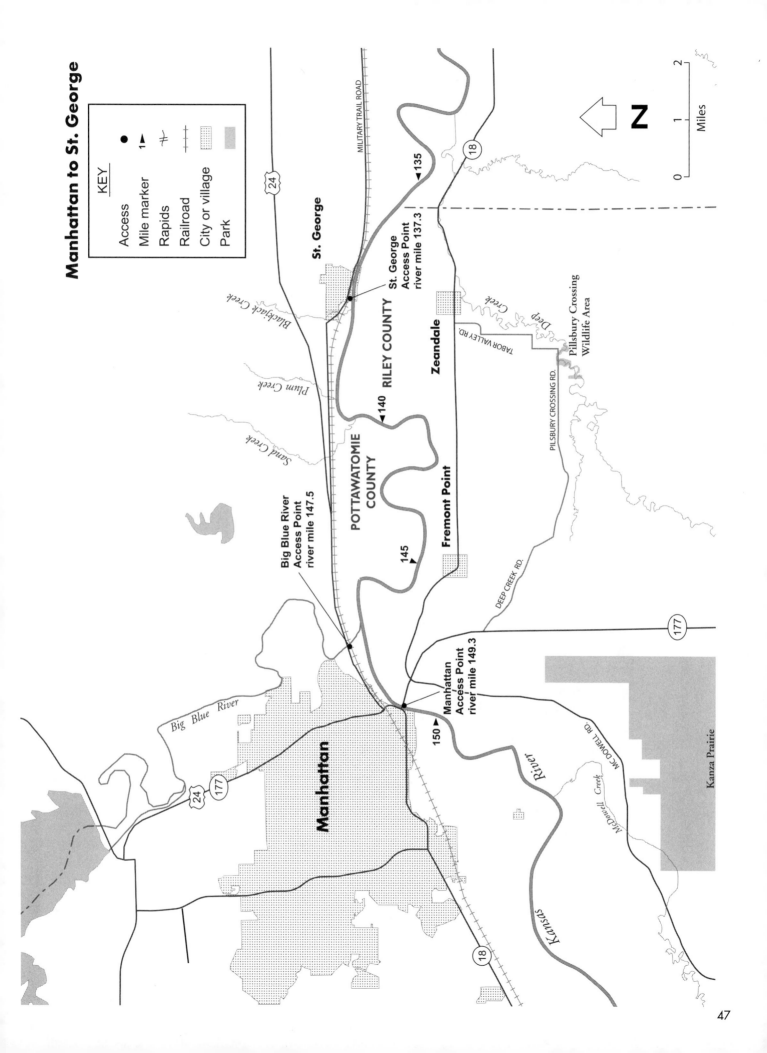

Manhattan to St. George

KEY

- ● Access
- ▲ Mile marker
- ‡ Rapids
- ┼┼┼ Railroad
- City or village
- Park

N

0 1 2
Miles

MILITARY TRAIL ROAD

St. George

▼135

St. George Access Point
river mile 137.3

24

Blackjack Creek

Plum Creek

Sand Creek

RILEY COUNTY

POTTAWATOMIE COUNTY

Zeandale

Deep Creek

TABOR VALLEY RD.

Pillsbury Crossing
Wildlife Area

18

▼140

Fremont Point

PILSBURY CROSSING RD.

▼145

Big Blue River
Access Point
river mile 147.5

DEEP CREEK RD.

Manhattan
Access Point
river mile 149.3

177

Manhattan

Big Blue River

24
177

150 ▶

Kansas River

18

McDowell Creek

MC DOWELL RD.

Kanza Prairie

KANSAS RIVER: ST. GEORGE TO WAMEGO

10.3 miles, Class I difficulty
St. George Access at river mile 137.3 to Wamego at river mile 127

The float from St. George, at river mile 137.3, to Wamego, at river mile 127, is often combined with the Manhattan to St. George section to make either a long day or a great multi-day trip.

The recommended **minimum flow below Manhattan is 1,100 CFS**. Use the USGS **gauging station** on the Kansas River at Wamego. The average **gradient** for this segment is 1.7 feet per mile. **Canoes and kayaks can be rented** at Tuttle Creek State Park, located below Tuttle Creek Lake Dam ([785] 539-7941). Kansas State University also rents canoes, but a student or faculty ID is required ([785] 532-6980).

Put in at **Bogg's Landing in St. George**. To get there from Manhattan, go east 4 miles on U.S. Highway 24 to Military Road. Continue 4 miles east on Military Road. The entrance to the park is on the right side of the road, as you enter the St. George downtown area. The 14-mile **round-trip shuttle** route takes you east on Military Trail Road to Lincoln Street (aka State Highway 99). Turn south (right) on Lincoln Street, then turn west (right) on Valley Road, then south (left) on Elm Street. The last I looked, Elm was not marked, but it is the first road west of Lincoln (not the alley). The access is under the Lincoln Street/Highway 99 bridge.

Once back in St. George, take a walk through the downtown area and check out the size of those trees. Wow! The park was named after Charlie Boggs, who was instrumental in the development of this beautiful river access park. Inspired and organized by Friends of the Kaw, Boggs Landing was the first of many new access points on the river, and it became the pattern for similar community efforts to build new river access points up and down the river and then throughout the state.

The river near St. George is a relatively straight and stable part of the river that begins a very slow bend to the southeast. Near river mile 134, the river begins a giant oxbow to the north and then it makes a series of two more bends in rapid succession. The river, through these bends, accelerates and scours the outside of each turn, cutting deep channels and depositing the eroded sand on the inside banks. Anywhere that a river morphologist would be tempted to talk about the instability of a river reach, paddlers will be equally tempted to talk about how easy it is to follow channels and to find great camping spots. Such is the case here. To make the river even more interesting, Deep Creek enters on river right, about halfway through the second meander. The mouth of Deep Creek is wide and makes an interesting diversion.

Once past these two quick meanders, good campsites become somewhat scarce all the way to Wamego. As the river nears Wamego, the landscape begins a very gradual transition from the hilly landscape of the Flint Hills into a flatter, broader floodplain. The broad floodplain has kept development along the river at bay. Neither tarmac nor railway approaches the river until mile 128, just before you enter Wamego. **Take out** on river left, under the **Lincoln Street/Highway 99 bridge**. A new boat ramp is planned for this location at this writing.

Carol Brown slaps another one on the barbie
(photo by Suzanne Murphy).

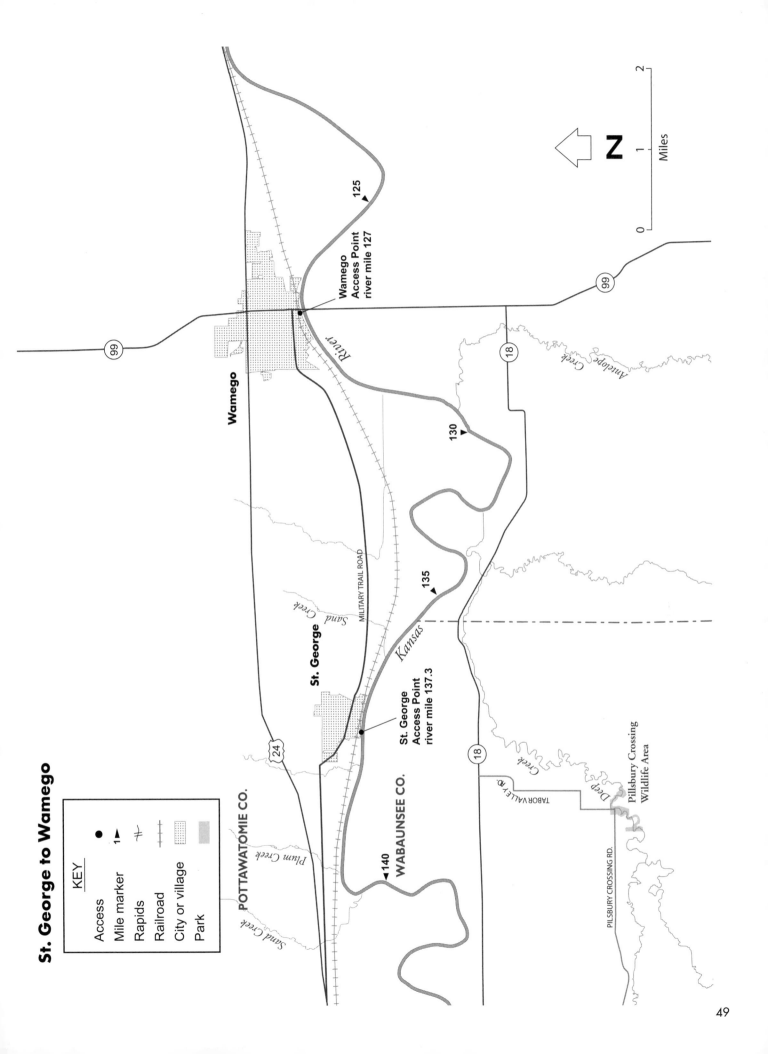

St. George to Wamego

KEY

- ● Access
- ▲ Mile marker
- ⊣⊢ Rapids
- ┼┼┼ Railroad
- ▦ City or village
- ▧ Park

Wamego Access Point river mile 127

St. George Access Point river mile 137.3

125

130

135

140

Wamego

St. George

River

Kansas

Sand Creek

Sand Creek

Plum Creek

Sand Creek

MILITARY TRAIL ROAD

Antelope Creek

Deep Creek

Pillsbury Crossing Wildlife Area

PILSBURY CROSSING RD.

TABOR VALLEY RD.

POTTAWATOMIE CO.

WABAUNSEE CO.

99

99

18

18

24

N

Miles

0 1 2

KANSAS RIVER: WAMEGO TO BELVUE

12 miles, intermediate access available, Class I difficulty
Highway 99 at river mile 127 to the Shoeman Bridge at river mile 118.5

The 12-mile float from Wamego, at river mile 127, to the Belvue Access, at river mile 115.5, is an easy, single-day float. It can easily be combined with either of the adjacent segments to create a multi-day trip. This part of the river is less-often traveled than the segments above it and, except near the confluence of Vermillion Creek, civilization has largely left this part of the river alone. If you are looking for a place to get away from it all and you have a strong back to carry your boat up a steep bank at the take-out, this is your spot.

The **minimum recommended flow for this segment is about 1,200 CFS** and the closest USGS **gauging station** is for the Kansas River at Wamego. The average **gradient** for this segment is 2.1 feet per mile. **Canoes and kayaks can be rented** at Tuttle Creek State Park, located below Tuttle Creek Lake Dam ([785] 539-7941). Kansas State University also rents canoes, but a student or faculty ID is required ([785] 532-6980).

To get to the **put-in** at the **Wamego Access** from I-70, go north on State Highway 99 (exit 328). After crossing the bridge into Wamego, take the first left turn (west) onto Valley Road. Go one block (past the alley) to Elm Street. Turn south (left) and park along the street so as not to block traffic for the neighbors. The access is under the north side of the Lincoln Street/Highway 99

Sophia Moore, Samantha Brown, and Nicole Sweet make good use of Kansas River sand (photo by Suzanne Murphy).

bridge. Do not confuse this with the private ramp that is just downstream of the bridge. A new boat ramp is planned, but not developed at this writing. The 21.6-mile **round-trip shuttle** route, from Wamego to the Belvue Access and back, goes north on Highway 99 less than a mile to U.S. Highway 24, then east about 7 miles past the town of Belvue and about a mile and a half to Schoeman Road, and then south on Schoeman Road to the north edge of the Schoeman Road bridge, which connects Belvue with Paxico.

Put in at Wamego and then stay left as the river finishes its first meander through this section. Though the river continues to meander constantly, the bends are wider and the straights are longer. Thus, the channel can be a little harder to follow when the water is low. The sandbars and camping spots are, in accordance, much farther apart. A good bet for a prime camp is at the first big bend near river mile 125.5. The downstream end of that sandbar has some good, late-afternoon shade. Between mile 125 and 122, at least five small creeks drop into the river from the hill country that borders the south edge of the valley.

Watch for the Vermillion Creek Diversion Channel on river left, at about mile 121.5. A railroad bridge crosses about 100 yards or so up the channel; upstream of that is the bridge for U.S. 24. The diversion channel makes a reasonably good, intermediate access. There is a good spot to park near the highway and, with some effort, it is possible to skinny up the bank next to the railroad bridge with your boat. This shortens the trip by 6 miles.

The real Vermillion Creek enters more than a mile farther downstream. The river bends are tighter now and closer together, so plenty of good sandbars will present themselves. The best of these might be near river mile 118.5, about three miles upstream from the Belvue Access. A camp here would provide a nice paddle out the following morning. Several small creeks enter the river from both sides just above the Schoeman Road bridge. **Take out** on river left, at the Belvue Access under the **Schoeman Road bridge**, near river mile 115.5, river left. This steep, undeveloped access is not for the weak of heart.

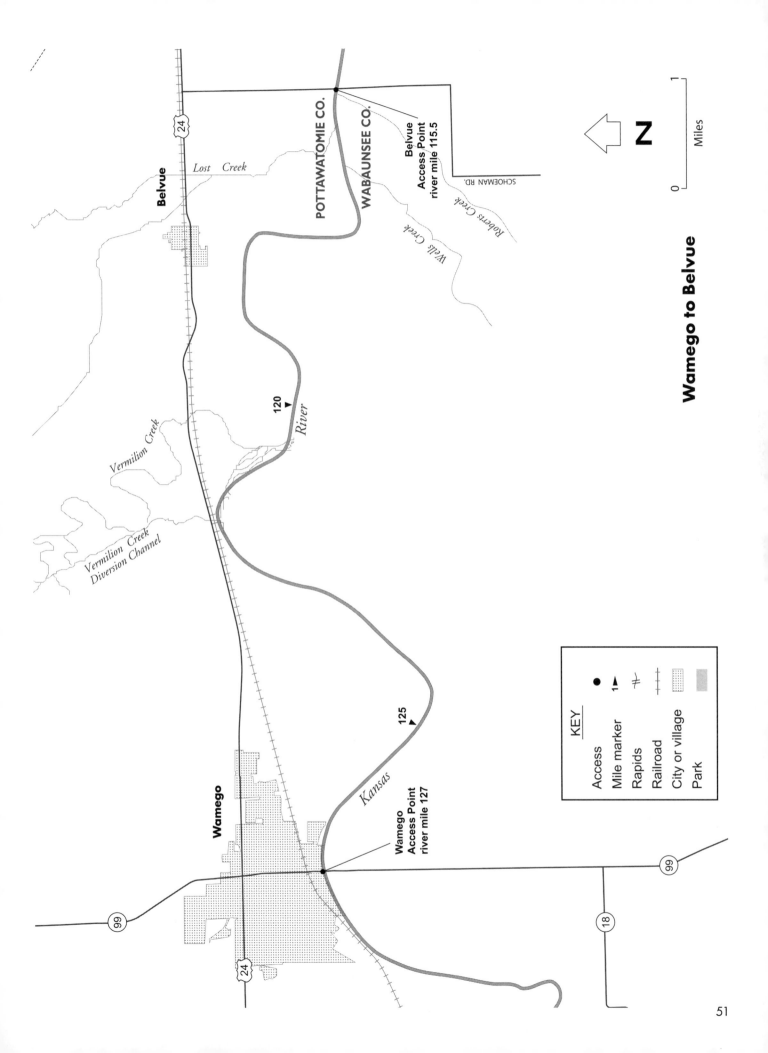

Wamego to Belvue

Belvue

Lost Creek

POTTAWATOMIE CO.

WABAUNSEE CO.

Belvue
Access Point
river mile 115.5

SCHOEMAN RD.

Roberts Creek

Wells Creek

River

120 ▶

Vermilion Creek

Vermilion Creek
Diversion Channel

Kansas

125 ▶

Wamego

Wamego
Access Point
river mile 127

KEY

● Access
▲ Mile marker
≠ Rapids
╫ Railroad
▦ City or village
▨ Park

N

0 ___ 1 Miles

99

18

99

24

KANSAS RIVER: BELVUE TO MAPLE HILL

9.5 miles, Class I difficulty
Belvue Access at river mile 115.5 to Maple Hill at river mile 106

The 9.5-mile float from Belvue, at river mile 115.5, to Maple Hill, at river mile 106, cuts through a broad valley of farmland that lies at the foot of rolling hills. A good float for the physically fit, stubborn, or both, the put-in and the take-out require a steep portage. A rope and an extra pair of hands can be useful. Although this part of the river is beautiful, its distance from larger population centers and its difficult access draw fewer, but more adventurous visitors.

The **minimum recommended flow for this river segment is 1,200 CFS**. Use the USGS **gauging station** on the Kansas River near Belvue. The average **gradient** for this segment is 3.1 feet per mile. **Canoes and kayaks can be rented** at Tuttle Creek State Park, located below Tuttle Creek Lake Dam ([785] 539-7941). Kansas State University also rents canoes, but a student or faculty ID is required ([785] 532-6980).

The **put-in** at the **Belvue Access** is on the north side of the Schoeman Road bridge that runs between the towns of Belvue and Paxico. The 26.8-mile **round-trip shuttle** route, from the Belvue Access to the Maple Hill Access, goes north on Schoeman Road, then east on U.S. Highway 24 through St. Marys about a mile to Maple Hill Road. Go south on Maple Hill to Sandy Crook Road and then follow it east to Maple Hill Road

again. Go south about two miles to Maple Hill Road bridge; the access is under the bridge at the northwest edge. To get to the Maple Hill Access from I-70, take the Maple Hill Exit 341 and go north on State Highway 30 (aka Maple Hill Road) through Maple Hill to the north side of the bridge.

Put in at Belvue. The river channel, over the next 3 miles, has long been unstable. You can see the history of past meanders along the old county lines that were drawn to follow the center of the river (see the map). Although the river is now somewhat straight, its recent meanders have built nearly 4 miles of sandbars on one side of the river or the other. At river mile 110.5, a large island has formed on river right, near the apex of a meander to the south.

This meander looks innocent enough on a map, but the southern exposure on a windy day can make the next 1.5 miles feel like a wind tunnel. The strong prevailing southwest winds can come storming up the broad, open valley to hit you square in the face. I have heard horror stories of paddlers who ignored the wind forecast and set out on this river thinking, "How bad could it get?" Common sense would be to avoid such situations, but if you paddle very much in Kansas, you'll get stuck in the wind sooner or later. Winds are often calmer in the mornings, rise in the middle of the day, then subside somewhat in the evenings. If you are taking a mid-day beating, you might consider sparing yourself the fight by waiting for a break in the evening. It usually works, but not always. For more advice about boating under windy conditions see the topic on "Wind" at the beginning of this book.

The wind, if any, may subside somewhat as the river begins a slight bend to the southeast. Although the protective hills are not close enough to help much, the main channel is close to the south (river right) bank, where the trees and the riverbank may provide a little protection.

Near river mile 108.5, Riley Creek enters on river left. At river mile 107 an island presents the last, best opportunity for a campsite. **Take out** at Maple Hill, near river mile 106, on river left under the **Maple Hill Road Bridge**. Get out wherever you can find a place to climb up the bank.

Kansas River Sandbar—Brent Maxwell, Brooks Fountain, and Mark Moore practice a game of balance.

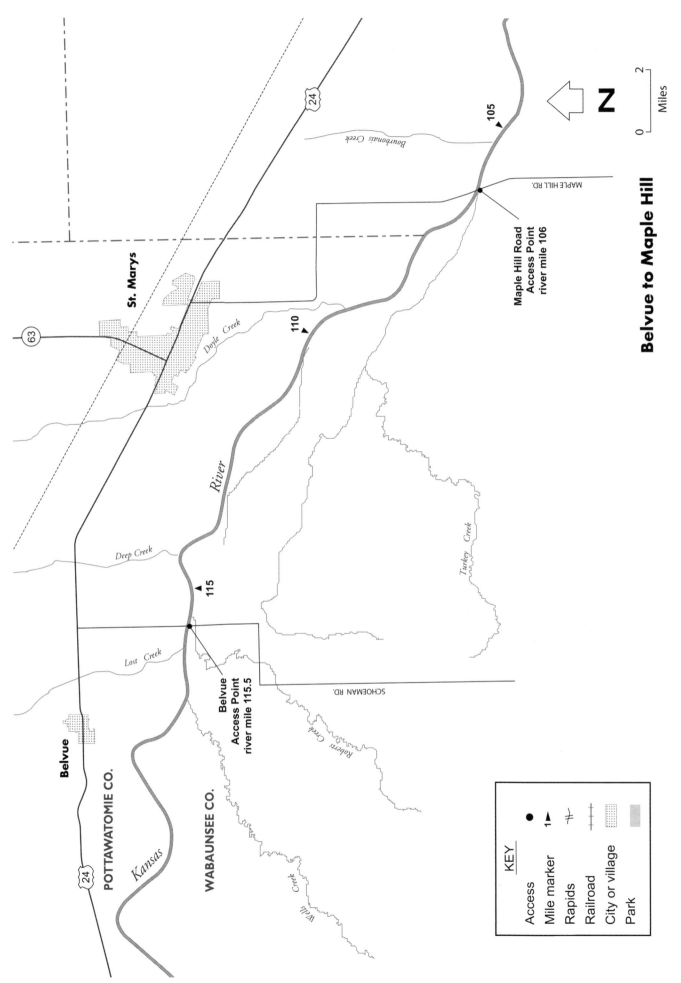

Belvue to Maple Hill

St. Marys

Belvue

POTTAWATOMIE CO.

WABAUNSEE CO.

Maple Hill Road
Access Point
river mile 106

Belvue
Access Point
river mile 115.5

MAPLE HILL RD.

SCHOEMAN RD.

Bourbonais Creek

Doyle Creek

Deep Creek

Lost Creek

Roberts Creek

Wells Creek

Turkey Creek

River

Kansas

105

110

115

24

63

24

N

0   1   2
Miles

KEY

Access
Mile marker
Rapids
Railroad
City or village
Park

KANSAS RIVER: MAPLE HILL TO TOPEKA

29.5 miles, Class I difficulty, one portage required
Maple Hill at river mile 106 to Seward Ave. Boat Ramp at river mile 76.5

CAUTION! THE TOPEKA AREA CAN BE HAZARDOUS TO BOATERS!

The Topeka Waterworks has a very dangerous cofferdam that is located at river mile 87, just one mile downstream of the new Kaw River State Park and a half mile downstream of the U.S. Highway 75 bridge. This low-head dam must be portaged on river left. When the river is low, you can begin your portage just upstream of the cofferdam. When the river is high it is best to pull ashore well upstream of the cofferdam to scout your portage options. Do not paddle over this structure or attempt to run the slot on the south side. A new maintained portage trail is planned for this site thanks to the work of Friends of the Kaw.

Sand dredgers sometimes have their booms and cables stretched across the channel. These can create hazardous, river-wide obstructions. Approach the railroad bridge along the south edge (river mile 83.7) to avoid the pilings and steel posts in the riverbed. Various pieces of equipment, including an old train car and posts the size of telephone poles, dot the riverbed. Keep your eyes on the water and watch for obstructions at and just below the surface. On river right, at river mile 82.5, the Oakland Wastewater Treatment Facility dumps treated sewage in the river. The discharge from this facility can be dramatically worse after a hard rain.

The float from Maple Hill Access, at river mile 106, to the Seward Boat Ramp in Topeka, at river mile 76.5, is a trip recommended for veteran paddlers with plenty of experience and time on their hands.

With the exception of one very poor access and some manmade river hazards, you have 29.5 miles of uninterrupted river ahead of you. Once you are on the river, you are fairly well committed. With 2,000 CFS or more under your boat, this trip will take about two days, but could be stretched to three days or more depending on flows, winds, and dawdling time. **A minimum recommended flow of 1,200 CFS** should be enough to clear most of the sandbars, but if you don't have a lot of experience on sandy-bottomed rivers, you should opt for 1,500+ CFS. Check the **gauging stations** on the Kansas River at Belvue and at Topeka. The average **gradient** for this segment is 2 feet per mile.

There are no **canoe rentals** available in the area.

This segment has the fewest and possibly the worst boat access points on the river. Yet if you are hearty enough to heft your boat and gear up and down steep river banks and around dangerous low-head dams, the first half of this float has a wonderful feeling of a wilderness river and the second half will keep most paddlers rubber-necking between the cityscape and the manmade river hazards.

To get to the **put-in** at the **Maple Hill Access from I-70**, take the Maple Hill Exit 341 and go north on State Highway 30 through the town of Maple Hill and continue on Maple Hill Road north, then east, and then north again to the Maple Hill Road bridge. The access is at the NW edge of the bridge. The 62.8-mile **round-trip shuttle** route, from the Maple Hill Access to the Seward Avenue Boat Ramp and back, goes north on Maple Hill Road to U.S. Highway 24, then east through the north Topeka area to State Highway 4, then south to Seward Avenue (just south of the municipal airport), and then east to the take-out at the Seward Avenue Boat Ramp.

The town of Maple Hill was named at the time of its founding by the local acting postmaster, Mrs. Higgenbotham, after a grove of trees she admired.

The difficulty of this leg comes not from the river, but from the somewhat inaccessible length of the segment and from manmade obstructions in the river. From the Maple Hill Access at river mile 106, the next public access is the Seward Avenue Boat Ramp east of Topeka, 29.5 miles downstream, at river mile 76.5.

Mill Creek enters on river right above river mile 104 and then Cross Creek enters from river left, below river mile 103. Both creeks have wide mouths and may provide good shelter on a windy day. An emergency access is available under the Willard Bridge, at river mile 101, river right, where Carlson Road crosses the river. To get to this access by road, from Carlson Road 64 turn east in Willard on 1st Street, then north (left) on Darling Street to the trailer court, then turn west (left) and follow the rutted dirt road under the Willard Bridge and over the railroad tracks (no warning signs) to the river. Although locals use this spot regularly, the path to the access crosses the private railroad right-of-way. This is the last, best place to get off the river for more than 24 miles.

The next few miles have some decent campsites, but large sandbars become scarce farther downstream. The river is not approached by roads or other development until near river mile 96, along the north bank (river left). The creek that drains Silver Lake enters from river left, at the beginning of that meander. If you can land your boat in the mouth of the creek, there is a small road directly north of the river. Although it requires a little bushwhacking, this spot has been used as an emergency exit before.

Near river mile 90.5, there is a large island and a series of sandbars. You are now immediately north of the intersection of SW Urish and SW Murray Hill Roads, just west of the Topeka area. As you proceed downstream of the island, watch for the sand dredge and its cables and equipment that may be stretched across the river from river right. DO NOT PROCEED DOWNSTREAM WITHOUT READING AND FOLLOWING ALL OF THE PRECAUTIONS OUTLINED IN THE SIDEBAR IN THIS SECTION.

At river mile 81, a large island has formed. The banks are steep except on the upstream side. Soldier Creek enters on river left at the bottom of the island.

Depending on the water level, the Grantville Sandbar, at river mile 78.5, may be your last useable sandbar before you reach the Seward Avenue Boat Ramp.

Take out at the **Seward Avenue Boat Ramp** at river mile 76.5, on river right. See the directions in the next segment for driving directions to this ramp.

WARNING! If you float past the Seward Avenue Boat Ramp, please see the additional hazard warnings in the next section of this book.

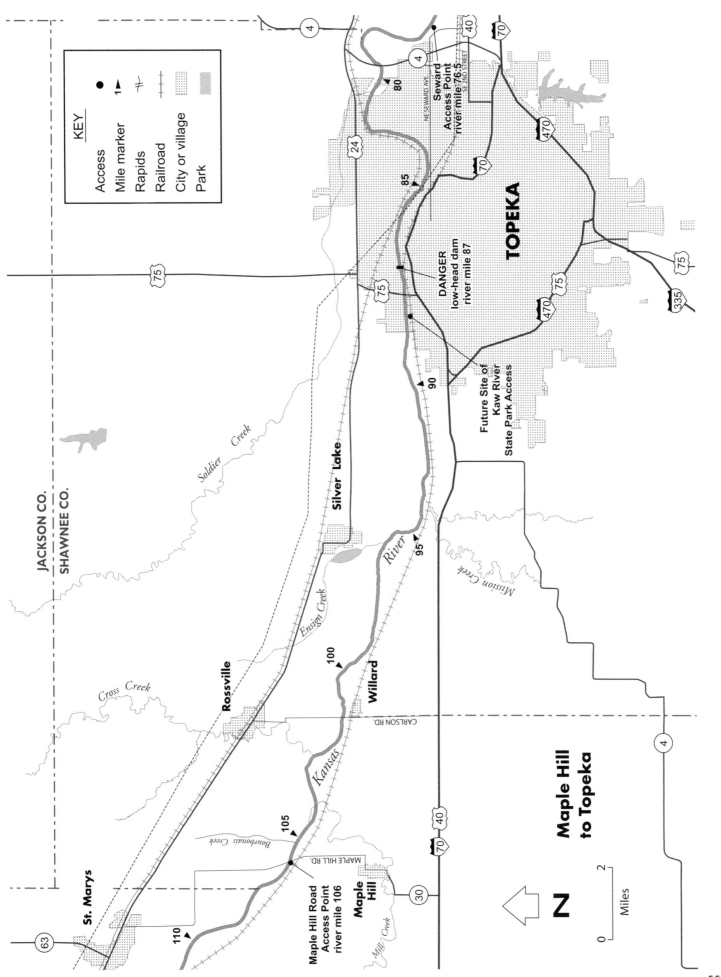

KEY

Access

Mile marker

Rapids

Railroad

City or village

Park

JACKSON CO.
SHAWNEE CO.

Soldier Creek

Silver Lake

Cross Creek

Rossville

Ensign Creek

Willard

Kansas River

Bourbonais Creek

Maple Hill Road
Access Point
river mile 106

MAPLE HILL RD.

St. Marys

Maple Hill

Mill Creek

Mission Creek

CARLSON RD.

TOPEKA

Seward Point
Access Point
river mile 76.5

SE 2ND STREET

NE SEWARD AVE.

DANGER
low-head dam
river mile 87

Future Site of
Kaw River
State Park Access

80

85

90

95

100

105

110

4

40

70

470

70

75

470

75

75

335

24

75

75

30

70

40

4

63

N

Maple Hill
to Topeka

0   2
Miles

55

KANSAS RIVER: TOPEKA TO PERRY

10.5 miles, Class I difficulty, one portage required
Seward Avenue Boat Ramp in Topeka at river mile 76.5 to the Perry Boat Ramp at river mile 66

The endangered least tern is native to the larger and higher sandbars and islands that are characteristic of this reach. In recent years, these rare birds have been spotted nesting on Franks Island and downstream. This rare bird requires open beach areas that are clear of vegetation. Please avoid hiking and camping on these high, bare, sandy areas during the nesting season from late May through the end of June.

This is one of the most enjoyable floats on the Kaw and is characterized by good access, plentiful islands, sandbars, and excellent camping. The river moves through flat farmland within the roughly 3-mile-wide floodplain and, once you leave the Topeka area, the mark of man is rarely visible.

Optimum flows in the range of 1,500 to 2,000 CFS and favorable winds will get you through this leg in four to five hours, but there is much to enjoy, so take your time. The **minimum recommended flow for a fun day is about 1,200 CFS**. With that, you can clear all of the sandbars if you stay alert and know how to read the river. Use the USGS **gauging station** for the Kansas River at Topeka. The average **gradient** for this segment is 2.6 feet per mile. **Canoe and kayak rentals** are available at the Lawrence KOA and Kansas River Canoe Company ([785] 842-3877) and at Anderson Rentals, 1312 West 6th Street, Lawrence ([785] 843-2044). The Lawrence KOA also runs a shuttle service It is located on the southeast side of the Lawrence area, just east of the intersection of U.S. Highways 24 and 40.

The Seward Avenue Boat Ramp is on the east side of Topeka and on the south side of the river. From I-70, take Exit 366 at State Highway 4. Go north to the Seward Avenue Exit. Go east on Seward to where it begins to bend south. Watch for the gravel road to the access. The 28.6-mile **round-trip shuttle** route, from Topeka to Perry, goes back to Highway 4, then north to U.S. 24, and then east to Thompsonville Road. Turn south (right) on Thompsonville Road and continue south to the boat ramp. Both the Seward Avenue Boat Ramp and the Perry Ramp were cut too deep into the river bank, so they tend to get silted over with mud after each high-water event.

Put in at the **Seward Avenue Boat Ramp**. From the ramp it is only 0.7 mile to the confluence with Shunganunga Creek, on river right. **Danger**—0.3 mile below Shunganunga Creek the Tecumseh Power Station has a low-head dam that can be very dangerous at all but high water levels. At low to normal levels, this concrete ledge does not look threatening as you approach it, but don't be deceived. The hydraulic can flip your boat, then trap and drown you. The banks are steep, so the portage can be difficult at some water levels. The author has portaged on river right (south side), but judge for yourself.

Beginning at river mile 74.5 and for the next 8.5 miles, sandbars are almost continuous, one after another, all the way to the confluence with the Delaware River. The best of these are in the first four miles of that range. The first and largest of these big islands and sandbars is Franks Island, which starts at river mile 74.5. Whetstone Creek flows into the river, just downstream of Franks Island, on river right. Then Muddy Creek enters on river left near river mile 72.3.

The river segment from Topeka to Lawrence is called Eagles Row for good reason. You will probably see bald eagles perched in the cottonwood trees along the river. If you are lucky, you will also get a glimpse of a least tern. This little bird is on the endangered species list and needs your help (see sidebar).

If you plan to camp along the river, remember that railroad tracks and a small road run intermittently along the south edge of the river at several locations. Unless you enjoy the rumble of freight trains at night, your most peaceful campsites will be from river miles 73 to 72 and from 66 to 65. Spring Creek enters on river right at river mile 68.5. **Take out** at the **Perry Boat Ramp**, on river left at river mile 66. It is easy to lose track of time and distance, so don't forget to keep a sharp eye out for the take-out as you approach the area. If you miss it, the next public access is the **Rising Sun Boat Ramp**, 2.5 miles downstream, on river left, just above the Perry-Lecompton Bridge.

DANGER! Portage the low-head dam one mile below the Seward Avenue Boat Ramp.

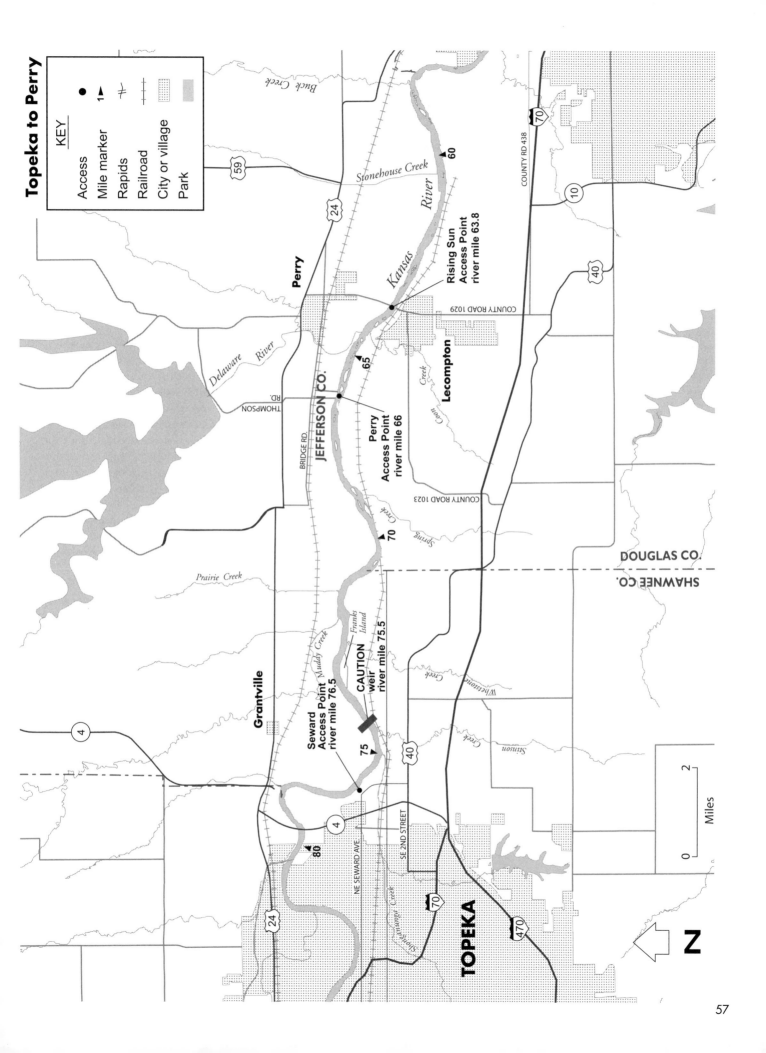

Topeka to Perry

KEY

- ● Access
- ▲ Mile marker
- ⌿ Rapids
- ┼┼ Railroad
- ▦ City or village
- ▨ Park

Buck Creek

Stonehouse Creek

Kansas River

▲ 60

Rising Sun
Access Point
river mile 63.8

Delaware River

Perry

JEFFERSON CO.

THOMPSON RD.

BRIDGE RD.

▲ 65

Perry
Access Point
river mile 66

Coon Creek

Lecompton

COUNTY ROAD 1029

COUNTY RD 438

COUNTY ROAD 1023

Spring Creek

▲ 70

Prairie Creek

DOUGLAS CO.

SHAWNEE CO.

Muddy Creek

Franks Island

CAUTION
weir
river mile 75.5

Grantville

Seward Access Point
river mile 76.5

▲ 75

Whetstone Creek

Stinson Creek

NE SEWARD AVE

SE 2ND STREET

▲ 80

Stonewinga Creek

TOPEKA

59

24

4

40

10

70

470

N

0   2
Miles

57

KANSAS RIVER: PERRY TO LAWRENCE

12.5 miles, intermediate access available, Class I difficulty
Perry Access at river mile 66 to North Riverfront Park at river mile 53.8

Lecompton, once named Bald Eagle, was one of the first settlements in Kansas and was forecast to be "the great metropolis of Kansas." In 1855, the pro-slavers made it the Kansas Territorial Capitol. With the triumph of free-state forces, the territorial capitol was moved to Topeka. You can beach your boat on the south side of the river (opposite the Rising Sun Access) and take a short hike to the Kansas Territorial Capitol Museum, Constitution Hall State Historic Site, and the local shops.

The float from the Perry Boat Ramp, at river mile 66, to the North Riverfront Park Boat Ramp in Lawrence, at river mile 53.3, is part of a relatively undisturbed reach of the river known as Eagles Row that extends upstream to Topeka and downstream to Lawrence.

Optimum flows in the range of 1,500 to 2,000 CFS and favorable winds will get you through this leg in four to five hours, but some paddlers, especially on windy days, prefer to shorten their float, by either taking out or launching 2.5 miles downstream at the Rising Sun Access.

The **minimum recommended flow for a fun day is about 1,200**. With that, you can clear all of the sandbars if you stay alert and know how to read the river. Use the USGS **gauging station** for the Kansas River at Topeka. The average **gradient** for six-mile leg of this segment is about 2 feet per mile, but the pool above Bowersock Dam reduces the average to only 1 foot per mile. You can **rent canoes and kayaks** at the Lawrence KOA and Kansas River Canoe Company ([785] 842-3877) and at Anderson Rentals, 1312 West 6th Street, Lawrence ([785] 843-2044).

To get to the put-in at the Perry Boat Ramp from U.S. Highway 24, go west from Perry to Thompsonville Road and then south on Thompsonville Road to the boat ramp. The 30-mile **round-trip shuttle** route, from the Perry Access to the North Riverfront Park Access and back, goes north on Thompsonville Road to U.S. 24, then east and south to the North Riverfront Park River Access at the north edge of the city of Lawrence. The turnoff is on the west side of an intersection called Teepee Junction, where U.S. 24 and 40 and State Highway 32 turn east, just west of the Municipal Airport.

Put in at the **Perry Boat Ramp**. This 13-mile segment is not as well blessed with large sandbars as the prior segment, but it has traditionally been one of the most popular stretches on the river. Typically a nice six-hour float, which you can shorten by using the Rising Sun Boat Ramp at Lecompton.

As you approach the Delaware River, near river mile 64.6, stay close to the north shore. At the confluence, the Delaware River and the Kaw have formed a small island. The main channel stays right of the island but, just for fun, you can usually slip around the north side of the island to follow the current of the Delaware the short distance around the island. At that point you will see the Perry-Lecompton Bridge right in front of you. The **Rising Sun Boat Ramp** is on river left, just upstream of the bridge, at mile 63.8.

Stonehouse Creek enters on river left near river mile 60.4. Beginning at river mile 60, on river right and farther downstream on river left, a system of levies was built to protect surrounding property from floodwaters. This system of levies and dikes are intermittent, both near and far along the river, all the way through Lawrence. The two most popular campsites on this part of the river are at river miles 59 and 58, left and right respectively. The first of these is Patty's Sandbar, named after Patty Boyer, one of the founders of Friends of the Kaw and the wife of the adjoining landowner in the 1990s. Patty Two is just around the bend, on river right.

At river mile 55.3, Westar Energy has a weir on river left that was built to force the river over to the south shore for the water intakes of its power plant. The main channel goes to the right, around a small island. The weir, on river left, is normally not a hazard. At moderate flows, a short riffle is formed between the gaps of the weir. If in doubt, or if you want a better view of the Westar Energy power plant, stay in the main channel and go around the right side of the island.

Once past the power plant, the river turns southward and into the prevailing wind. **Take out** at the **North Riverfront Park Boat Ramp** at river mile 53.5. To avoid missing it, keep your eyes peeled toward river left shore. By the time you can first see the I-70 Bridge, you should already be on river left and at the ramp.

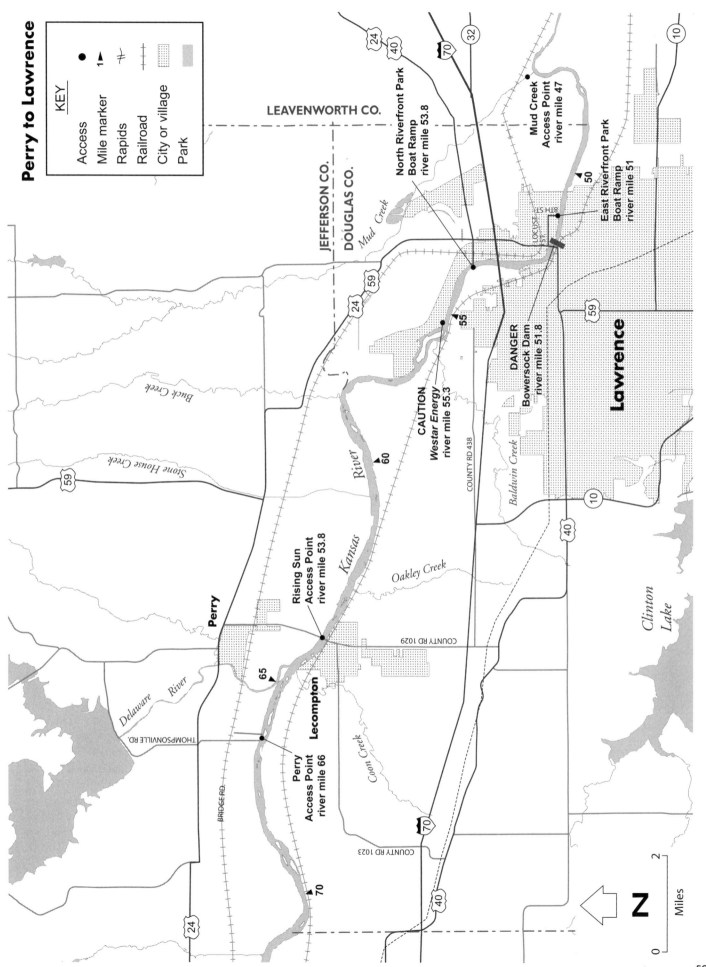

Perry to Lawrence

KEY

- Access ●
- Mile marker 1▲
- Rapids ⊬
- Railroad ┼┼┼
- City or village
- Park

LEAVENWORTH CO.

JEFFERSON CO.

DOUGLAS CO.

Mud Creek

Buck Creek

Stone House Creek

North Riverfront Park
Boat Ramp
river mile 53.8

Mud Creek
Access Point
river mile 47

East Riverfront Park
Boat Ramp
river mile 51

8TH ST.

LOCUST ST.

50

55

CAUTION
Westar Energy
river mile 55.3

DANGER
Bowersock Dam
river mile 51.8

Baldwin Creek

COUNTY RD 438

60

Lawrence

Kansas River

Perry

Rising Sun
Access Point
river mile 53.8

Oakley Creek

Clinton
Lake

65

Lecompton

COUNTY RD 1029

Delaware River

THOMPSONVILLE RD.

Perry
Access Point
river mile 66

BRIDGE RD.

Coon Creek

COUNTY RD 1023

70

N

Miles

0 2

59

KANSAS RIVER: LAWRENCE TO EUDORA

11.9 miles, alternate access available, Class I difficulty, one portage
North Riverfront Park at river mile 53.8 to Wakarusa River Access at river mile 42

The float from the North Riverfront Park Boat Ramp to the East Riverfront Boat Ramp requires the long and difficult portage of Bowersock Dam; however, boaters can safely portage the dam. The dam is immediately downstream of the Massachusetts Avenue (U.S. 40/59) bridge. Pull your boat out of the water, river left (north), a safe distance above the dam. A trail runs along the river, on top of the levee. Use caution carrying your boat across busy Massachusetts Avenue and then portage your way back down to the edge of the river, below the dam.

If you wish to paddle from the North Riverfront Park Boat Ramp instead of the East Riverfront Boat Ramp, please see the insert along the margin of this page. Otherwise the put-in for this segment is at the East Riverfront Park Boat Ramp (aka East Riverfront Park).

The segment from Lawrence to Eudora has been one of the most popular floats in this part of the state. Good access points are conveniently located for half-day or full-day trips. The **minimum recommended flow is 1,200 CFS**. Use the USGS **gauging stations** on the Kansas River at Perry and the Kansas River at DeSoto. The average **gradient** for this segment is 2.4 feet per mile. You can **rent canoes and kayaks** at the Lawrence KOA and Kansas River Canoe Company ([785] 842-3877) and at Anderson Rentals, 1312 W 6th Street, Lawrence ([785] 843-2044).

The **put-in** at the **East Riverfront Boat Ramp** is at river mile 51. It is located south of 8th and Oak Streets. To get there from the East Lawrence Exit off I-70, go south on Massachusetts Locust. Go east on Locust to 8th Street, then go south on 8th Street to the river. The 27-mile **round-trip shuttle** route, from the East Riverfront Park to the Eudora Boat Ramp and back, takes you west to Massachusetts Street, north past I-70 to U.S. Highway 24/40 east past the airport to State Highway 32, then east to 222nd Street, then south over the Kansas River and to the southwest edge of the bridge over the Wakarusa River on the northern edge of the town of Eudora. This access is on the Wakarusa River (not the Kaw), about 0.8 mile by boat from the Kansas River.

Put in at East Riverfront Park. The float from East Riverfront Park to Mud Creek is marred by concrete rubble and trash dumped along the south riverbank. It is sad to see how little some people care for rivers. At river mile 47, just upstream of Mud Creek, the river splits, creating a large island and two routes. If you want the faster channel, go right. That is the newer and narrower channel, but there aren't any sandbars for the next few miles. If you want a quick campsite, take the left fork and camp near the head of the island, straight across the river from Mud Creek. **The Mud Creek Boat Ramp** is 200 yards up the creek. Public access is limited to those who have a key to the road gate. Contact the Lawrence Parks and Recreation Department ([785] 832-3450) if you want a key ($10 deposit and a valid ID). Anglers use this site a lot.

Past Mud Creek, the low hills of eastern Kansas begin to rise slowly along the southern horizon. Picture-perfect campsites are well situated. The railroad tracks move farther from the north banks and the south side is very natural.

The first and only bridge you will come to is the Eudora Bridge. Remember: you will **take out** one mile up the **Wakarusa River** (not the Kansas River). From the river, your turn up the Wakarusa is easy to miss if you aren't paying attention. After you cross under the bridge, move to river right (south side) and start watching for your turn up the Wakarusa, about three-quarters of a mile downstream of the bridge. The turn up the river can be a challenge for novice paddlers. The current is fairly fast at the confluence and fallen tree limbs can partially blockade your approach.

The Wakarusa is usually a pleasant, shady little stream and a pleasure to paddle, but if the Wakarusa is really moving (300 CFS or more), it can be difficult to reach the take-out. In that case, you should plan to paddle down the Kaw to the next boat ramp, in **DeSoto**, at river mile 31.3. Check the flow on the USGS gauging station on Wakarusa River near Lawrence ahead of time, but be aware that the Corps of Engineers sometimes has unscheduled releases from Clinton Lake, southwest of Lawrence, that can come screaming down the Wakarusa without preamble.

If you miss the turn up the Wakarusa River, as others have, the next access is the Linwood Access at river mile 35, seven more miles downstream, and the DeSoto Boat Ramp, another four miles farther, at river mile 31. The Linwood Access is not developed, but it is usable in a pinch. The access is about 200 yards up Stranger Creek, at the railroad bridge in **Linwood**. This access may be impossible to reach if the creek is running fast.

Rod Snyder surfs and squirts the Kansas River below Bowersock Mill in Lawrence (photo courtesy of Dan Irvin)

Lawrence to Eudora

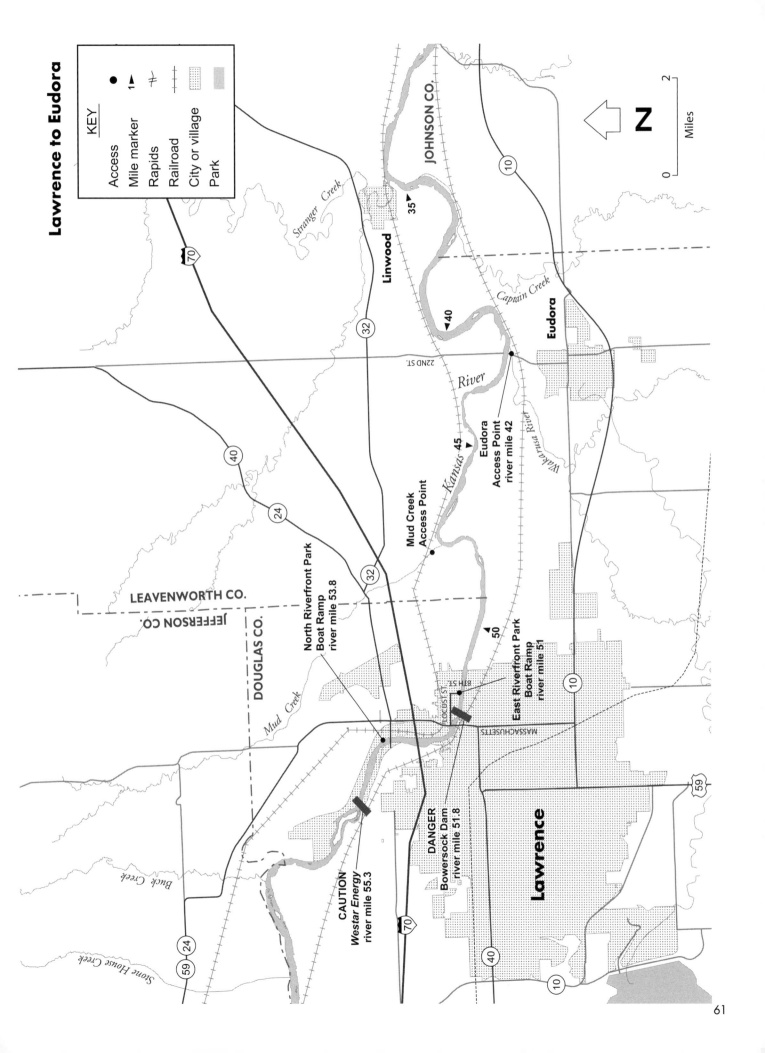

KEY
- ● Access
- ▲ Mile marker
- ≠ Rapids
- ┼┼┼ Railroad
- ▦ City or village
- ▨ Park

N

Miles
0   2

Stranger Creek

70

32

Linwood

JOHNSON CO.

35 ▶

◀ 40

10

Captain Creek

River

22ND ST.

Eudora

Eudora
Access Point
river mile 42

Kansas 45 ▶

Wakarusa River

40

24

32

Mud Creek
Access Point

LEAVENWORTH CO.
JEFFERSON CO.

DOUGLAS CO.

North Riverfront Park
Boat Ramp
river mile 53.8

Mud Creek

50 ▶

8TH ST.

LOCUST ST.

East Riverfront Park
Boat Ramp
river mile 51

10

MASSACHUSETTS

CAUTION
Westar Energy
river mile 55.3

DANGER
Bowersock Dam
river mile 51.8

Lawrence

59

Buck Creek

24

70

40

Stone House Creek

59

10

61

KANSAS RIVER: EUDORA TO DESOTO

11 miles, no good intermediate access, Class I difficulty
Wakarusa River Access at river mile 42 to DeSoto Boat Ramp at river mile 31.3

The City of DeSoto was laid out in the spring of 1857 and was named for the Spanish explorer, Hernando de Soto. The land was part of the Louisiana Purchase and cost the United States three cents per acre. It was given to John Possum, a Shawnee Indian, who sold the first tract at $15 per acre. In 1858, John Possum and Hattie Possum sold 80 acres to John F. Legate, S. Todd, and Stratton and Williams for $1,200. The next sale was 80 acres to the DeSoto Town Co. in July 1861 for $1,176. Originally, the main street was Shawnee Street, because it ran down to the river and the ferry crossing. The town museum, located at 83rd Street and Peoria Street, is in Abbot Hall, which was built by Major James B. Abbott, one of the town's pioneer landowners.

With the addition of the DeSoto Boat Ramp in 2006, the 11-mile float from Eudora has become more popular with local boaters. More than most of the river, this segment is blessed with sandbars and campsites. In the fall, the hills along the south shore are filled with spectacular reds, yellows, and browns.

The **minimum recommended flow is 1,200 CFS**. Use the USGS **gauging station** for the Kansas River at DeSoto. The average **gradient** for this segment is 2.7 feet per mile. **Canoes and kayaks can be rented** at A-1 Rentals, 14891 East Highway 40, Kansas City, MO ([816] 373-0234); Anderson Rentals, 1312 West 6th Street, Lawrence, KS ([785] 843-2044); and the Lawrence KOA and Kansas River Canoe Company, 1473 Highway 40, Lawrence, KS ([785] 842-3877).

The Eudora boat ramp is located on the Wakarusa River, at the north edge of Eudora, under the southwest edge of the Wakarusa Bridge on Main Street (aka County Road 222 if you're coming from the north). The 18-mile **round-trip shuttle** route, from Eudora to DeSoto and back, goes south to N 1400th Road (East Main Street), east to State Highway 10 and then to the DeSoto Exit, and then north on Lexington Avenue into DeSoto, turning left (north) at Ottawa Street. The boat ramp is located where Ottawa Street becomes 79th Street, just northwest of town, a third of a mile upstream of the DeSoto Bridge (Wyandotte Street).

Put in at the **Eudora Boat Ramp** on the Wakarusa River. Normally a small, peaceful, shady lane of a river, the Wakarusa can come up fast when the Corps of Engineers is releasing a lot of water from Clinton Lake; the resulting surge can sweep you downstream and into the current of the Kansas River in short order. When you reach the Kaw, hang a right. The squeeze between the island and the south shore can be loaded with downed trees, making passage a trick as you try to maneuver the swirling water where the currents of the Kansas and the Wakarusa Rivers meet. If that narrow channel is too congested, paddle upstream and then around the other side of the island.

The main channel, over the first 8 miles, is easy to follow. Contained within one of the narrowest parts of its valley (1.5 miles wide), the river ricochets from one meander to another, cutting fairly clear paths through the sandy riverbed. Huge sandbars with great campsites are found at the inside of each bend and sometimes in between. Captain Creek enters from river left at river mile 37 and then Stranger Creek enters on river left just below river mile 35. Stranger Creek is substantial and has a wide mouth and a good channel. The town of Linwood is only a few hundred yards up the creek, so if the creek isn't running too fast, you can paddle upstream to the railroad bridge for a short visit. Don't leave your belongings unattended.

Railroad tracks follow along both edges of the river valley, so the best campsites will be at least a few hundreds yards or more from the tracks.

Take out at the **DeSoto Boat Ramp**, on river right (south side), just upstream of the DeSoto Bridge.

The Kansas River hugs the right bank at about 500 CFS downstream of its confluence with the Wakarusa River.

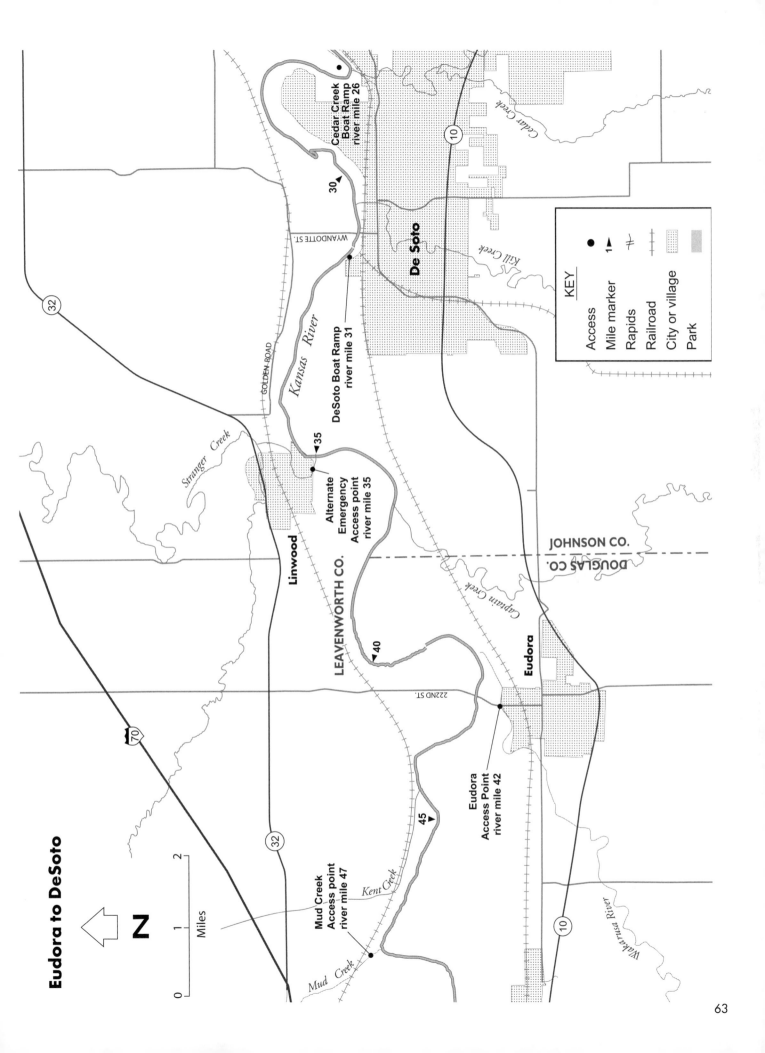

Eudora to DeSoto

N

Miles
0   1   2

KEY

●   Access
▲   Mile marker
  Rapids
  Railroad
  City or village
  Park

Cedar Creek
Boat Ramp
river mile 26

30 ▼

De Soto

DeSoto Boat Ramp
river mile 31

35 ▼

Alternate
Emergency
Access point
river mile 35

Kansas River

GOLDEN ROAD

WYANDOTTE ST.

Stranger Creek

Linwood

LEAVENWORTH CO.

JOHNSON CO.

DOUGLAS CO.

Captain Creek

40 ▼

222ND ST.

Eudora

Eudora
Access Point
river mile 42

45 ▼

Mud Creek
Access point
river mile 47

Kent Creek

Mud Creek

Wakarusa River

Kill Creek

Cedar Creek

32

70

32

10

10

KANSAS RIVER:
DESOTO TO WILDER ROAD
15.3 miles, intermediate access available, Class I difficulty
DeSoto Boat Ramp at river mile 31.3 to Mill Creek Access at river mile 16

You will see things on this segment that you haven't seen elsewhere on the river. The trip from the DeSoto Boat Ramp, at river mile 31.3, to the Wilder Road Access, at river mile 16, will take you through almost every kind of habitat you will find on the Kaw—in the span of only a few miles. Already confined between hills, the channel grows narrower and the river makes a final charge over a limestone riverbed then into a 5-mile long, steep-sided pool. Although this segment is a bit long, the first 10 miles of river go by very quickly and there are two intermediate access points available to shorten it up.

The **minimum recommended flow is 1,200 CFS**. Use the USGS **gauging station** for the Kansas River at DeSoto. The average **gradient** for this segment is only .6 feet per mile, due to the pool behind the Johnson County Water One cofferdam.

The Kansas River looking downstream from the DeSoto Bridge

Canoes and kayaks can be rented at A-1 Rentals, 14891 East Highway 40, Kansas City, MO ([816]-373-0234); Anderson Rentals, 1312 West 6th Street Lawrence, KS ([785] 843-2044); and the Lawrence KOA and Kansas River Canoe Company, 1473 Highway 40, Lawrence, KS ([785] 842-3877).

The **put-in** is in DeSoto a third of a mile upstream of the **Wyandotte Street bridge** and located at the intersection of 79th Street and Ottawa Street, just northwest of town. The 28-mile **round-trip shuttle**, from DeSoto to the Wilder Road Access and back, goes east on 83rd Street to State Highway 7, then north to West 47th Street, and then east to Mill Creek. Park in the paved parking lot on the south (right) side of the road, just before the Wilder Road bridge over Mill Creek. The small canoe access is southeast of the parking lot.

Put in at the DeSoto Boat Ramp. The straightaway

of the first mile downstream of the DeSoto Bridge is an open, lazy pool, but as the river makes its first bend, the next four miles gain character and sandbars. Through these four miles, this sandy-bottomed prairie river cuts its last two elegant meanders in grand style. The banks are low and the sandbars are high, with beautiful campsites and shallow areas for shore birds and beachcombers.

If you prefer an intermediate access or a shorter day on the river, there is a good **boat ramp on Cedar Creek**. As you pass river mile 27, move over to river right and watch for Cedar Creek just past the apex of the tightest bend in the entire river. It's a very small stream, so watch carefully or you'll miss it. Paddle up the creek about 100 yards to the boat ramp. If the creek is blocked with trees, the parking lot is accessible via a portage of about 100 yards along the west edge of the creek.

Once past Cedar Creek, the river begins to flow against limestone bluffs along the south shore. As the river approaches Bonner Springs, the limestone rises on both sides. Between these bluffs, the river narrows. Here, a stone shelf creates a natural dam and an unusually rocky riverbed. These next four miles will go by very fast as the river accelerates over and down the rock shelf.

Near the bottom of that slide, near river mile 22, there are two large sandbars, on either side of the river. The sandbar/campsite of choice is on river right. These will be the last sandbars and the last campsites on the river. From Bonner Springs to Kaw Point, the river has been badly degraded by sand dredging and the effects of the Missouri River's bed degradation. Even so, the river maintains a distinct majesty, battered but not beaten, as it moves slowly and quietly past the trees and skyscapes as you enter the Kansas City area. The first bridge you come to is Highway 7, which goes into Bonner Springs to the north.

At this writing, Bonner Springs is considering constructing a river access at about river mile 20.7, on the north side (river left). From Highway 7 to just downstream of the I-435 Bridge (river mile 15.3), the river forms a five-mile long lake behind the Johnson County Water One cofferdam. The next access is the **Edwardsville Boat Ramp** on river left, at river mile 17. The boat ramp is located at 9th Street (aka 102nd Street) and Woodend Road in Edwardsville.

Take-out on **Mill Creek**, on river right, a half mile upstream of the I-435 Bridge. The creek can become a maze of downed trees, but with a little ingenuity, you can work your way one mile upstream to a small concrete pad that is just past the Wilder Road bridge.

DeSoto to Wilder Road

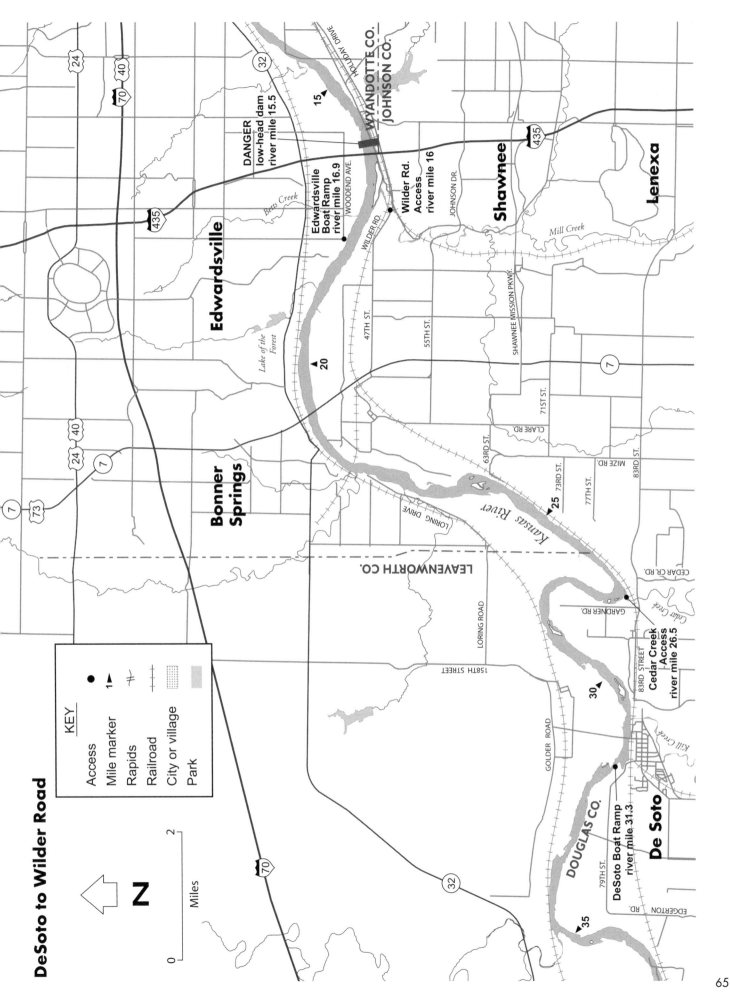

KEY

- ● Access
- 1 ▲ Mile marker
- ≠ Rapids
- ‡‡‡ Railroad
- ⬚ City or village
- ▧ Park

N

Miles
0 | 2

DANGER
low-head dam
river mile 15.5

Edwardsville Boat Ramp
river mile 16.9

Wilder Rd. Access
river mile 16

Betts Creek

Lake of the Forest

Edwardsville

Bonner Springs

WYANDOTTE CO.
JOHNSON CO.

Shawnee

Lenexa

Mill Creek

LEAVENWORTH CO.

Kansas River

Cedar Creek Access
river mile 26.5

Kill Creek

DeSoto Boat Ramp
river mile 31.3

De Soto

DOUGLAS CO.

Cedar Creek

HOLIDAY DRIVE
WOODEND AVE.
WILDER RD.
47TH ST.
55TH ST.
JOHNSON DR.
SHAWNEE MISSION PKWY.
71ST ST.
63RD ST.
CLARE RD.
73RD ST.
77TH ST.
MIZE RD.
83RD ST.
CEDAR CR. RD.
GARDNER RD.
83RD STREET
79TH ST.
GOLDER ROAD
LORING DRIVE
LORING ROAD
158TH STREET
EDGERTON RD.

15 ▼
20 ▼
25 ▼
30 ▼
35 ▼

24
70 40
32
435
7
73
24 40
7
70

KANSAS RIVER: WILDER ROAD TO KAW POINT

17 miles, Class 1 difficulty, one portage required
Mill Creek Access at river mile 16 to Kaw Point Boat Ramp at river mile 0.1

The 17-mile float from the Wilder Road Access, at river mile 16, to Kaw Point, near river mile 0, is the last leg in the river's graceful, 170-mile journey across central and eastern Kansas. Some of these waters have traveled from as far away as Colorado and Nebraska. Other waters have been released from decades or even centuries of storage in the soil.

Water backs up above the Johnson County Water One cofferdam and then again from the Missouri River, creating lakelike conditions all the way to Kaw Point. The Kansas River Water Assurance District maintains a **flow of 400 CFS or greater** at all times by controlling releases from reservoirs upstream. Thus, this last part of the river is floatable at all flows. Use the USGS **gauging station** for the Kansas River at DeSoto. Not including the elevation loss at the Johnson County Water One cofferdam, the average **gradient** for this segment is .5 feet per mile. These rental stores are not close but, if you must, you can **rent canoes and kayaks** at A-1 Rentals, 14891 East U.S. Highway 40, Kansas City, MO ([816] 373-0234); Anderson Rentals, 1312 West 6th Street, Lawrence, KS ([785] 843-2044); and the Lawrence KOA and Kansas River Canoe Company, 1473 Highway 40, Lawrence, KS ([785] 842-3877).

The **put-in** on **Mill Creek**, at the Wilder Road Access, is open dawn to dusk. The park is at the northernmost end of the Mill Creek Streamway Park that runs 17 miles from Olathe to the Kansas River. To get there, from I-435, take the Holliday Drive Exit 8A, turn west on Holliday Drive, go about one mile on Holliday, and then turn north on Wilder Road and cross Mill Creek. The parking lot is on the left (southwest) side of the Mill Creek Bridge (Wilder Road bridge). A small concrete pad, southeast of the parking lot, is only suitable for canoes and kayaks. The 29-mile **round-trip shuttle**, from the Wilder Road Access to Kaw Point and back, goes back to I-435, north to I-70, and then east to the James Street Exit (Exit 423). Follow the signs to Fairfax Trafficway. As you come to the bottom of the ramp, turn east (right) into the first parking lot and follow the signs to the access. As you come down to the bottom of the ramp, turn east (right) into the first parking lot and follow the signs to the access. The Kaw Point boat ramp is located at the northwest tip of the Kansas River's confluence with the Missouri River.

Put in at the Wilder Road Access on Mill Creek. The first mile of this float is an enjoyable trip down the creek to its confluence with the Kaw. Be careful of strainers on this little creek. **Caution:** Once on the Kaw, move to the north (river left) side immediately so that you can safely portage the Water One cofferdam a quarter mile downstream of the I-435 bridge. The water district maintains a small landing and a safe and fairly easy portage route on river left.

For this section of the Kaw, it is the best of times and

the worst of times. More than 60 years of sand dredging have transformed this reach of the river into a large, channeled ditch, with steep banks lined with riprap. Unless the water is very low, it is very difficult to find a place to get out of your boat, except at the cofferdam. Yet this part of the river has much to offer. Anglers are rewarded with large stringers of catfish and carp. Paddlers enjoy it for a multitude of reasons, as you will discover.

In addition to the landing and portage route, Johnson County Water One maintains a fish ladder for pallid sturgeon in the main jetty. The fast water below the jetty can create some nice surfing waves at moderate flows. This is a dangerous place for unskilled paddlers. The water is fast, the hydraulics are powerful, and the rocks are sharp. Do not approach the fast water unless you have the requisite skills, equipment, and paddling partners. KDWP has shown interest in providing a public access for anglers and boaters. If built, it would be located off Woodend Road and just east of I-435.

Below the cofferdam, backwater from the Missouri River creates a 15.5-mile-long pool, the elevation of which depends on water levels in the Missouri. The remaining miles gradually and increasingly contrast a somewhat surreal cityscape against the ageless beauty of the river. The trees of the riparian and urban forests softly frame the steel, concrete, and glass of the city.

In order, the Turner Bridge (State Highway 32) is at mile 9.5, the I-635 bridge is at mile 7.2, and the Kansas Avenue bridge (Highway 32) is at mile 5.8. A rocky island rises from the river at mile 5.5. The 18th Street bridge (U.S. Highway 69) is at mile 5; then comes the 12th Street bridge at mile 4.4. As you round the bend at mile 3, have your camera ready to capture downtown Kansas City rising up from the river. There is a deteriorating boat ramp under the north side of the 7th Street bridge (U.S. Highway 169) at river mile 3.5. At this writing, the Fairfax Drainage District has closed the gate to this boat ramp due to illegal trash dumping. You can try to get a key from the Kaw Valley Drainage District office by calling (913) 342-2382.

Now the bridges come at you fast. There are nine bridges between mile 2.5 and Kaw Point and anglers seem to enjoy their shelter, come rain or shine.

Take out at **Kaw Point**, at river mile 0.1, on river left. The boat ramp is located at the northwest tip of the Kansas River's confluence with the Missouri River. **Caution:** Do not proceed downstream to the confluence with the Missouri River unless you have the skill to negotiate the turbulence at the meeting of these rivers. The Missouri River moves along at about 6 miles per hour. If you flip your boat, you could be in for a long and dangerous swim.

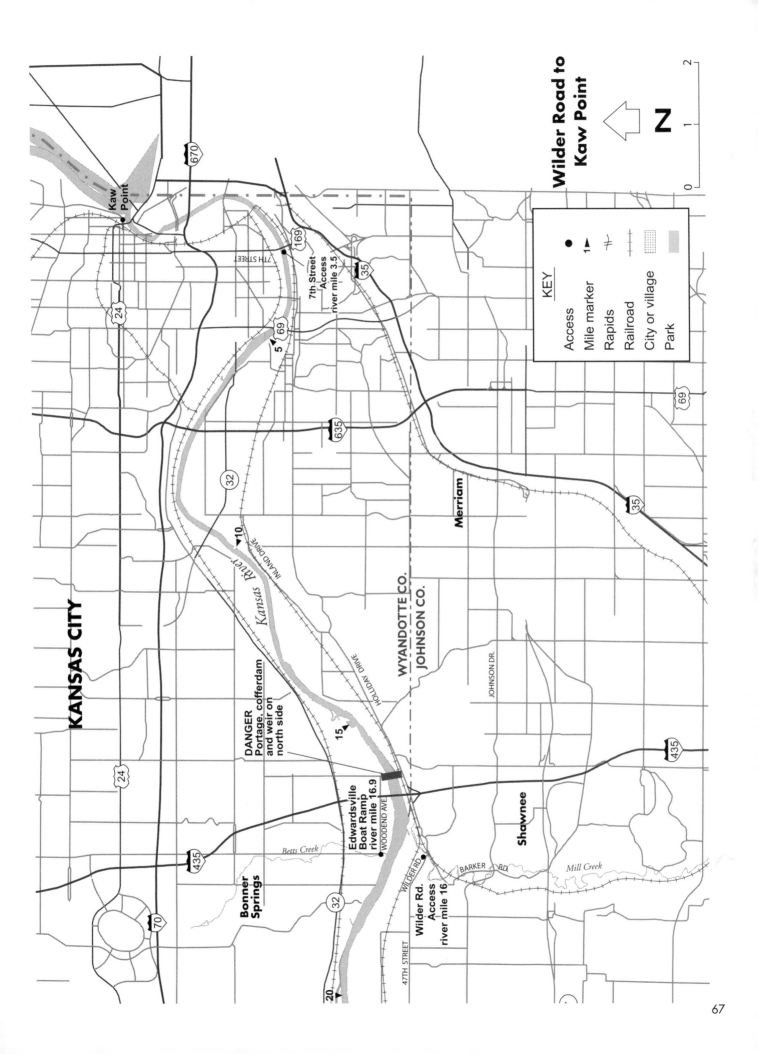

KANSAS CITY

Kaw Point

7th Street Access river mile 3.5

DANGER Portage, cofferdam and weir on north side

Edwardsville Boat Ramp river mile 16.9

Betts Creek

Bonner Springs

WYANDOTTE CO.

JOHNSON CO.

Merriam

Shawnee

Wilder Rd. Access river mile 16

BARKER RD.

Mill Creek

JOHNSON DR.

Kansas River

INLAND DRIVE

HOLLIDAY DRIVE

WOODEND AVE.

47TH STREET

7TH STREET

Wilder Road to Kaw Point

N

KEY

Access
Mile marker
Rapids
Railroad
City or village
Park

REPUBLICAN RIVER: ABOVE MILFORD LAKE

5 miles, intermediate access available, Class I difficulty
Broughton Bridge Access to Gatesville Boat Ramp

This beautiful, wildlife-rich segment of the river takes you through the 19,000-acre Milford Wildlife Area. The float from Broughton Bridge to the Gatesville Boat Ramp should take only two to four hours. The river is accessible all year long and the wildlife area is open for public hunting during the various seasons. The riverbed is mostly sandy, so, except after precipitation, the water is fairly clear to slightly turbid and the most common "hazard" is getting stuck on a shallow sandbar when the river is low.

The Republican River was named after a band of Pawnee Indians whom French explorers thought used a republican form of government. In more recent times, Milford Lake is best known by anglers for its crappie and walleye, but the lake also supports a good population of catfish and white bass. The crappie and white bass move up into the river during their spawning period. Angers who have fished the river for many years tell me the fishing is especially good when the water is running clear.

Although the Republican River watershed is huge—24,900 square miles, agricultural pumping in Nebraska has brought the flows that cross the Nebraska-Kansas border to a trickle compared with what they should be. A lightly loaded canoe can make it down the river with **100-150 CFS**. Use the **gauging station** at Republican River at Clay Center to determine flows and the Corps lake gauge to determine the lake level. The average **gradient** for this section, before you encounter the backwater of the lake, is 3 feet per mile.

Camping is not permitted along the river, but Milford Lake, the state's largest lake, has some nice campgrounds. You can reserve a campsite in the Corps' campgrounds by calling (877) 444-6777 (National Recreation Reservation Service) and you can contact the Milford State Park office at (785) 238-3014. (See the Milford Lake map in the Appendix.) You can find **canoe and kayak rentals** at Tuttle Creek State Park, below Tuttle Creek Lake Dam, ([785] 539-7941), and at Kansas State University, Manhattan, ([785] 532-6980 or [785] 532-6894); a KSU student or faculty ID is required.

The **put-in** is at the **southeast edge of Broughton Bridge**, located where Redwood Road (aka County Road 837) crosses over the river. The 22.6-mile **round-trip shuttle** route, from Broughton Bridge to the Gatesville Boat Ramp and back, is north on Redwood (County Road 837) to Broughton Road, east on Broughton Road to Valleyview Road (County Road 859), south on Valleyview Road to 10th Road, then west on 10th Road to the Gatesville Boat Ramp. The shortcut on Thunder Road (south from Broughton Road about a mile west of Valleyview Road) is either dusty or muddy, but always more scenic. The boat ramp area is not well marked, so it may not be obvious when you first drive by it.

From Broughton Bridge, it is 2.5 miles by river to **Beichter Bottom**, 5 miles to the Gatesville Boat Ramp, and 9.2 miles to the **Wakefield Clay County Park Access** on the lake. After unloading your boats at the Broughton Bridge Access, leave your vehicle in the parking area south of the bridge.

Put in at the Broughton Bridge Access. The steady current will carry you along through riparian forests of cottonwoods and sycamores and upland woods full of hickories, oaks, elms, and walnuts. The 1,100-acre **Steve Lloyd Wildlife Refuge** begins on river right near river mile 1 and extends roughly 4 miles along the west side of the river. Although the river is still accessible all year, the refuge is closed to all access from the opening day of the waterfowl hunting season until March 1 of each year. During the migratory season and deer season, the animals seem to know that they are safe in this area, so the late fall and winter months are a great time to paddle this segment.

At normal pool, Milford Lake backs up to just above the Gatesville Boat Ramp. This gives the paddler about five miles of moving water to play on before encountering the slower backwater from the lake. In the spring, when the white bass make their run upstream, the Beichter Bottoms area is a good place for anglers, especially when the river is running fairly clear. When the river gets high and the riverbed gets stirred up, the catfish move out of the lake and into this reach looking for food along the banks and around deep holes.

Take out at the **Gatesville Boat Ramp** on river left. The Corps maps show this part of the river as a broadening part of the lake, but the water hasn't been that high in years, so start watching for the boat ramp well before the lake begins to widen.

If you plan to paddle the additional 4 miles downstream to the Clay County Park (Wakefield), be aware that a giant muddy delta has choked the mouth of the lake just downstream of the Gatesville Boat Ramp. The river is passable when the river or the lake is high, but under lower water levels this reach is impassable. Do not attempt to paddle downstream of the Gatesville Boat Ramp unless you have either river flows in excess of 300 CFS or a lake surface elevation at least one foot above conservation pool. This last segment will be on open water and into the prevailing wind. If you get stuck in the middle of the mud flats, the only way out may be to paddle back upstream (maybe) or a very expensive helicopter ride after a miserable day spent floundering in mud. Always let someone know where you are going and when to expect you back. Take extra water and some way to signal for help. (Been there, done that—almost.)

Local Contacts: Army Corps of Engineers, (785) 238-5714; Milford Wildlife Area, (785) 461-5402.

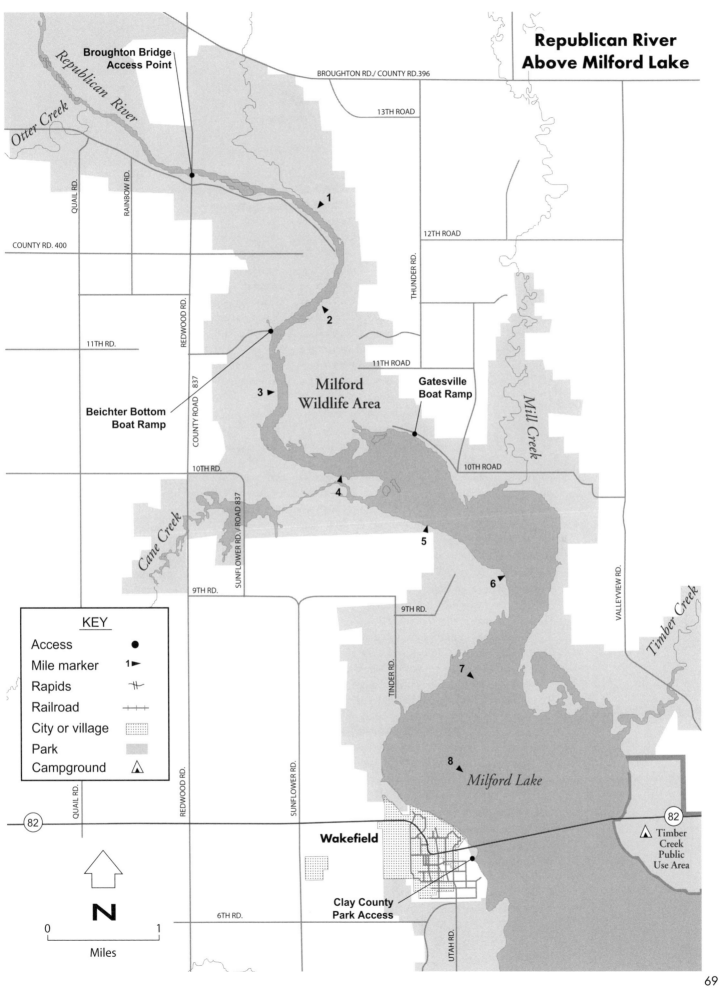

Republican River
Above Milford Lake

Broughton Bridge
Access Point

BROUGHTON RD./ COUNTY RD.396

13TH ROAD

Republican River

Otter Creek

QUAIL RD.

RAINBOW RD.

COUNTY RD. 400

12TH ROAD

THUNDER RD.

REDWOOD RD.

11TH RD.

11TH ROAD

COUNTY ROAD 837

Beichter Bottom
Boat Ramp

*Milford
Wildlife Area*

Gatesville
Boat Ramp

Mill Creek

10TH RD.

10TH ROAD

Cane Creek

SUNFLOWER RD./ ROAD 837

9TH RD.

9TH RD.

VALLEYVIEW RD.

Timber Creek

KEY

Access ●

Mile marker 1 ▶

Rapids ✜

Railroad ┼┼┼

City or village ▦

Park ▨

Campground ⚠

TINDER RD.

Milford Lake

QUAIL RD.

REDWOOD RD.

SUNFLOWER RD.

82

82

⚠ Timber
Creek
Public
Use Area

N

0   1

Miles

6TH RD.

Wakefield

UTAH RD.

Clay County
Park Access

REPUBLICAN RIVER: BELOW MILFORD LAKE

7.3 miles, intermediate access available, Class I difficulty
Milford Dam to Grant Avenue Park

THE KANSAS RIVER

The Kansas River is only about a hundred yards downstream of the Grant Avenue Park Access. If you continue paddling downstream on the Kansas River, you will come to Ogden in another 7 miles (another two to three hours), to Manhattan in 21 miles (two days recommended), or the Missouri River in 170.5 miles (about 10 to 15 days). See the section on the Kansas River for more details. It's a trip!

The cool, clear water from the bottom of Milford Lake will carry you swiftly through long pools and over rocky shoals toward its rendezvous with the Smoky Hill River in Junction City, where these two rivers converge to become the beautiful Kansas River.

You'll need **200 CFS or more** to squeak down, but with 300 CFS or more this float goes by quickly. Check the **gauging station** on the outflow of Milford Lake, but remember that the flows in this river segment are completely under the control of the Corps of Engineers and they can change that flow very quickly and very dramatically. Even though you may have checked their gauging station at the outfall, it is a good idea to call the Corps ([785] 238-5714) just before you launch, just to be sure. The average **gradient** on this segment is over 6.5 feet per mile, so the miles go by very easily.

Camping is not permitted along the river, but Milford Lake, the state's largest lake, has some nice campgrounds. You can reserve a campsite in the Corps' campgrounds by calling (877) 444-6777 (National Recreation Reservation Service) and you can contact the Milford State Park office at (785) 238-3014. (See the Milford Lake map in the Appendix.)

You can find **canoe and kayak rentals** at Tuttle Creek State Park, below Tuttle Creek Lake Dam, (785) 539-7941; Kansas State University, Manhattan, (785) 532-6980 or (785) 532-6894 (a KSU student or faculty ID is required); and Fort Riley Outdoor Recreation Center, on Fort Riley Military Reservation, in Building 9011 (785) 239-6368 or (785) 239-2364 (a military ID is required).

The **put-in** is at the south edge of the base of **Milford Dam in the Milford Dam South Outlet Park**. The 12.6 mile **round-trip shuttle** route, from the Milford Dam South Outlet Park to the Grant Avenue Park Access in Junction City and back, is east on State Highway 57 to 18th Street. Go east on 18th Street. Eighteenth Street becomes Grant Avenue. Continue east on Grant to Grant Avenue Park. The Grant Avenue Boat Ramp is located under the Republican River bridge at the east end of Grant Avenue Park. You'll know you have

gone too far if you pass over the river or come to the gates of Fort Riley. The take-out is at the end of the dirt track that leads down to the river. If you plan to leave your car overnight, consider moving it to an area with better lighting and security.

Put in at the base of Milford Dam. The banks there are steep and rocky, but manageable. Due to the danger of fast-rising water from the base of the dam, keep boats tied up and attended while loading and running shuttles and while on the river. Do not approach the base of the dam by boat under any circumstances.

As you move downstream, you will float between steep hills on both sides of the river. You will be tempted, but don't plan to camp along this segment of the Republican River. It isn't allowed—and for good reason: A nighttime release from Milford Dam could wash you and your belongings away very suddenly. Similarly, releases from the base of Milford Dam may also be turned off very quickly. When the Corps turns off the water, the river begins to drop fast. Your best bet is to keep moving, especially if the flows seem to be receding.

The outer banks of the river are high enough to contain the maximum releases from the dam and the rocky riverbed is fairly well swept clear of large vegetation. Without obstruction, the cool, clear water moves right along and the gravel bars provide inviting spots for swimming, skipping rocks, or eating lunch.

The first bridge you come to is U.S. Highway 77. **Access points** at either end of the bridge make good alternate take-outs or put-ins. Shortly after you cross under the Highway 77 bridge, the river begins to spread out and slow down a little and the property line for Fort Riley appears on river left. The Fort's property is off limits and extends the rest of the way to the take-out and beyond.

Near river mile 5, you will pass under the Washington Street bridge (G Street from Fort Riley). As you pass by Junction City, you will see junk cars, tires, concrete rubble, and other trash piled along the banks and sometimes in the river. Very sad!

Take out at **Grant Avenue Park** at river mile 7.3. The park is under your third bridge. If you pass this access by, you will come to the confluence of the Smoky Hill River, where the Republican and Smoky Hill join to form the Kansas River (aka the Kaw).

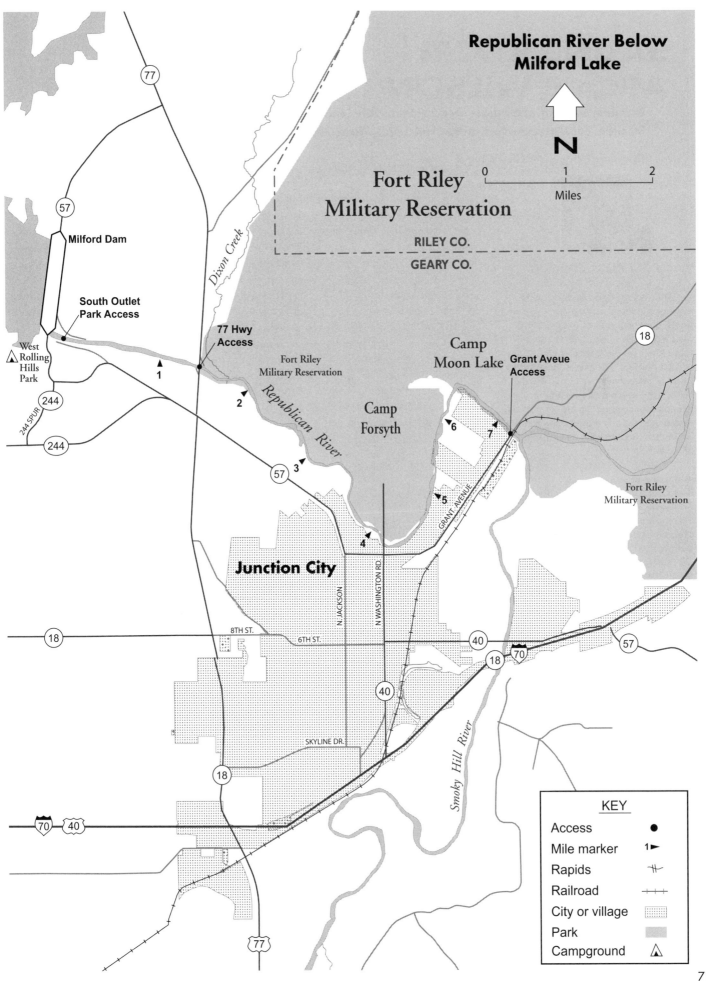

Republican River Below Milford Lake

N

0   1   2
Miles

Fort Riley
Military Reservation

RILEY CO.

GEARY CO.

Milford Dam

South Outlet
Park Access

77 Hwy
Access

Dixon Creek

Fort Riley
Military Reservation

Camp
Moon Lake

Grant Aveue
Access

West
Rolling
Hills
Park

Republican River

Camp
Forsyth

GRANT AVENUE

Fort Riley
Military Reservation

Junction City

N. JACKSON

N WASHINGTON RD.

8TH ST.

6TH ST.

SKYLINE DR.

Smoky Hill River

244 SPUR

KEY

Access   ●

Mile marker   1▶

Rapids   ╫

Railroad   +++

City or village

Park

Campground   △

SALINE RIVER: ABOVE WILSON LAKE

6 miles, with intermediate access available, Class I difficulty
Decker Road Access to Bunker Hill-Lurey Road access

POST ROCK COUNTRY AND TRAILS

This is Post Rock Country. Early European settlers, lacking trees for fence posts, quarried and cut the limestone rock from nearby deposits to use as fence posts on the treeless plains. Even after more than 100 years, miles and miles of stone fence posts still stand. Here is the original "home on the range" that inspired Dr. Brewster Higley to write one of the most lasting refrains and what came to be the state song of Kansas.

There are several good hiking and/or biking trails in Wilson State Park. Burr Oak Nature Trail (0.75 miles), the Rocktown Trail (3 miles), and the Switchgrass Mountain Bike Trail (4 miles) are near the lake and very scenic. The Dakota Trail has a one-mile and a half-mile interpretive loop (pick up a guide at the trailhead) that will help you learn about the native plants and habitat.

This float is in one of the most scenic parts of the Smoky Hills. This is a land of rolling grassland prairies and hills, wind-sculpted rock formations, buttes, and long vistas. French explorers named the river "Saline" because of the salt it picks up across north-central Kansas. With a grassland watershed of over 1,900 square miles, Wilson Lake is the clearest, coolest, and deepest lake in the state. It also sports the best fishing and the largest variety of fish species in the state. The lake is stocked with millions of fish, including walleye, white bass, smallmouth bass, and striped bass. The striped bass, a nonnative oceanic species, reach weights of over 40 pounds in the lake's salty waters. In the spring and fall, the Wilson Wildlife Area, through which the Saline flows, attracts many thousands of waterfowl. Bald eagles often winter around the lake.

Tamarisk (salt-cedar) plants just began sprouting along the shoreline. Unless control measures are implemented, the banks will soon be covered with these obnoxious, intrusive, nonnative plants.

The Decker Road Access to the Cedar Flats Boat Ramp will require **200 CFS or more**. You actually only need about 50 CFS for the first 3 to 4 miles, but there are two problems that will confront you with such low flows. The riverbed has been covered with three feet of stinking, black, anaerobic muck. With low flows you will have a hard time getting in and out of your boat without sinking knee deep, or worse, into this nasty stuff. Further down, the mouth of the river forms a broad delta that has also been filled with this muck. Once in that delta, you want to be very sure that you can float over it without stepping out of your boat. I made that mistake once—and I won't do it again. If the lake's surface elevation is at 1,516 feet or more you should have enough water to float the entire segment with only about 50-100 CFS. The average **gradient** is only 1.3 feet per mile, but it is enough to carry you along nicely until you hit the backwater of the lake.

Determining whether you will have enough water in the Saline River or on Wilson Lake to do a good float trip takes more thought than for most rivers. First check the **gauging station** at the Saline River near Russell and the Corps lake elevation gauge on

Wilson Lake. The interpretation of those numbers is the trick. By way of example, you could have 1,000 CFS coming down the river in Russell, but have only 10 CFS left in the river by the time it reaches the Wilson Wildlife Area. If the area has been dry, the high flows can run up the dry creek beds and disappear into the dry, highly permeable sandy soils of the riverbed. The best way to interpret the gauge is to look at the history of recent flows, precipitation, and lake levels. If the river has been holding water for more than a week, the lake is rising, and the immediate area has been getting some rain, then you can be sure that the river will not peter out on you.

There are no **canoe or kayak rentals** in the area and **camping** is not allowed on the river, but you will find very nice campgrounds around the lake. You can reserve a campsite at the Corps' campgrounds ([877] 444-6777) (National Recreation Reservation Service) or at Wilson State Park ([785] 658-2465) from April 1 to October 31. (See the Wilson Lake map in the Appendix.) The state park also rents camping equipment at the park office.

To get to the **put-in** on **Decker Road** from I-70, take the Bunker Hill exit (Bunker Hill-Luray Road, a.k.a. 193rd Street). Go north on Bunker Hill-Luray Road past Bunker Hill and about five or six miles more (it changes name from 193rd to 192nd) until you cross the Saline River; then turn west (left) on Decker Road and follow it until it bends right, about a mile. The 12.2-mile **round-trip shuttle** from the Decker Road Access to the **Cedar Creek Boat Ramp** goes east on Decker Road to 193rd Road, then south about 1.4 miles to Land Road (aka Rogg Road), then east to the end of the road, where a smaller road takes you north to the river and the Cedar Creek Boat Ramp.

Put in at the Decker Road Access. It is on a single-track "road" that can become deeply rutted. Low-clearance vehicles might want to take special care. Access to the river may take a little bushwhacking. As you float downstream, you might feel as if you were just dropped into an old Western movie. Refrains of "Home on The Range" may come to mind. The river is small, but the sky and view are huge. Watch for bobwhites, coyotes, greater prairie chickens, thirteen-lined ground squirrels, pocket gophers, collared lizards, cliff swallows, cormorants, geese, ospreys, sandhill cranes, golden and bald eagles, white-tailed deer, mule deer, cottontail deer, and ring-necked pheasants.

As you pass under the Bunker Hill-Luray Bridge, you will begin to get a better view of the bluffs and wind-carved red Dakota sandstone rock outcroppings that rim the valley. This valley was full of large cottonwood trees until 1990, when floodwaters drowned them. Most of the old trees have now fallen down and new vegetation has taken hold.

Take out at Cedar Creek Boat Ramp. Watch for it near river mile 6, where the hills that you have been passing by on the right side of the river begin to flatten out a little.

Local Contacts: Army Corps of Engineers, (785) 658-2551; Wildlife Area Office, (785) 483-5615.

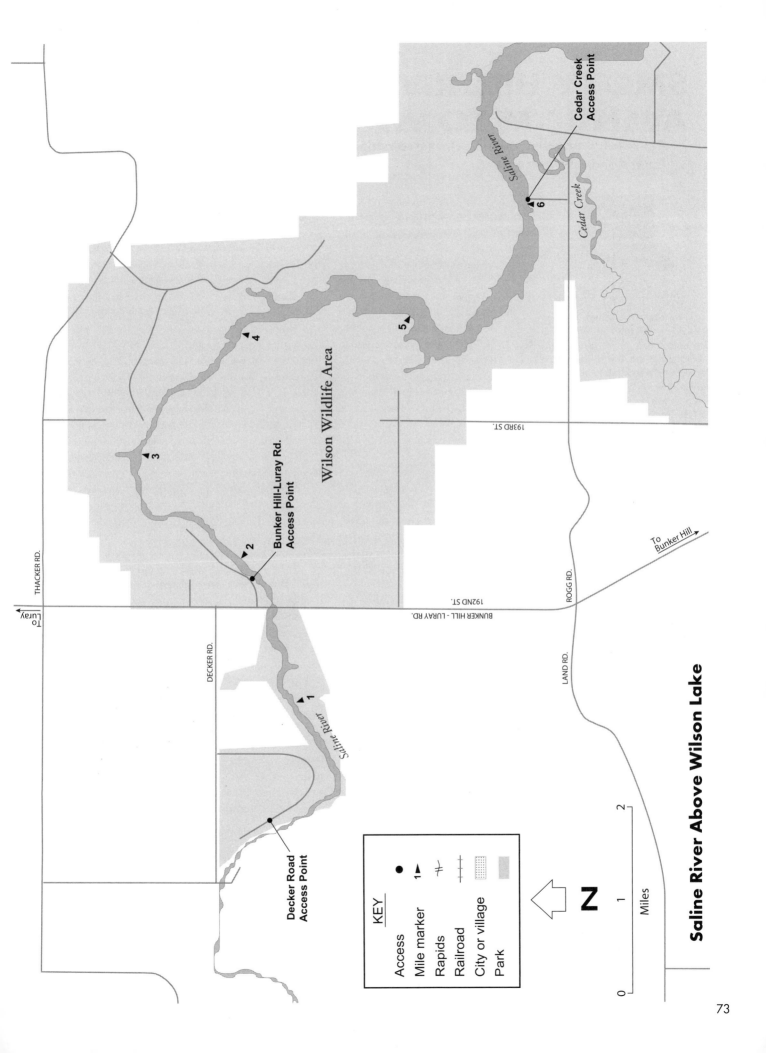

Cedar Creek
Access Point

Saline River

Cedar Creek

6

5

4

Wilson Wildlife Area

3

193RD ST.

Bunker Hill-Luray Rd.
Access Point

2

To Bunker Hill

THACKER RD.

To Luray

DECKER RD.

192ND ST.

BUNKER HILL - LURAY RD.

ROGG RD.

LAND RD.

1

Saline River

Decker Road
Access Point

KEY

● Access
▲ Mile marker
⊁ Rapids
╫ Railroad
City or village
Park

N

0   1   2
        Miles

Saline River Above Wilson Lake

SMOKY HILL RIVER: AVENUE M TO WHITE BASS RUN

8.5 miles, with intermediate access available, Class I difficulty
From Kanopolis Access

THE FORT HARKER GUARDHOUSE MUSEUM

This historic building is on the west side of the town of Kanopolis. First named Fort Ellsworth, it provided protection for the Kansas Stage Line and the military wagon trains that traveled the Fort Riley Road and Smoky Hill Route to Denver. The post was renamed Fort Harker in 1866.

In 1866, young Bill Cody took his first scouting job at the fort. While hunting buffalo for the railroad the next year, he became known as "Buffalo Bill."

Fort Harker served as a supply depot and distribution point for the forts in Arizona, Colorado, New Mexico, and northern Texas.

Today, most of what was Fort Harker is private property and is managed by the Ellsworth County Historical Society.

This is the first of two segments on one of the prettiest small-stream floats in Kansas. Because of its length and convenient access, the river is easily divided into two roughly equal segments. The first of these is this **8.5-mile segment** that runs from just west of the town of **Kanopolis** to the **White Bass Run Access**. This upper section and the **11.7-mile** lower section, covered in the next chapter, can be combined to make a great, multi-day float.

The average **gradient** is 3 feet per mile. This upper reach can be paddled in three to six hours with a **minimum recommended flow of 100 CFS**. Calculating flows takes some work. First check recent and current flows on the gauging station on the Smoky Hill River at Ellsworth. Then check **the Corps lake gauge**. The interpretation of those numbers is the trick. For example, you could have 1,000 CFS coming down the river at Ellsworth, but have only 10 CFS left in the river by the time it reaches the Kanopolis Wildlife Area. If the area has been dry, the high flows can run *up* the dry creek beds and disappear into the highly permeable sandy soils before they reach this part of the river. If the river has been holding water for several days, the lake is rising and the immediate area has been getting some rain, then you can be sure that the river is not disappearing into the sand. If in doubt, call the Kanopolis Wildlife Area manager at the number below.

Camping is not allowed along the river, but campsites are available at the state and Corps campgrounds around the lake. The reservation number for the Corps area is (877) 444-6777 (National Recreation Reservation Service) and the State Park

number (Horsethief Area) is (785) 546-2779. There are no **canoe or kayak rentals** in the area. See lake map in next segment.

To get to the **put-in** at the **Avenue M Access** from the town of Kanopolis, go west on West Ohio Street (aka Avenue L) to 18th Road. Go south on 16th Road to Avenue M and then east on Avenue M to the access. If the cable is not across the trail, you can drive the short distance to the river, unload, and then drive outside the gate and park on the *road* (off the grass). Otherwise, carry your boat about 200 yards from the road. The 21.2-mile **round-trip shuttle**, from the Avenue M Access to White Bass Flats and back, is west on Avenue M to 18th Road, north to Avenue L (aka Ohio Street), east through the town of Kanopolis and out the other side to 22nd Road. Go south on 22nd Road, follow the jog on Avenue M, and continue south on 22nd Road to Avenue N. Go west on Avenue N. You will find the White Bass Run Access where the road turns north, on the way to Faris Caves.

Put in at the Avenue M Access. For the first mile or so downstream, you'll find large iron relics in the river but soon almost all of the signs of man disappear. To the north and east, the riverbanks grow steeper and sandstone outcroppings begin to appear more regularly. As the river meanders through the 11,000-acre Kanopolis Wildlife Area, the riverbanks are a linear forest of cottonwood and sycamores.

There are plenty of places to get out and hike. When the river is low, you may even prefer hiking to paddling. The sandy riverbed is beautiful and you will enjoy the cool water, the forested landscape, and the many birds, fish, mussels, and tadpoles. Near river mile 2, the 18th Road Access is on river left. The banks are very steep, so I recommend this as an emergency exit only. If you use it, park on the gravel at the end of the road (off the grass) and carry your boat. Just downstream of here, the river will make a sharp bend back to the northeast. The bluffs on river right are known as Eagles Roost.

Near river mile 5.4, the **Grubb Access** provides another emergency access, but it is another steep and overgrown site hardly worthy of the term "access." **Faris Caves** are about 75 yards east of the river and about a half mile upstream of Hummel Bridge. The caves, built around 1890, aren't much more than small rooms carved into the sandstone rock, but early European settlers used them as homes, as storage, and even as a small schoolhouse.

Your first good intermediate access, the **Hummel Bridge Access**, is near river mile 8. If you use this access and the ground is wet, park on the road and carry your boat.

Take out at **White Bass Run**, on river left near river mile 8.5. If you didn't already find a good spot to climb the banks to see Faris Caves, it is an easy walk up the trail. If you wish to paddle all or part of the next river segment, carefully read the information about minimum flows and lake levels in the next section to be sure you will have enough water to complete your trip.

Local Contacts: Kanopolis Wildlife Area Office, (785) 546-2279.

The Smoky Hill River with about 50 CFS near Hummel Bridge

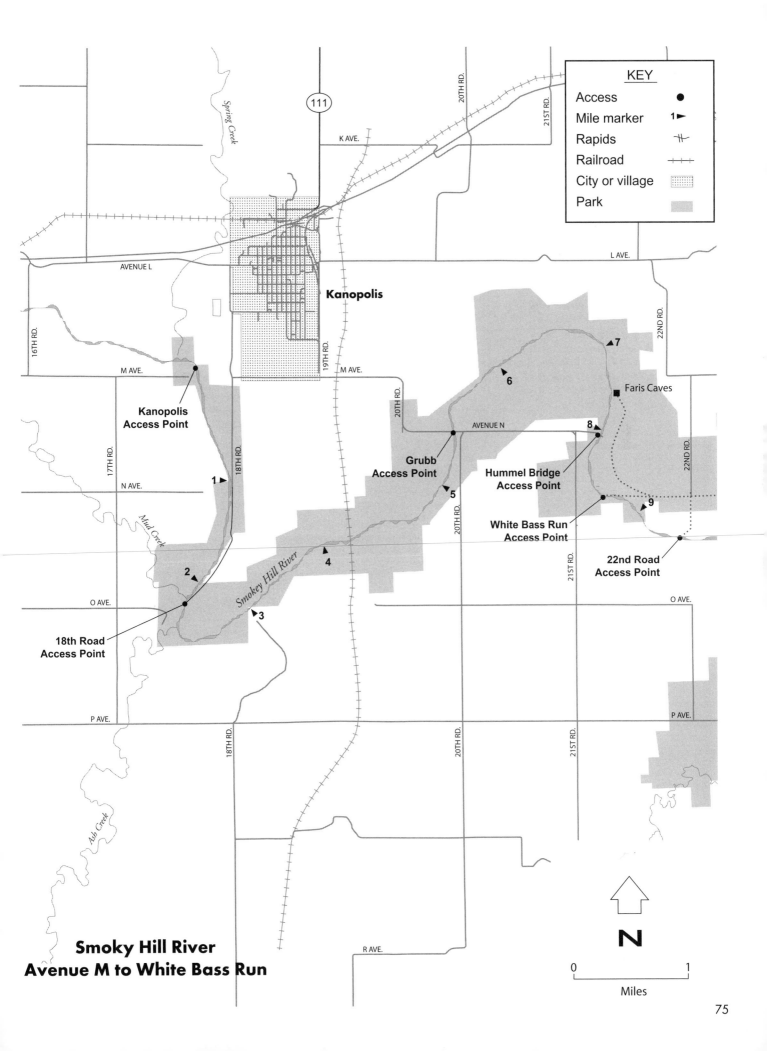

KEY

Access ●
Mile marker 1▶
Rapids ＃
Railroad ┼┼┼
City or village
Park

Kanopolis

Kanopolis
Access Point

Grubb
Access Point

Hummel Bridge
Access Point

Faris Caves

White Bass Run
Access Point

22nd Road
Access Point

18th Road
Access Point

Spring Creek

Mud Creek

Ash Creek

Smokey Hill River

K AVE.

AVENUE L

M AVE.

M AVE.

N AVE.

O AVE.

P AVE.

AVENUE N

L AVE.

O AVE.

P AVE.

R AVE.

16TH RD.

17TH RD.

18TH RD.

18TH RD.

19TH RD.

20TH RD.

20TH RD.

20TH RD.

21ST RD.

21ST RD.

22ND RD.

22ND RD.

22ND RD.

111

**Smoky Hill River
Avenue M to White Bass Run**

N

0   1
Miles

SMOKY HILL RIVER: WHITE BASS FLATS TO KANOPOLIS STATE PARK

11.7-miles, intermediate access available, Class I difficulty
White Bass Run Access to Horsethief Area Ramp

MUSHROOM ROCK STATE PARK

Mushroom Rock State Park is a five-acre park that is located north of Kanopolis Lake and a few miles west of State Highway 141. The Dakota formations are the remains of sandy beaches and sediments of the Cretaceous Period, about 144 to 66 million years ago. The rocks look like giant mushrooms, the largest of which measures 27 feet in diameter.

This is the second segment on one of the prettiest rivers in Kansas. The lake and this lower segment are known for their white bass; the lake is also home to walleye and wipers (hybrid cross between the white bass and the striped bass). The time needed to paddle to the Big Bottoms Access or the Horsethief Area will vary dramatically, depending on lake levels and river flows. If the river is high and the lake is low, you can make it all the way to the Horsethief Area in two to four hours, but river and wind conditions on the lake can lengthen your trip time substantially.

At the put-in, the river is as narrow as the reaches upstream, but as you approach the Big Bottoms Area, the river becomes wider and shallower and you will need a proportionally larger volume of water to float it comfortably. By the time you reach the mouth of the lake, your progress downstream will require either **200 CFS** or enough water in the lake to cover the delta area. A lake surface elevation two feet above conservation pool or higher should do the job. Any less than that and you will have an 8-mile walk through a muddy delta to reach your take-out.

Determining whether you will have enough water in both the river and the lake to do a good float trip takes more thought than for most rivers. To calculate the flow, first check recent and current flows on the **gauging station** on the Smoky Hill River at Ellsworth. Then check the **Corps lake gauge**. You could, for example, have 1,000 CFS coming down the river at Ellsworth, but have only 10 CFS left in the river by the time it reaches the Kanopolis Wildlife Area. If the area has been dry, the high flows can run up dry creek beds and soak into sandy soils before they get to this part of the river. To ensure adequate flow, check to see if the river has been holding water for several days, the lake is rising, and the areas upstream have been getting some rain. If in doubt, call the Kanopolis Wildlife Area manager at the number below. The average **gradient** above the delta is about 6 feet per mile, but that gradient effectively disappears when the river meets the lake.

Camping is not allowed along the river, but the camps are very nice at the state and Corps campgrounds around the lake. The reservation number for the Corps campground is (877) 444-6777 (National Recreation Reservation Service); the Kanopolis State Park number (Horsethief Area) is (785) 546-2779. (See the Kanopolis Lake maps in the Appendix.)

To get to the **put-in at the White Bass Run Access** from Kanopolis, go east on Ohio Street out of town to 22nd Road and head south. Follow the jog on Avenue M but continue south on 22nd Road to Avenue N. Go west on Avenue N. You will find the White Bass Run Access where the road turns north, on the way to Faris Caves. Your 46-mile **round-trip shuttle**, from White Bass Run to the Horsethief Canyon area, will be 6 miles shorter when they reopen 22nd Road, but at this writing the roads that would take you directly north to State Highway 140 are washed out. So for now, from White Bass Run go back to the town of Kanopolis, then north on State Highway 11 (Missouri Drive) to Highway 140, then east to State Highway 141, and then south to Kanopolis State Park. Turn into the park area and follow the signs to the boat ramp that is nearest the Worthier Canyon area. This will be next to Trailhead B on the Kanopolis State Park map that you will get when you enter the park.

Put in at White Bass Flats. The riverbed is still narrow, but as the river meanders through the Smoky Hills and the 11,000-acre **Kanopolis Wildlife Area**, the nearby riparian landscapes of cottonwoods and sycamores are increasingly displaced by Dakota sandstone outcroppings that rise up along the north edge of the river and lake. Pheasant, quail, prairie chicken, rabbit, white-tailed deer, and mule deer are the most abundant game species, but there are also plenty of ducks, geese, coyotes, fox, mink, and beaver.

The river gradually widens as the hills and sandstone cliffs rise higher along the north shore. You are now entering the Big Bottoms Area near river mile 12.5. When the lake is four feet below conservation pool, this is also where the river and lake meet. At or below conservation pool, the reach downstream of the **Big Bottoms Access** becomes a widening delta. As the river becomes a lake, your vista of the hill country and rugged terrain begins to broaden. A waterfowl refuge begins along the eastern shore, where the river begins to make a giant turn to the south. Below the **Buckeye Fishing Access**, the rest of the river, the upper end of the lake and both shores are closed to all access from October 1 through March 1 of each year. With little wind and enough water, the delta and lake over the next 8.7 miles are very enjoyable.

Take out in the **Horsethief Area**, at Kanopolis State Park. Be sure to allow two to six hours to hike Horsethief Canyon, Red Rock Canyons, and the Alum Creek Trail areas. Don't cut yourself short on time, camera film, or drinking water. There are several stream crossings and 24 miles of trails that wind through tallgrass prairies, small canyons, and interesting rock formations.

Local Contacts: Kanopolis Wildlife Area Office, (785) 546-2779.

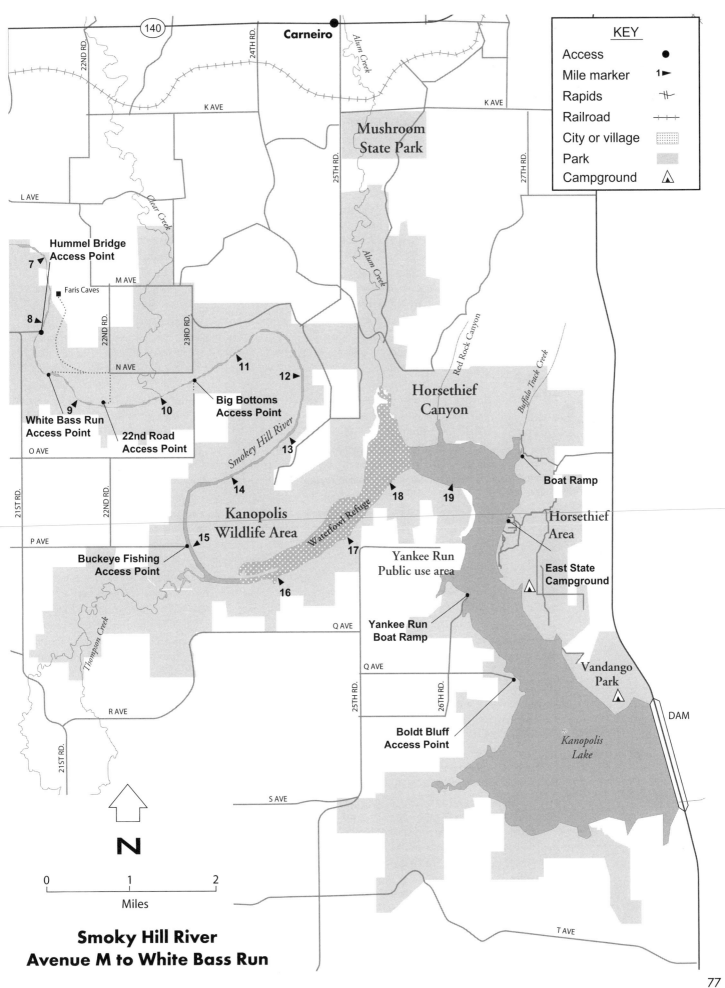

KEY

Access	●
Mile marker	1▶
Rapids	╫
Railroad	┼┼┼┼
City or village	▦
Park	▨
Campground	⛺

140

Carneiro

Alum Creek

Mushroom State Park

K AVE

K AVE

22ND RD.

24TH RD.

25TH RD.

27TH RD.

L AVE

Clear Creek

Hummel Bridge Access Point

7▼

Faris Caves

M AVE

8▼

22ND RD.

23RD RD.

N AVE

11▼

12▶

White Bass Run Access Point

9

10▼

Big Bottoms Access Point

22nd Road Access Point

Smokey Hill River

13▼

O AVE

14▼

Alum Creek

Red Rock Canyon

Buffalo Track Creek

Horsethief Canyon

Boat Ramp

21ST RD.

22ND RD.

Kanopolis Wildlife Area

18▼

19▼

Horsethief Area

P AVE

15▶

Waterfowl Refuge

17▼

East State Campground ⛺

Buckeye Fishing Access Point

16▼

Yankee Run Public use area

Thompson Creek

Q AVE

Yankee Run Boat Ramp

Q AVE

25TH RD.

26TH RD.

Vandango Park ⛺

DAM

R AVE

Boldt Bluff Access Point

Kanopolis Lake

21ST RD.

N

S AVE

0   1   2
Miles

T AVE

Smoky Hill River
Avenue M to White Bass Run

77

BIG BLUE RIVER: BLUE RAPIDS TO THE BLACK VERMILLION RIVER

11 miles, intermediate access available, Class I difficulty
Highway 77 to 14th Road

TRAIL GUIDE FOR THE AREA

The 4.5-mile Fancy Creek Mountain Bike Trail offers challenging terrain and is one of the state's best trails of its kind. There are 5 miles of loop trails in Carnahan Creek Park and a 12-mile linear trail that goes to Garrison Lake. Randolph State Park has over 12 miles of scenic loops through prairie and wooded ravines. The Spillway Cycle Area is a popular, 45-acre ATV and motorcycle park. The Tuttle Creek Off-Road Vehicle Area is a 310-acre park that is open to all vehicles. It features many miles of steep, rugged terrain. The Konza Prairie, the largest tallgrass prairie in the country, is located southwest of Manhattan, west of State Highway 177 on McDowell Creek Road. Some of the fossils in the rocks below Tuttle Creek Spillway are also pretty neat.

The 21.1-mile float from Blue Rapids to the Swede Creek Marsh Boat Ramp can be easily divided into two-day trips, the first of which is covered here.

The fishing, wildlife, and beauty of the Tuttle Creek Lake State Wildlife Management Area, combined with somewhat dependable flows and abundant sandbars, make the Big Blue River a local favorite. The crappie run can be excellent. The turbidity of the water and the somewhat muddy riverbed provide good conditions for channel and flathead catfish. The area around Tuttle Creek Lake also has nice hiking, equestrian, and mountain bike trails.

The **minimum recommended flow on the Big Blue is 300 CFS** or more. To calculate the flow at the put-in, add the flow from the USGS **gauging station** on Big Blue River at Marysville to the flow from the Little Blue at Barnes. The .6 foot per mile **gradient** provides a steady 1- to 2-mile-per-hour current until the river meets the backwater of the lake, near the Irving Bridge Access.

Camping is not allowed except in park areas, but good campsites are available at the state or federal park areas around the Tuttle Creek Reservoir. (See a Tuttle Creek Lake map for more detail.) You can make campsite reservations in Stockdale Park by calling (877) 444-6777 (National Recreation Reservation Service) or online at www.recreation.gov. The Tuttle Creek State Park's number is (785) 539-7941.

You can find **canoe and kayak rentals** at Tuttle Creek State Park, below Tuttle Creek Lake Dam, (785) 539-7941; Kansas State University, Manhattan, (785) 532-6980 or (785) 532-6894 (a KSU student or faculty ID is required); and Fort Riley Outdoor Recreation Center, (785) 239-6368 or (785) 239-2364 (a military ID is required).

To get to the **put-in** at the **Blue Rapids Access** from the town of Blue Rapids, go a half mile east on U.S. Highway 77 across the bridge to the small dirt road on the northwest side. Follow this road under the bridge to the river. This access is steep, muddy, and infested with poison ivy and stinging nettles. Long pants, a shirt, and socks can help reduce poison ivy exposure. If this access road is muddy, park your car at the state historical marker that is located east of the bridge on the south side of the road. Your 24-mile **round-trip shuttle** will take you east on State Highway 9 to 13th Terrace. Go south on 13th Terrace to Zenith Road. Follow 13th Terrace/Zenith Road south to 14th Road and across the Black Vermillion. After you cross the river, turn west (right) onto the first dirt road. Park on firm ground near the bridge. The take-out is near the bridge. The dirt road downstream along the Black Vermillion is suitable only under dry conditions. Walk or drive the half-mile fair-weather trail down to the confluence so that you are sure to be able to identify it from the river.

Put in at the Blue Rapids Access. Here the river flows between forested hills of hardwoods, past the wetlands, and views of distant, rolling, tallgrass prairie hills. These areas are chock-full of wildlife, including deer, wild turkeys and waterfowl, coyotes, and bobcat. With only a few exceptions, the woods along either bank within this segment are in the project lands of the Tuttle Creek Lake and are fair game for exploration. You will rarely find more beavers per river mile than you will here. Have your camera ready as you float by their large holes in the riverbanks. Irving Marsh begins on river right, near river mile 4, just downstream of a railroad bridge. Near river mile 5.7, the stone bridge pilings on river left and the concrete pillar at midstream are the remnants of the old Zenith Road bridge. The banks are steep and the footing is poor, but in an emergency you can scramble out on river right and hike 100 yards west to a small dirt road.

Intermittent high water from the lake and the activity of beavers cause the banks to be rather steep, yet there are plenty of good sandbars in the upper and middle reaches. In the lower reaches, the sandbars are silted over with mud when not inundated by the lake.

As you approach river mile 10.5, keep a sharp eye on river left for the mouth of the Black Vermillion River. Follow it and **take out** a **half mile upstream**.

Local Contacts: U.S. Army Corps of Engineers, (785) 539-8511; Kansas Department of Wildlife and Parks, (785) 363-7316; Tuttle Creek State Park, (785) 539-7941; Tuttle Creek Wildlife Area, (785) 363-7316.

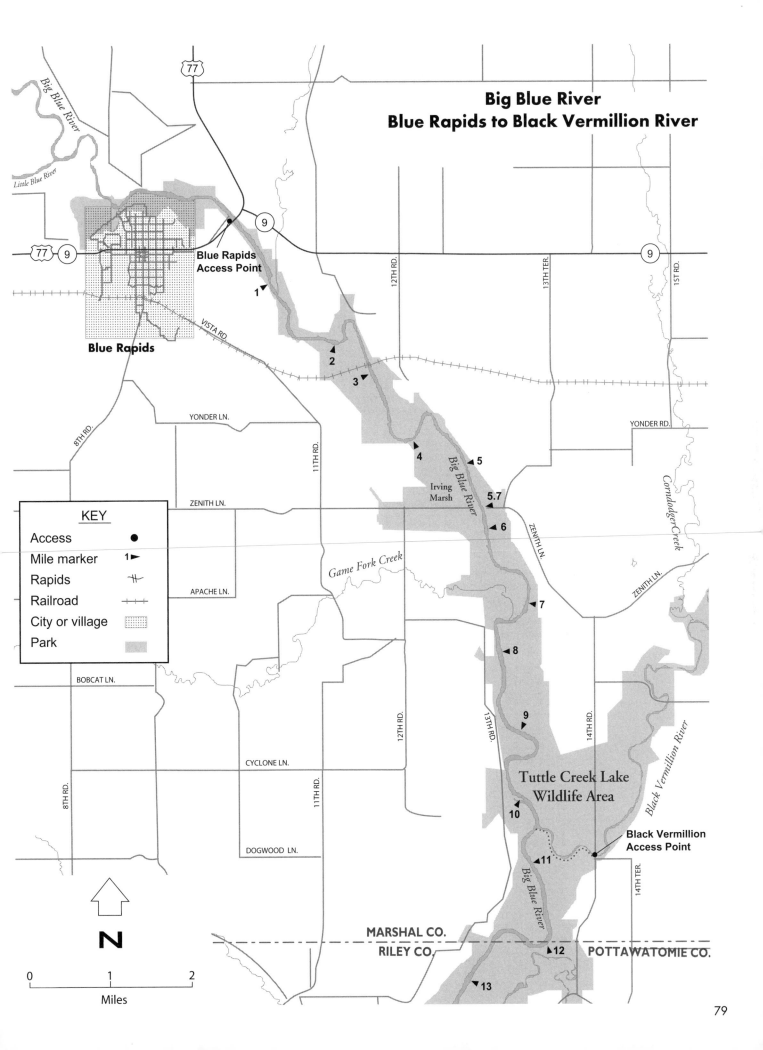

Big Blue River
Blue Rapids to Black Vermillion River

Blue Rapids

Blue Rapids
Access Point

KEY

Access	●
Mile marker	1▶
Rapids	┼┼
Railroad	┼┼┼
City or village	▦
Park	▨

Big Blue River

Little Blue River

Big Blue River

Irving Marsh

Game Fork Creek

Corndodger Creek

Tuttle Creek Lake
Wildlife Area

Black Vermillion River

Black Vermillion
Access Point

MARSHAL CO.
RILEY CO.
POTTAWATOMIE CO.

N

0   1   2
Miles

VISTA RD.
8TH RD.
YONDER LN.
11TH RD.
ZENITH LN.
APACHE LN.
BOBCAT LN.
8TH RD.
CYCLONE LN.
11TH RD.
DOGWOOD LN.
12TH RD.
13TH RD.
14TH RD.
13TH TER.
1ST RD.
YONDER RD.
ZENITH LN.
ZENITH LN.
14TH TER.
12TH RD.

79

BIG BLUE RIVER: BLACK VERMILLION RIVER TO SWEDE CREEK

10.1 miles, intermediate access available, Class I difficulty
14th Road to Carlson Road

This segment from Black Vermillion to Swede Creek is the second part of a 21.1-mile, two-day float from Blue Rapids to Swede Creek Marsh Boat Ramp.

The fishing, wildlife, and beauty of the Tuttle Creek Lake State Wildlife Area, combined with somewhat dependable flows and backwater from Tuttle Creek Lake, make this segment popular with anglers. The crappie run can be excellent, particularly in this lower reach. The turbidity of the water and the somewhat muddy riverbed provide good conditions for channel and flatheads catfish. The area around Tuttle Creek Lake also has nice hiking, equestrian, and mountain bike trails. (See the sidebar on area trails in the previous section.)

When the lake is at conservation pool or above, this part of the Big Blue is floatable whenever not frozen. Check the **lake gauge** for Tuttle Creek Reservoir. Even if the lake is low, if the Big Blue is running **400 CFS** or more, you can still get through. To make a rough calculation of flow at the put-in, add the flow from the USGS **gauging station** on Big Blue River at Marysville to the flow from the Little Blue at Barnes and add a little more for the tributaries that are downstream of those gauges. Unless the lake is low, the river is now entirely in the backwater of the lake; there is no **gradient** to this river segment.

Camping is not allowed except in park areas, but good campsites are available at the state or federal park areas around the Tuttle Creek Reservoir. (See a Tuttle Creek Lake map for more detail.) You can make campsite reservations in Stockdale Park by calling (877) 444-6777 (National Recreation Reservation Service) or online at www.recreation.gov. The Tuttle Creek State Park's number is (785) 539-7941.

You can find **canoe and kayak rentals** at Tuttle Creek State Park, below Tuttle Creek Lake Dam, (785) 539-7941; Kansas State University, Manhattan, (785) 532-6980 or (785) 532-6894 (a KSU student or faculty ID is required); and at Fort Riley Outdoor Recreation Center (785) 239-6368 or (785) 239-2364 (a military ID is required).

The **put-in** at the **Black Vermillion Access** is located just southwest of the 14th Road bridge over the Black Vermillion River. The 68-mile **round-trip shuttle**, from the put-in to the Swede Creek Marsh Boat Ramp and back, goes south on 14th Road, then curves right (west) on Shannon Creek Road briefly and then south again on Four Mile Road, and then south (right) on Spring Creek Road to State Highway 16. Turn west on Highway 16, pass Olsburg, and then cross the bridge over Tuttle Creek Lake to U.S. Highway 77 (aka Tuttle Creek Boulevard). Go north on Highway 77 to Rose Hill Road (aka County Road 897); then turn east (right), following its bend to the north to Carlson Road (aka County Road 362). Turn right (east) on Carlson Road and follow it to the boat ramp. For a shorter float, use the Redbud Boat Ramp in the Timber Creek Marsh Area, south of Dial Road where it hits 3400 Road W and Vilander Road. Note that the road signs and odd-angled intersections can make road navigation tricky. A compass and/or a GPS can be handy, especially on a cloudy day or at night.

Put in at the southwest edge of the Black Vermillion Bridge at 14th Road and float a half mile to its confluence with the Big Blue (Big Blue river mile 10.5). The banks of the Black Vermillion are steep and often muddy, as are the banks of the Big Blue. Moving downstream, the paddler will find little or no current and fewer places to get off the river, yet the broadening valley provides long vistas of the surrounding Flint Hills and rolling grasslands. Though this reach is usually all backwater from the lake, it is still narrow and follows the original meandering river channel. At river mile 14.2, Spring Creek enters on river left. The activity of beavers is everywhere. Keep your camera ready as you approach the dens that look like basketball-size holes in the banks, but don't get too close. Large families of 30- to 50-pound beavers can make quite an upset if you block their path to the water. Notice how they keep the banks "grazed" short.

The **alternate take-out** at the **Redbud Boat Ramp** is on river right at river mile 16.5. Shannon Creek enters at about river mile 18 from river left.

The **take-out** at the **Swede Creek Marsh Boat Ramp** is at river mile 20.1, on river right. A waterfowl refuge is located immediately downstream of the take-out. The entire river is open to the public all year long, but the adjacent shoreline and wetland within the 1,500-acre waterfowl refuge below Swede Creek Marsh are closed October 1 to January 15 each year. The river downstream of Swede Creek is silted over and filled with logjams. Passage downstream is not possible unless the lake is very high.

Local Contacts: U.S. Army Corps of Engineers, (785) 539-8511; Tuttle Creek State Park, (785) 539-7941; Tuttle Creek Wildlife Area, (785) 363-7316.

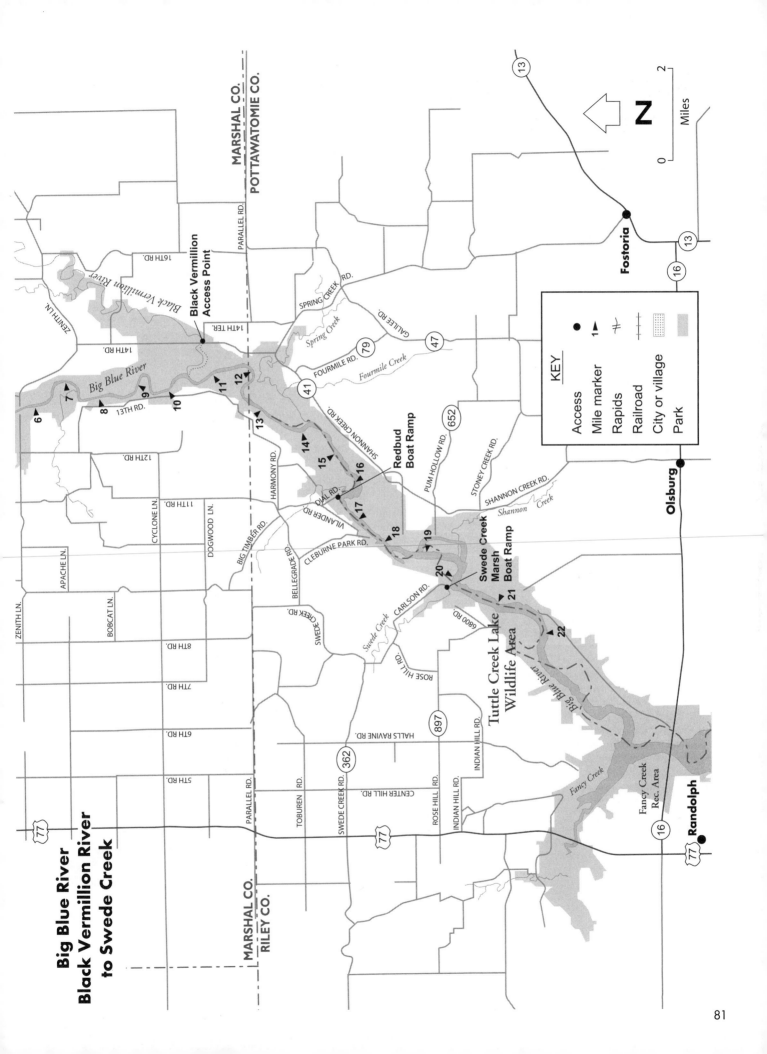

Big Blue River
Black Vermillion River
to Swede Creek

81

BIG BLUE RIVER:
AT THE ROCKY FORD RIVER PARK
1/10 mile, Class I-III difficulty
At Rocky Ford Road

Rocky Ford's history dates back to the Indians and pioneers who crossed the river here because of its natural shale bottom. In 1988, during a renovation of the site, the Kansas Department of Wildlife and Parks teamed up with members of the Kansas Canoe Association (now the Kansas Canoe and Kayak Association) to improve the aeration of the water, provide better fish habitat, and create a whitewater course where paddlers could learn and practice their river skills. KCA provided its expertise and rented huge dump trucks and the Army Corps of Engineers supplied giant boulders that were placed in the riverbed. Local paddlers T.J. Hittle and Rex Replogle worked with KDWP staff and construction crews to see that the boulders were placed strategically. The result was the first whitewater park in Kansas.

The new park provided world-class whitewater features and KDWP began to promote the use of the area by paddlers. In 1990, a dramatic and unprecedented emergency release of floodwaters from Tuttle Creek Reservoir moved many of the boulders downstream along with a large island that had previously divided the river and a pond area. Although it's no longer a world-class paddling site, paddlers still come from all over the state to practice their skills among the remaining boulders and cool, fast water.

After a snafu that temporarily put this land in private hands, KDWP is developing a Rocky Ford Master Plan that we hope will include the restoration of our whitewater park.

The Rocky Ford Recreation Area is a park-and-play spot for boaters and anglers alike. Coming from the bottom of Tuttle Creek Lake, the water is cool and fairly clear all year long. The fish spawn here is incredible and the large rocks and fast water make waves and "holes" where boaters learn and practice whitewater skills such as surfing and ferrying.

You'll get the **best surfing at flows between about 1,000 and 1,500 CFS**, with 1,200 to 1,300 CFS being the best. Above 1,300 CFS, the holes wash out and below 1,000 CFS the holes collapse. This is a good place for novice paddlers to begin trying out whitewater skills. Start by practicing your ferries at about 800 CFS and work your way up. Use the USGS **gauging station** on the Big Blue River near Manhattan.

DANGER—Do not paddle near the spillway. The hydraulic is strong and dangerous.

To get to the **Rocky Ford Fishing Area** from Manhattan, go north on U.S. Highway 24 to Barnes Road (County Road 404), then east and north to the Rocky Ford Fishing Area sign and follow the signs to the parking lot. The **put-in** and **take-out** are at the same spot.

Camping is not allowed except in park areas, but good campsites are available at the state or federal park areas around the Tuttle Creek Reservoir. (See a Tuttle Creek Lake map for more detail.) You can make campsite reservations in Stockdale Park by calling (877) 444-6777 (National Recreation Reservation Service) or online at www. recreation.gov. The Tuttle Creek State Park's number is (785) 539-7941.

Do not paddle downstream from Rocky Ford. The river crosses private property between Rocky Ford and the Highway 24 bridge, 8 miles downstream. The privilege of using the park comes with an equal responsibility to stay in the park. This request comes from landowners, your fellow paddlers, the KDWP, and local officials. Be cool.

Other Fun Stuff: Pillsbury Crossing is a natural ford on a beautiful prairie stream. Deep Creek runs through the scenic Flint Hill and through the 59-acre Pillsbury Crossing Wildlife Area. A native Elmont limestone rock layer creates a natural waterfall, about 40 feet across and about five feet high. The stone shelf serves as both a dam and a road crossing that forms a long pool above the dam. The impounded stream is all flat water and is floatable all year long, except when frozen over. Channel cats and spotted bass are popular in the 5/8-mile-long channel. Swimming, hunting, and alcoholic beverages are not allowed. To get to Pillsbury Crossing from Manhattan, go 1.8 miles south on State Highway 177 to Deep Creek Road (County Road 911). Go east on Deep Creek Road 6 miles (it becomes Pillsbury Crossing Road) to the crossing. The Konza Prairie, the largest tallgrass prairie in the country, is located southwest of Manhattan. To get there take Highway 177 south of the Kansas River to McDowell Creek Road. Turn west on McDowell Creek Road and follow it south and west about 6 miles to the **Kanza Prairie** (south side of road).

Local Contacts: U.S. Army Corps of Engineers, (785) 539-8511; Tuttle Creek State Park, (785) 539-7941; Tuttle Creek Wildlife Area, (785) 539-7941.

Paddling legend T.J. Hittle surfs the Big Blue River at Rocky Ford (photo courtesy of Bob Sinnett)

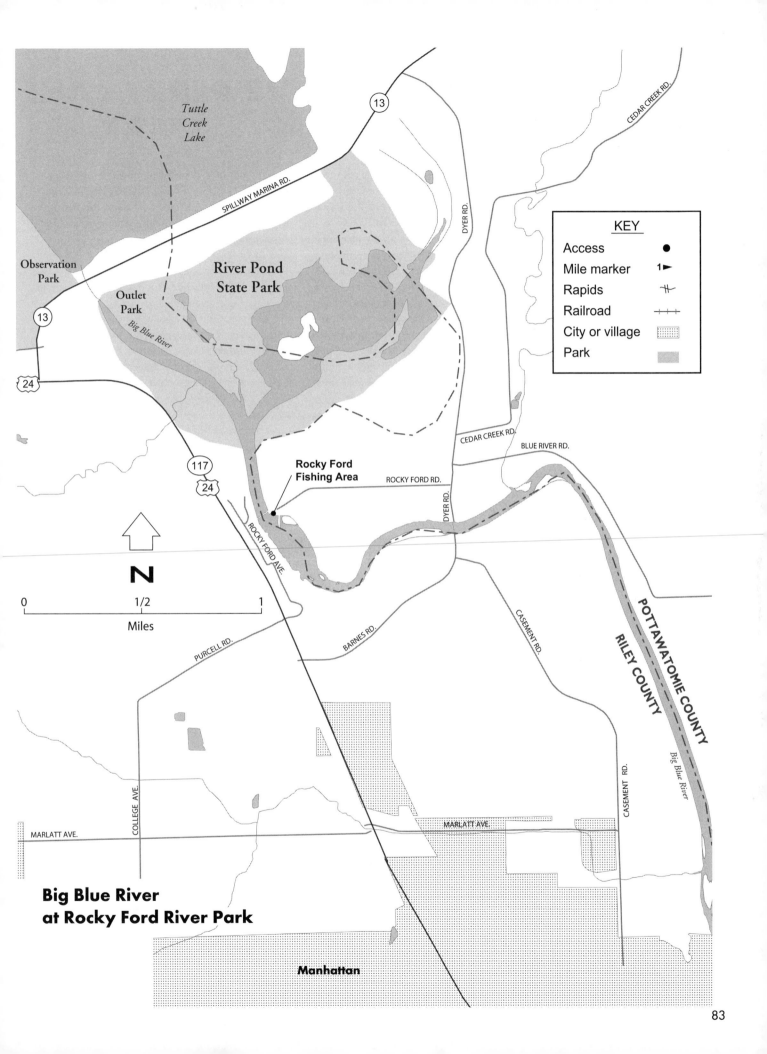

Tuttle
Creek
Lake

SPILLWAY MARINA RD.

Observation
Park

River Pond
State Park

Outlet
Park

Big Blue River

(13)

(24)

(117)

(24)

DYER RD.

CEDAR CREEK RD.

CEDAR CREEK RD.

BLUE RIVER RD.

**Rocky Ford
Fishing Area**

ROCKY FORD RD.

DYER RD.

ROCKY FORD AVE.

PURCELL RD.

BARNES RD.

CASEMENT RD.

CASEMENT RD.

POTTAWATOMIE COUNTY

RILEY COUNTY

Big Blue River

COLLEGE AVE.

MARLATT AVE.

MARLATT AVE.

KEY

Access	●
Mile marker	1▶
Rapids	╫
Railroad	┼┼┼
City or village	▦
Park	▨

N

0   1/2   1
Miles

Big Blue River
at Rocky Ford River Park

Manhattan

DELAWARE RIVER ABOVE PERRY LAKE

6.5 miles, Class I difficulty
Half Mound Fishing Access to Valley Falls Boat Ramp

HIKING, BIKING, AND ATVS

Hikers may want to explore the 30-mile Perry Recreation Trail. This hiking/biking trail makes a large loop that goes up Big Slough Creek, along a dirt road, down Little Slough Creek, then along the edge of the lake. Find the trail map at www.perrylaketrail.net/TrailMaps.html. Perry State Park also has a separate mountain bike trail and the Corps has an ATV trail located south of the dam, adjacent to the Outlet Park.

This float would be used more if it were not so hard to catch at other than very high or very low water levels. When the river is up and Perry Lake is low, this is a nice day trip. Alternately, when the lake is high, this section is more prized by fishermen and hunters than by paddlers, due to the lakelike conditions, turbid water, and steep, muddy banks. Except for the Delaware River Boat Ramp in Valley Falls, none of the accesses on the river have been developed; most are very steep and infested with poison ivy. The access "roads" to most access points are covered with more mud than gravel. If all of this sounds very negative, don't be turned away too easily. The riverbed and sandbars are sandy and even moderate flows help carry you along through the first three miles or more. Anglers enjoy the crappie spawn in the spring and, as in most Kansas streams, catfish are plentiful anytime.

The river was once called the Grasshopper River, but plagues of grasshoppers made the name unpopular. The name was changed to Delaware, after the Indians living in the area.

Although this is an easy Class I float, downed trees and strainers are common. Depending on the usual factors, you can make it from Half Mound to Valley Falls in two to four hours. The **minimum recommended flow is 100 CFS**. The nearest USGS **gauging station** for this part of the Delaware is near Muscotah. It is good to check this gauge, but it is too far upstream to provide accurate flows for this segment of the river. Local streams between Muscotah and Half Mound can add a lot of flow for several days after a hard rain. If the Muscotah gauge is starting to bottom out, but the local area is wet, you can feel fairly confident that you'll find enough water in the river. On the other hand, if the Muscotah gauge is high or climbing, the flow at the put-in could be much higher. The average **gradient** between Half Mound and Valley Falls is 1.5 feet per mile.

Camping is not allowed along the river, but nine state and federal parks surround Perry Lake, with over 1,000 campsites. Camping areas may be reserved in the Corps park ([877] 444-6777) (National Recreation Reservation Service) and at Perry State Park ([785] 246-3449). (See the Perry Lake map in the Appendix.) **Canoes and kayaks can be rented** in Lawrence at Anderson Rentals ([785] 843-2044) and the Lawrence KOA and Kansas River Canoe Company ([785] 842-3877).

The **put-in** at the **Half Mound Fishing Access** is west of the small town of Half Mound (on Half Mound Road, aka County Road 382) and about a quarter mile northwest of the Delaware Bridge. The 13-mile **round-trip shuttle** takes you 2.5 miles east on Half Mound Road to Coal Creek Road, then south about 4 miles to the Delaware River bridge just before the town of Valley Falls. The Valley Falls Boat Ramp is on the downstream side of the bridge, along the southeast bank.

The put-in at Half Mound is somewhat of a steep bushwhack down to the river. A rope and a second person can be helpful. Once on the river, paddlers are quickly immersed in the **Perry Wildlife Area**, a wonderfully rich habitat surrounded by bluestem prairie, hills of oak and hickory, meadows, old fields, cropland, riparian woodland, marshes, and mudflats. The current here is steady but gentle. For the first three miles, sandbars build along the inside of each bend and the sandy riverbed feels good between your toes. Although 190th Road approaches the river on the right, the banks are too steep and muddy at that spot to use it for access.

Numerous small creeks enter from left and right. Near river mile 2, sandy and clear Coal Creek enters on river left. The current slows down where the river meets the pool from the lake, near river mile 3. From there down, the sandy riverbed becomes smothered in mud and the banks become barren and steep from long periods of flooding. Still, the next three miles go by very easily and the beavers and soft-shelled turtles become more common.

On the approach to Valley Falls, a church steeple first appears through the trees. Cedar Creek, a nice side trip, is now on river right. Around the next bend, the Delaware River bridge and Walnut Creek come into view. The **take-out** at the **Valley Falls Boat Ramp** is on river right, just past the bridge.

If you have the stamina and the time, it is 9 more miles to the **Paradise Point Area** and just a little farther to the **Sunset Ridge Area**. Be advised that there are not any good intermediate access points available in that reach. The Delaware Boat Ramp off 150th Road is mudded in and the Walker Bridge Access is too steep and muddy for use. Despite the appearance of the Corps' maps, the last few miles of water upstream of Paradise Point are still more riverlike than the map shows and are well worth the time, especially for anglers. As you approach Paradise Point, the river begins to widen, forming a broad, muddy delta downstream.

Local Contacts: The Corps of Engineers, (785) 597-5144; KDWP Perry Wildlife Area, (785) 945-6615.

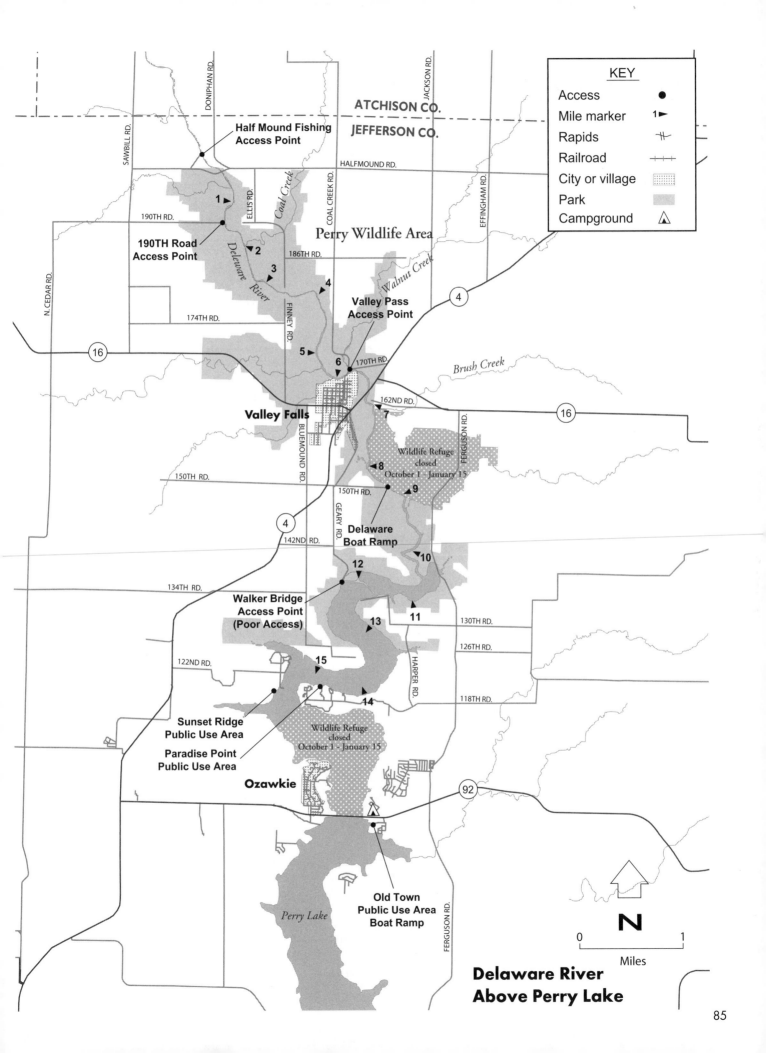

KEY

Access ●
Mile marker 1▶
Rapids
Railroad
City or village
Park
Campground ⛺

ATCHISON CO.
JEFFERSON CO.

DONIPHAN RD.
SAWBILL RD.
JACKSON RD.
HALFMOUND RD.
EFFINGHAM RD.

Half Mound Fishing
Access Point

Coal Creek
ELLIS RD.
COAL CREEK RD.

190TH RD.

1▶

190TH Road
Access Point

Delaware River

2▼

3▼

186TH RD.

Walnut Creek

4▼

Perry Wildlife Area

Valley Pass
Access Point

N.CEDAR RD.

174TH RD.

FINNEY RD.

4

16

5▶

6▼

170TH RD.

Brush Creek

16

Valley Falls

BLUEMOUND RD.

162ND RD.

7▼

FERGUSON RD.

150TH RD.

150TH RD.

8◀

Wildlife Refuge
closed
October 1 - January 15

9▼

4

142ND RD.

GEARY RD.

Delaware
Boat Ramp

10▼

12▼

134TH RD.

11▼

130TH RD.

Walker Bridge
Access Point
(Poor Access)

13▼

126TH RD.

HARPER RD.

122ND RD.

15▼

118TH RD.

14▼

Sunset Ridge
Public Use Area

Paradise Point
Public Use Area

Wildlife Refuge
closed
October 1 - January 15

Ozawkie

92

⛺

Old Town
Public Use Area
Boat Ramp

FERGUSON RD.

Perry Lake

N

0   1
Miles

**Delaware River
Above Perry Lake**

WAKARUSA RIVER ABOVE CLINTON LAKE

14.6-miles, intermediate access available, Class I difficulty
Through the Clinton Wildlife Area

NEARBY PADDLING, HIKING, BIKING, AND PRIMITIVE CAMPING

Rock Creek—This neat little creek, right next door (coming into Clinton Lake from the southwest), should be run in the spring or right after a hard rain. (See below.)

The Waka Wave—This rodeo hole is downstream of the Clinton Lake spillway.

Trails—The north and south sides of the lake sport good hiking/mountain biking/horse trails. (See the Clinton Lake map in the Appendix.) You can get trail maps at www.nwk.usace.army.mil/cl/.

The Woodridge Area—At the west end of Clinton Lake (easy access by boat from the Wakarusa River or Bloomington Park), you can camp around the edge of the lake in designated primitive camp sites that are tucked into the woods and accessible only by foot or boat.

Depending on where you start, which direction you go, and whether you paddle one way or round trip, you can make this a short float or a full-day workout. The float from the Wakarusa River Boat Ramp to the upper reach of the public use area and back is the most common route, but the float can be shortened to 7.3 miles if you set up a shuttle and paddle only one way. Touring boaters sometimes paddle from the Clinton State Park Boat Ramp and back, a 29.2-mile day if you go all the way. The Wakarusa River collects water from the south-central edges of the Kansas River Valley from as far east as Topeka. Having already lost its gradient, by the time it reaches the floodplain of Clinton Lake the Wakarusa is in no hurry as it meanders through the forest above the lake.

Unless the lake is very low, this part of the river is floatable whenever it is not frozen over. **At lower flows**, the mouth of the river is filled with mud and passage becomes difficult. You can check the USGS **gauging station** on the Wakarusa near Richland. Unless the lake is very low, there is no appreciable **gradient** for this river segment since it is all within the backwater from Clinton Lake. Anglers use this delta area and the river upstream in pursuit of the lake's long-reputed white bass, crappie, and catfish. The turbid water and deep holes can hold nice size cats and the lake is also known for good populations of largemouth bass and walleye.

Wakarusa looks more like a creek near the Richland Access, but widens quickly in the backwater of Clinton Lake

Canoes and kayaks can be rented in Lawrence at Anderson Rentals ([785] 843-2044) and the Lawrence KOA and Kansas River Canoe Company ([785] 842-3877).

Camping is not allowed along the river, but you can reserve a Corps campsite in Bloomington Park on Lake Clinton at (877) 444-6777 (National Recreation Reservation Service) or online at www.recreation.gov. The number for camping in Clinton State Park is (785) 842-8562. You can also camp in a wilderness setting in the Woodridge Area. The campsites in that area are only accessible by backpack or boat. A trail rings the peninsula and along that trail are designated spots with fire pits. Some of them are very near the water's edge. There are no fees for using this area. (See the Clinton Lake map in the Appendix.)

To get to the Wakarusa River Boat Ramp from Lawrence, go south on U.S. Highway 59 (aka South Iowa Street and East 1300 Road) to County Road 458. Turn west on Road 458 following the curves south, then west, and then northwest to N 851 Road (aka County Road 1023), opposite the turnoff to Clinton. Go southwest on N 851 Road to N 950 Road, the first right. Follow 950 west to E 100 Road; turn right (north) and follow the signs to the boat ramp.

Put in and take out at the **Wakarusa River Boat Ramp**. The best way to enjoy this section is to paddle upstream from the ramp. It is 5.5 miles to the Richland Access and another 1.8 miles beyond to the end of the public use area. The 14.6-mile round-trip is the best way to enjoy the Wakarusa without having to run a shuttle or paddle over to it from the Lake. There is no shortage of wildlife along the river, especially beaver. From about one mile downstream of the put-in to about one mile past the County Road 1023 bridge, the river flows through the Clinton Wildlife Area. This area is open to hunting during the appropriate seasons.

If you prefer to launch upstream at the **Richland Access**, go west from the Wakarusa Boat Ramp on N 950 Road (aka N 1000th Road, aka Camp Creek Road). The road changes its name several times as it crosses the county line and winds its way west: continue west to Shawnee Heights Road. Turn north on SE Shadden Road (aka Shawnee Heights Road) to the river.

The best time to paddle the Wakarusa is in the fall or spring, when the water and air are cool. The river is deeply entrenched between fairly steep and muddy banks. Downed trees and beaver dams can block your path in the upper reaches.

Local Contacts: U.S. Army Corps of Engineers, (785) 843-7665; Kansas Department of Wildlife and Parks, (785) 842-8562.

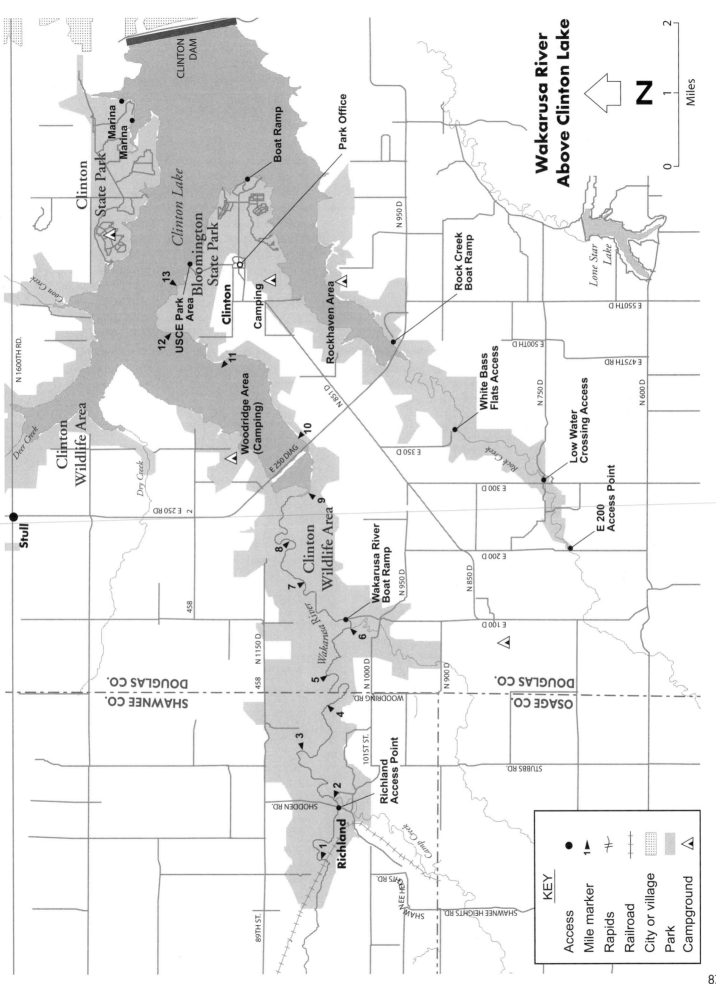

Wakarusa River Above Clinton Lake

N

0   1   2
Miles

CLINTON DAM

Clinton State Park

Marina

Marina

Boat Ramp

Clinton Lake

Park Office

Bloomington State Park

USCE Park Area

Clinton

Camping

Rockhaven Area

Rock Creek Boat Ramp

White Bass Flats Access

Low Water Crossing Access

E 200 Access Point

Clinton Wildlife Area

Deer Creek

Coon Creek

Dry Creek

Woodridge Area (Camping)

Stull

Rock Creek

Lone Star Lake

Clinton Wildlife Area

Wakarusa River

Wakarusa River Boat Ramp

Richland Access Point

Richland

Camp Creek

N 1600TH RD.

458   N 1150 D

458

101ST ST.

SHODDEN RD.

89TH ST.

OTIS RD.

SHAWNEE HEIGHTS RD.

STUBBS RD.

WOODRING RD.

N 1000 D

N 950 D

N 900 D

N 850 D

E 100 D

E 200 D

E 300 D

E 350 D

E 250 RD

E 250 DIAG

N 851 D

N 750 D

N 950 D

E 500TH D

E 475TH RD

E 550TH D

E 600 D

SHAWNEE CO.
DOUGLAS CO.

DOUGLAS CO.
OSAGE CO.

1 2 3 4 5 6 7 8 9 10 11 12 13

KEY

- ● Access
- 1 ▲ Mile marker
- ⊬ Rapids
- ┼ Railroad
- ▦ City or village
- ▨ Park
- △ Campground

ROCK CREEK

5.1 miles, intermediate access available, Class I-II+ difficulty above White Bass Flats, Class I below E 200 Road Access to Rock Creek Road Boat Ramp

ROCK CREEK FLOW CONVERSION

Using the upstream end of the pipes at the low-water bridge on East 300 Road, figure:

1/4 full pipe = 50 CFS
1/2 full = 200 CFS
3/4 full = 400 CFS
Full = 500 CFS
Over road = 600+ CFS

This seat-of-the-pants conversion table has not been scientifically verified and is intended for use only as a rough guide when all of the tubes are clear of obstruction.

This little creek pours off the southern hills of the Wakarusa watershed, then tumbles down the rocky ridges that border the Kansas River valley. The upper five miles of this little creek twist and turn their way through tight channels, over gravel bars, around brush-covered islands, and through hills of mature hardwood forest. Even after it settles into the backwater of Clinton Lake, Rock Creek is still a gem to paddle. Flatwater paddlers can approach from below, while whitewater boaters will enjoy it more from the top. Easy to access, this skinny arm of the lake is full of white bass and crappie during the spring run.

Catch Rock Creek in the spring while the ground is still wet or shortly after a good rain. The first gravel bar is a good indicator whether there is enough water for a float. If you don't mind a little walking, the bare-bones **minimum flow is about 50 CFS**, but I recommend 200 CFS or more for maximum fun. There are **no gauging stations**. (See the flow conversion chart above.) The average **gradient** is 6.7 feet per mile, but most of this is in the first five miles.

Always scout the low-water crossing on East 300 Road prior to launching from anywhere upstream, especially at high flows. At all flows this low-water crossing must be portaged. At high flows you will need to know how to identify your approach well in advance, where to take out, and how to negotiate your portage. The low-water crossing can be EXTREMELY dangerous and can be very difficult to portage when water is flowing over it. If in doubt, launch below the low-water crossing. (See the driving directions below.)

Camping is not allowed along the creek, but campsites are available at various parks around Clinton Lake.

You can **rent canoes** for use on the flat water section below White Bass Flats and on the lake in Lawrence at Anderson Rentals ([785] 843-2044) and at the Lawrence KOA and Kansas River Canoe Company ([785] 842-3877). These are flat water boats and are not suitable for the whitewater conditions on the upper reaches of Rock Creek.

To get to the **put-in** at the **E 200 Road Access** from Lawrence, go south on U.S. Highway 59 to County Road 458. Turn west on Road 458 following the curves south, then west, and then northwest to N 851 Road (aka County Road 1023), opposite the turnoff to Clinton. Turn left (southwest) following N 851 Road to E 200 Road. Turn south (left) on E 200 and go to the Rock Creek bridge. The access is under the

bridge. Please stay on the east side of the bridge, since the west side is private property. The 12.4-mile **round-trip shuttle** route, from the E 200 Road Access to the Rock Creek Boat Ramp, goes north on E 200 Road, then northeast on N 851 Road, then east on County Road 458, across the bridge over Rock Creek, then north on the lake road (E 535th Road) to the Rock Creek Boat Ramp.

From the **put-in** at the E 200 Road Access, the next 2.4 miles have a wide enough flood channel, but the creek often constricts as it splits into circuitous braids around tree-covered islands, strainers, and steep banks. The **gradient** from here to the low-water crossing at E 300 Road is 4 feet per mile. You will likely encounter strainers that block the entire channel and strong currents that try to push you into and under overhanging root wads and through brush and stinging-nettle-covered islands. If the water is pushy, you'll have to negotiate very tight turns and catch eddies to avoid trouble. If you cannot see a clear route through a thicket or log jam, scout it from the top and then, if still in doubt, portage. Expect strainers in the middle of rapids and blind turns. Even experts have difficulty with this section, so paddlers of all ability levels should either stay off it or be willing to portage.

Watch high on river left for road signs, then on river right for the ruins of an old bridge foundation. These landmarks are immediately upstream of the potentially very dangerous low-water crossing ahead.

The run from the low water crossing to the **White Bass Flats Access** is 2.3 miles and has a screaming gradient of 15.6 feet per mile. The increased speed of the current will hold your attention, but there are fewer strainers, blind turns, and sycamore jungles. Soon the space between riffles lengthen to become long pools. Eventually, the creek merges with the backwater of Clinton Lake, just upstream of the White Bass Flats Access. A better name for the White Bass Flats Access would be "Mud Slide." If you can manage the steep banks, this access off E 350 Road will cut about 2 miles of flat water off your trip. In the spring, white bass and crappie come upstream to spawn in this area. Some anglers paddle or drive their boats up here from the lake while others hike along the creek and fish from the banks.

Over the next 2 miles, the beautiful hills and forest pass more slowly. The banks grow farther apart and the tight turns become slow meanders. At one of these meanders an old channel goes left and a new channel goes right. Take the right channel. After the next big left turn, you'll see the highway bridge ahead. Cross under the bridge then **take out** at the **Rock Creek Boat Ramp**, on river right, just northeast of the bridge.

Local Contacts: U.S. Army Corps of Engineers, (785) 843-7665; Kansas Department of Wildlife and Parks (Clinton State Park), (785) 842-8562.

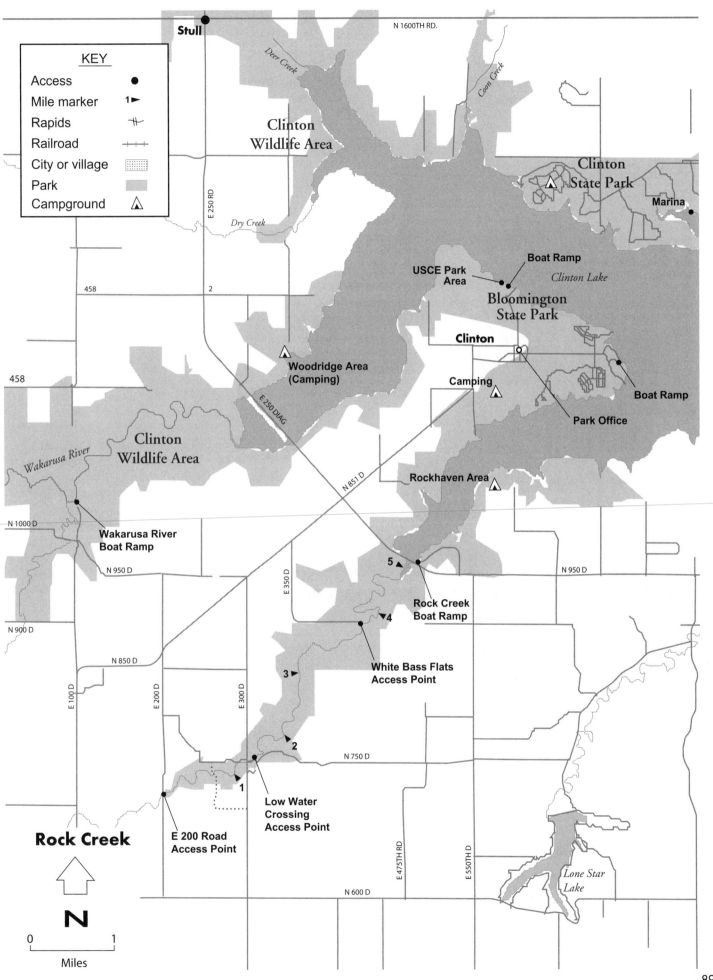

KEY

Access ●

Mile marker 1▶

Rapids

Railroad

City or village

Park

Campground ⛺

Stull

N 1600TH RD.

Deer Creek

Coon Creek

Clinton Wildlife Area

Clinton State Park

Marina

Dry Creek

E 250 RD

Clinton Lake

Boat Ramp

USCE Park Area

Bloomington State Park

458

2

458

Woodridge Area (Camping)

E 250 DIAG

Clinton

Camping

Boat Ramp

Park Office

Clinton Wildlife Area

Wakarusa River

N 851 D

Rockhaven Area

N 1000 D

Wakarusa River Boat Ramp

N 950 D

N 950 D

5 ▶

Rock Creek Boat Ramp

N 900 D

N 850 D

E 350 D

4

White Bass Flats Access Point

E 100 D

E 200 D

E 300 D

3 ▶

2

N 750 D

1 ▶

Low Water Crossing Access Point

Rock Creek

E 200 Road Access Point

E 475TH RD

E 550TH D

Lone Star Lake

N 600 D

N

0   1

Miles

THE WAKA WAVE
0 miles, Class III-VI difficulty (extreme danger at high flows)
Below the Clinton Lake Dam

This **park-and-play** spot is less than a half mile downstream of the Clinton Lake Dam. Here, the Wakarusa River drops over a five-foot high rock ledge. When the river is running over this drop at **850-1,000 CFS**, the effect is the Waka Wave, *the* destination for park-and-play rodeo-style boaters for hundreds of miles around. You name the move—enders, retendos, spins,

Shawn Tolivar (top) and Kate O'Connel (bottom) demos some rodeo moves on the Waka Wave on the Wakarusa River below Clinton Lake Dam (photos courtesy of Nicoya Helm).

cartwheels—if you've got the skill, you can find a spot to make it somewhere on the Waka Wave.

At the recommended water levels, this is a Class III play spot. Above 1,000 CFS, the wave starts to wash out. As the flow drops below 850 CFS, the hydraulic gradually becomes more intense. At 700 it gets really sticky. Between 500 and 600 CFS, the hydraulic is a drowning machine.

Water conditions can change very rapidly below the dam. Contact the Army Corps of Engineers office at (785) 843-7665 before entering this area. Get off the river immediately if you hear sirens going off at the dam. The same conditions that create great whitewater conditions for skilled paddlers also create a high level of danger for unskilled paddlers. Do not attempt to paddle in this area without the requisite skills or without other skilled paddlers to help if you get into trouble.

The Waka Wave is located in the **Outlet Park** area, just downstream of the Clinton Dam, and behind and slightly upstream of Shelter #8. This is a city park (City of Lawrence) and a popular spot for anglers. It is a good idea to carry a knife in case you need to cut yourself free from fishing lines. Be courteous to anglers.

The Army Corps of Engineers ([785] 843-7665) controls releases from the dam. Use the **Clinton Lake outflow gauge** at http://www.nwk.usace.army.mil/cl/daily.cfm.

Camping is available at various sites around the lake. (See the Clinton Lake map in the Appendix.) There are no businesses in Kansas that **rent canoes or kayaks** suitable for this kind of boating. However, Kansas City Paddler, in Peculiar, Missouri, sells them ([816] 779-1195, www.kcpaddler.com).

This park is for day-use only, but camping is available at numerous places around Clinton Lake or at Lone Star Lake. You can reserve a campsite at the Corps campgrounds at (877) 444-6777 (National Recreation Reservation Service) or online at www.recreation.gov or at Clinton State Park at (785) 842-8562.

Local Contacts: U.S. Army Corps of Engineers, (785) 843-7665; Kansas Department of Wildlife and Parks (Clinton State Park), (785) 842-8562.

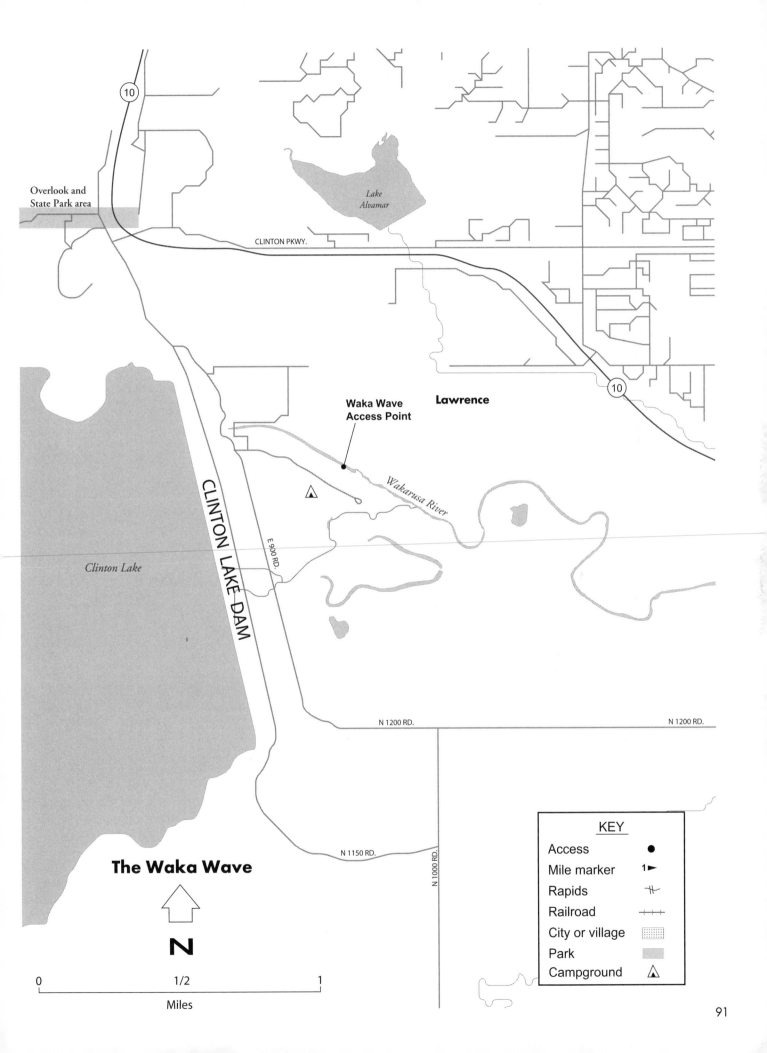

Overlook and
State Park area

Lake
Alvamar

CLINTON PKWY.

10

Waka Wave
Access Point

Lawrence

CLINTON LAKE DAM

Wakarusa River

E 900 RD.

Clinton Lake

N 1200 RD.   N 1200 RD.

N 1000 RD.

N 1150 RD.

The Waka Wave

N

KEY	
Access	●
Mile marker	1►
Rapids	⌗
Railroad	+++
City or village	▦
Park	▨
Campground	⧍

0   1/2   1

Miles

MILL CREEK THROUGH SHAWNEE MISSION PARK

3.5 miles, Class I-II+ difficulty
Midland Drive Access to Wilder Road Access

Mill Creek Streamway Park includes a paved walking and biking trail that follows Mill Creek for 15 miles from Olathe to the Kansas River. The trail passes through hardwood forests and fields of native grasses. Shawnee Mission Park also has hiking, mountain bike, and horse trails at various locations around the lake.

Mill Creek flows over beautiful, rocky ledges into deep pools, through hills, and past a mature hardwood forest that provides excellent habitat for deer and other wildlife. The water is surprisingly clear. Although only a short float, it is a lot of fun and the shuttle is easy. An annual Johnson County Parks and Recreation permit is required for your boat. The Shawnee Mission Park Office ([913] 438-7275) is at West 79th Street and Renner Road at the east edge of Shawnee Mission Park.

At **0-25 CFS** this is a Class I float with a dozen or so short portages. The long shaded pools are home to channel and bullhead catfish, bluegill, and green sunfish. In the spring or after a nice rain, leave your fishing poles in the garage and get out your whitewater helmet. Approaching **50-100 CFS** the riffles become more passable. A good downstream lean will help avoid swamping, flipping, and pinning if you broach on the many shallow rocks. At about **100 CFS** the broach risk goes down and the fun factor goes up. Sharp turns are punctuated by whitewater drops with even better surf below the ledges. As flows rise, the short drops combine to form complex rapids. At high flows this is no place for novice paddlers. As the creek rises, it gets pushy very quickly. Class II+ drops form at some of the ledges and rock gardens. High flows are only recommended for experienced paddlers.

Check the USGS **gauging station** for Mill Creek at Johnson Drive, Shawnee. This section of Mill Creek has an average **gradient** of 5 feet per mile. You can **rent canoes** at A-1 Rentals, Kansas City, MO, (816) 373-0234.

To get to the **put-in** at the **Midland Drive Access**, go west from city of Shawnee on Shawnee Mission Parkway. Go past I-435 about a mile to Midland Drive (traffic light). Turn south on Midland and then immediately west on Lawrence Road. Your 5.6-mile **round-trip shuttle** route takes you north on Midland Drive, crossing Shawnee Mission Parkway to continue on Barker Road to Holiday Drive, east on Holiday Drive, and then left (northwest) on Wilder Road for a little more than a quarter mile, crossing Mill Creak. The access is on the southwest side of the Wilder Road bridge and the tiny canoe access is located northeast of the parking lot. The take-out is just upstream of the Wilder Road bridge.

From the Midland Creek Access parking lot, carry your boat about 200 yards west, along the trail that parallels Little Mill Creek to the put-in. Continue straight past (not over) the walking bridge over Little Mill Creek. The creek access is where the trail turns right, at the confluence of Little Mill

Creek and Mill Creek. This unmarked access tends to be muddy after a rain.

Warm up on the long pools for the next half mile downstream. Clear Creek Island Rapids begins near river mile 0.7. This is the most technical rapids on the creek and potentially the most dangerous. It is immediately upstream of the first walking bridge overpass and just south of the Barker Road Access. As you come around a gentle curve, the river is suddenly split by a tall island. At this time, the left channel has several routes. The best route is next to the left edge of the island. The route to the right side of the island is only suitable at moderate to high flows and is recommended only for experienced boaters. It is a blind turn with the potential for stream-wide logjams. Once you're into the channel, the current accelerates and pushes you hard against the right bank. In 2005 the right channel was totally blocked by a potentially deadly strainer that was not visible at the head of the rapids. In 2007 the strainer was gone. If in doubt, scout.

Clear Creek enters from the left side and part way down the left route. The only access to the Barker Road Access is on river right, at the bottom of the rapids and about 15 yards up the right channel.

If you're accessing the creek from the Barker Road Access parking lot, the carry is about 100 yards south along the path, then down the bank on the left side of the trail, just before the walking bridge.

Over the next two miles you will encounter several Class I-II difficulty riffles. The named rapids include **Home Run** (stream mile 1.6) and **Last Chance Rapids 1, 2, 3, and 4** (stream mile 3.3). Last Chance is really a series of four closely spaced drops that span about 400 yards. Nice waves and holes form at some of these drops between about 50 and 300 CFS. Most of the rocks that form the rapids in this lower section were pushed over the edge of the railroad siding to stabilize the banks. These rocks have not been worn smooth by the river so stay right side up if you can. The Kansas River meets the creek just below Last Chance and will cover Last Chance 4 if the river is high. The **take-out** at the **Wilder Road Access** is immediately downstream of Last Chance 4 and just upstream of the Wilder Road bridge.

Once you get to Wilder Road, you have the option of continuing downstream about a mile to the Kansas River. From there you can paddle one mile upstream to the Edwardsville Boat Ramp, 5 miles upstream to the Bonner Springs Bridge, or 16 miles downstream to Kaw Point. If you paddle downstream, be aware of the **DANGEROUS** cofferdam that must be portaged. See the last section on the Kansas River for details.

Local Contacts: Johnson County Parks and Recreation, (913) 441-8669.

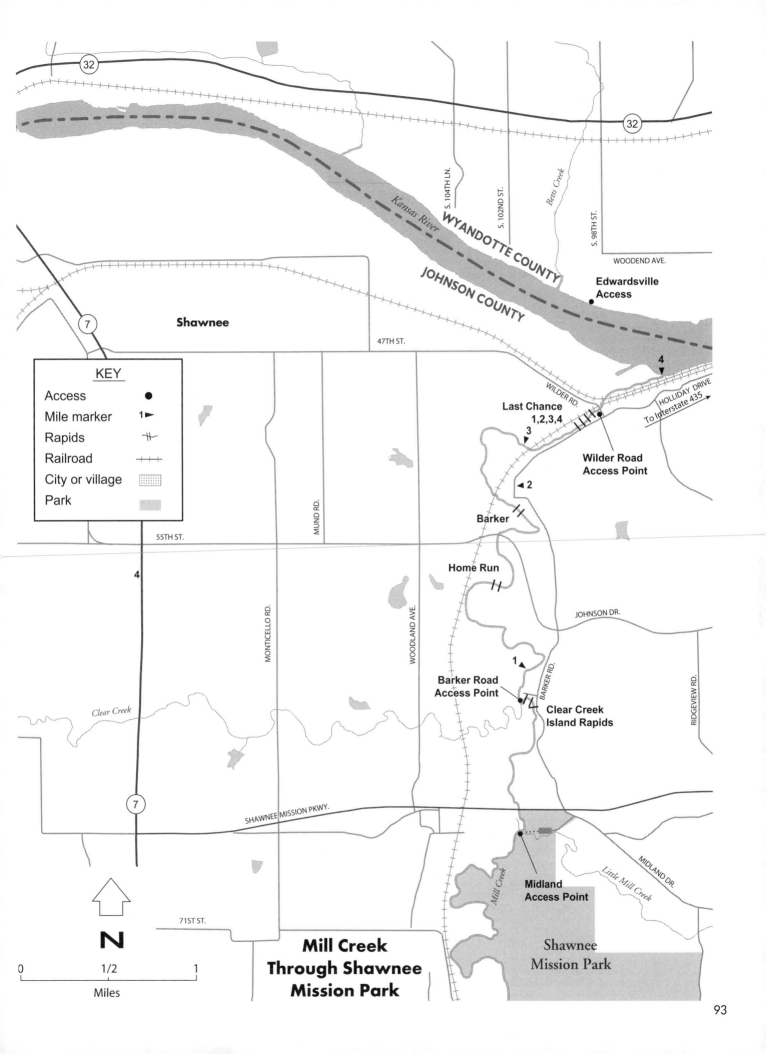

KEY

Access   ●
Mile marker   1 ▶
Rapids   ⫫
Railroad   +++
City or village
Park

Kansas River

WYANDOTTE COUNTY
JOHNSON COUNTY

S. 104TH LN.
S. 102ND ST.
S. 98TH ST.
Betts Creek

WOODEND AVE.

Edwardsville
Access

Shawnee

47TH ST.

WILDER RD.

HOLLIDAY DRIVE
To Interstate 435

4

Last Chance
1,2,3,4

3

Wilder Road
Access Point

2

Barker

Home Run

JOHNSON DR.

MUND RD.

WOODLAND AVE.

55TH ST.

4

1

Barker Road
Access Point

BARKER RD.

Clear Creek
Island Rapids

RIDGEVIEW RD.

MONTICELLO RD.

Clear Creek

7

SHAWNEE MISSION PKWY.

Mill Creek

MIDLAND DR.

Little Mill Creek

Midland
Access Point

Shawnee
Mission Park

71ST ST.

N

0   1/2   1
Miles

**Mill Creek
Through Shawnee
Mission Park**

DRAGOON CREEK ABOVE POMONA LAKE
6 miles, intermediate access available, Class I-II difficulty
Fairlawn Road to Highway 75

Part of the Marais des Cygnes Watershed, this neat float from the Fairlawn Road Access to Carbolyn Park takes you over gravely riffles and through narrow channels that are nestled in hills of hardwoods. The stream is sheltered by a rocky valley and large trees that provide excellent protection for those windy days when other rivers are impossible. The water is often fairly clear and pleasantly cool. Bald eagles frequent the area and are easy to spot soaring above the river or settling into the trees. Dragoon Creek flows through "the project lands" and are open to hunting and hiking. If Pamona Lake is a little bit low, this creek is a gem all the way to the take-out.

The creek was named when a young soldier was killed near the Santa Fe Trail crossing. State record flathead catfish and wipers (hybrid cross between the white bass and the striped bass) have been taken out of Pomona Lake, but the walleye, largemouth bass, and white bass are also good. If you are an angler, you don't need a boat to fish this creek. There are several turnouts along 205th Street that provide good access. Most of these spots are also suitable for canoe access if you can carry your boat a short distance. Of the available alternate accesses, the ones off Morrill Road and Lewelling Road are probably the most convenient. In the spring when the lake is high, some anglers launch at the Carbolyn Park Boat Ramp and motor upstream to white bass and crappie country.

A lightly loaded boat can float this stretch at 50 CFS, but **100 CFS or more is preferred**. Plan two to four hours for your float. The nearest **gauging station** is at Dragoon Creek near Burlingame. The average **gradient** for this section is 4 feet per mile.

The closest **canoe rentals** are in Lawrence (not really close at all): Anderson Rentals, (785) 843-2044,

This is the entrance to the first riffle on Dragoon Creek. As the channel narrows, it will try to push you into root wads and hanging limbs along the right bank (photo by Susan Kysela).

and Lawrence KOA and Kansas River Canoe Company, (785) 842-3877.

Camping is not allowed along the river, but the **campsites** at Pamona State Park are very nice, as are the park areas maintained by the Corps of Engineers. The State Park's office number is (785) 828-4933. Corps campsite reservations can be made at (877) 444-6777 (National Recreation Reservation Service). Campsites have electricity and water; some have sewer hookups. The state park has a swimming beach, a bathhouse, picnic shelters, horseshoe pits, volleyball courts, a nine-hole disc golf course, and trails. A marina near the dam provides full service to boaters, anglers, and skiers. (See the Pomona Lake map in the Appendix.)

The **put-in** is on **Fairlawn Road**, west of Pomona Lake. From the U.S. Highway 75 bridge over Dragoon Creek, go two miles north to 205th Street and then west (left) three miles to Fairlawn Road West 209th Street). Turn south (left) and go a few hundred yards to the old bridge. The 10-mile **round-trip shuttle** route, from the Fairlawn Road Access to Carbolyn Park and back, takes you three miles east on 205th Street to Highway 75, then south about two miles to Carbolyn Park (about 500 feet south of the bridge over Dragoon Creek). Turn east into Carbolyn Park and follow the signs to the boat ramp.

Put in at the Fairlawn Road Access. The fun starts right here. This isn't your usual Kansas stream. Launch from a rock ledge, under the old, broken-down iron bridge. Looking downstream, you'll see an island. At normal flows, the left channel has no water. The right channel accelerates around the island and tries to push you up against the bank, under root wads and low-hanging branches. That is just the start. The rest of the river is a series of S-turns, pools, and gravelly riffles. It has no more than its share of downed trees, tight turns, and strainers, but caution is advised, since the channel is fairly narrow.

The first and second bridges you come to are Lewelling Road at stream mile 1.3 and then Morrill Road at stream mile 3. The Corps map shows that the stream widens shortly after Lewelling Road, but that map is misleading. This little creek is still a little creek all the way to the take-out, except when the river or the lake is very high. **Take out** on river right, just downstream of the **Highway 75 bridge**.

Local Contacts: Pomona State Park, (785) 828-4933.

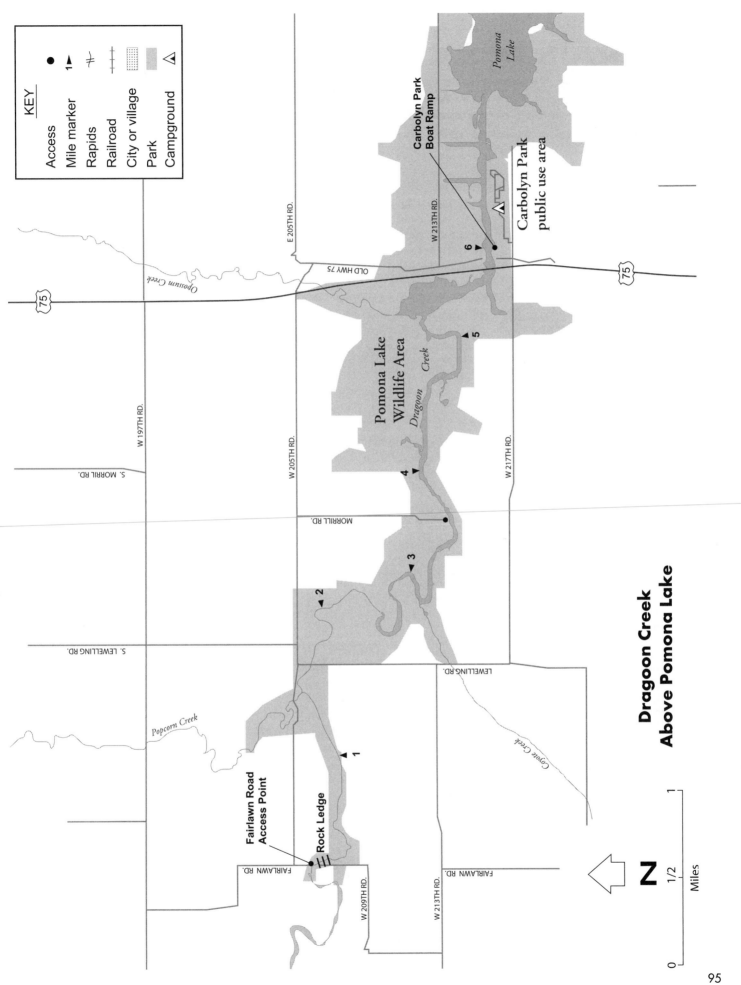

KEY

- • Access
- ▲ Mile marker
- ⊬ Rapids
- ╫ Railroad
- ▦ City or village
- ▨ Park
- ⛺ Campground

Dragoon Creek
Above Pomona Lake

N

0   1/2   1
Miles

Pomona Lake

Carbolyn Park
Boat Ramp

Carbolyn Park
public use area

Pomona Lake Wildlife Area

Dragoon Creek

Opossum Creek

Popcorn Creek

Coyote Creek

Fairlawn Road
Access Point

Rock Ledge

E 205TH RD.
W 197TH RD.
S. MORRIL RD.
W 205TH RD.
MORRILL RD.
W 217TH RD.
S. LLEWELLING RD.
LLEWELLING RD.
W 209TH RD.
W 213TH RD.
FAIRLAWN RD.
FAIRLAWN RD.
OLD HWY 75
W 213TH RD.

75

MARAIS DES CYGNES RIVER: ABOVE MELVERN LAKE

6 miles, intermediate access available, Class I difficulty
Coffman Crossing Access to 309th Road Boat Ramp

MARAIS DES CYGNES AND WATERSHED

Named by the early French trappers, Marais des Cygnes (pronounced "mare-de-zeen") means Marsh of the Swans and was a translation of the Osage Indian name for the region, Mixa-ckau-tse, which means "where white swans are plentiful." Trumpeter and tundra swans are now rare, but an abundance of other wildlife is found in this meeting of tallgrass prairie, hardwood forests, and wetland areas.

The Marais des Cygnes River Basin covers 4,304 square miles in east central and southeast Kansas. The area has three major reservoirs: Pomona Lake, Melvern Lake, and Hillsdale Lake. After the Kansas and Neosho Rivers, this river takes more water out of state than does any other stream. The trees along the shore are mostly cottonwood, sycamore, bitter pecan, elm, and maple. The hills are covered with hardwood forests of mostly walnut, hickory, pecan, oak, and ash.

The watershed is largely agricultural, but its population is growing. Like much of Kansas, bare soil farming practices, inadequate riparian protection, and small feedlots in and along stream banks in the watershed have negatively impacted water quality.

This is the uppermost publicly accessible reach of the Marais des Cygnes River. Arching trees shade the water and create a pleasant tunnel of green. You can expect to see plenty of wildlife such as deer, fox, coyotes, wild turkeys, bobcats, and especially beavers as the river flows through the center of the Melvern Wildlife Area. This backwater paradise is full of deep holes where nice-sized catfish hang out. It is a place to relax, watch the beavers slide down the bank, wet a hook, or just coast along in the shade of giant sycamore and cottonwood trees.

The **minimum recommended flow is 50 CFS**, or slightly less with a lightly loaded canoe. The 6-mile float from Coffman Crossing to the 309th Road Boat Ramp will take about two to four hours one way. That, of course, requires a shuttle. But if you don't want to mess with shuttles and if the river isn't running fast, it is quite easy to paddle upstream, from 309th Road all the way up to Coffman Crossing and back. You can check flows at the **gauging station** on Marais des Cygnes near Reading and the lake levels at the Corps Web site (see index) if in doubt. The average **gradient** for this part of the creek is 2.1 feet per mile.

Camping is not allowed along the river, but plenty of good campsites are available at Eisenhower State Park ([785] 528-4102) or at the Corps campgrounds ([877] 777-6777) (National Recreation Reservation Service). (See the Melvern Lake map in the Appendix.) No **canoe rentals** are available in this area.

To get to the **put-in** at the **Coffman Crossing Access** from the town of Reading, go 2 miles north on Carlson Road (aka Road Z) to West 285th Road (aka Road 270), then west to the southwest edge of the bridge, about 500 feet beyond Road YS. The fair-weather parking area is about 50 yards west of the bridge and can be overgrown but is fairly firm. The 10-mile **round-trip shuttle** route, from Coffman Crossing to the 309th Road Boat Ramp, takes you east on 285th Road to Carlson Road (aka Z Road), south on Carlson Road and through Reading to 309th Road, and east on 309th to the access. Three-hundred-ninth Road starts off as a dirt

road, but it gradually narrows to a dirt path that is not suitable for wet conditions. The dirt path that goes north to the river gets even worse.

Put in under the bridge. This takes a little bit of bushwhacking as you carry, drag, and lower your boat to the water's edge under the bridge. This is at the very upper limit of the **Melvern Wildlife Area**. Just upstream is a two-foot-high rock ledge, the original Coffman Crossing. The river is a series of long, deep pools that are interspersed with shallows, gravel, or rock ledges. Depending on the river's flow and the lake's level, the ledges and gravel bars may require a little finesse or dragging, but not when at or above the minimum recommended levels. Some of the banks are fairly steep, but there are plenty of good places to pull over.

The first bridge you'll come to, near river mile 2.7, is Carlson Road. Downstream of there, near river mile 4, you will find a riprap boat ramp on river right that leads up to a nice, grassy field. This middle-of-nowhere ramp is the best picnic spot on this river segment.

At mile 5, you'll pass under the State Highway 170 bridge. There is a parking area on the southeast side of the bridge that is used by anglers, but this is not a suitable canoe access. The banks are too steep to be convenient but, if you need an emergency exit, get out on river left if you can. The 309th Road Boat Ramp is only a mile farther downriver and is the take-out of choice.

Take out at the **309th Road Boat Ramp**. At this writing, you can only go another 400 yards or less beyond the boat ramp. A series of downed trees blockade the channel. Another logjam farther downstream, called "the Big Logjam," is a quarter mile long and is also impassible, but the river has cut a new channel and is now passable. Above the logjam, catfish are the angler's favorite. Downstream of the logjams, white bass and crappie congregate and become easy targets for savvy anglers.

If you would like to paddle downstream of the Davis Road Boat Ramp, you can launch at that ramp and paddle downstream to the **Docking Road Boat Ramp** or start at the Docking Ramp and proceed upstream. The Corps of Engineers map makes the river look very wide at the Docking Ramp, but in fact it is still fairly narrow and well protected. Most of the river and shore area between the Davis Road Boat Ramp and the Sun Dance Area is a Waterfowl Refuge that is closed to all access from October 21 to January 15 of each year.

Local Contacts: U.S. Army Corps of Engineers (Melvern Lake), (785) 549-3318.

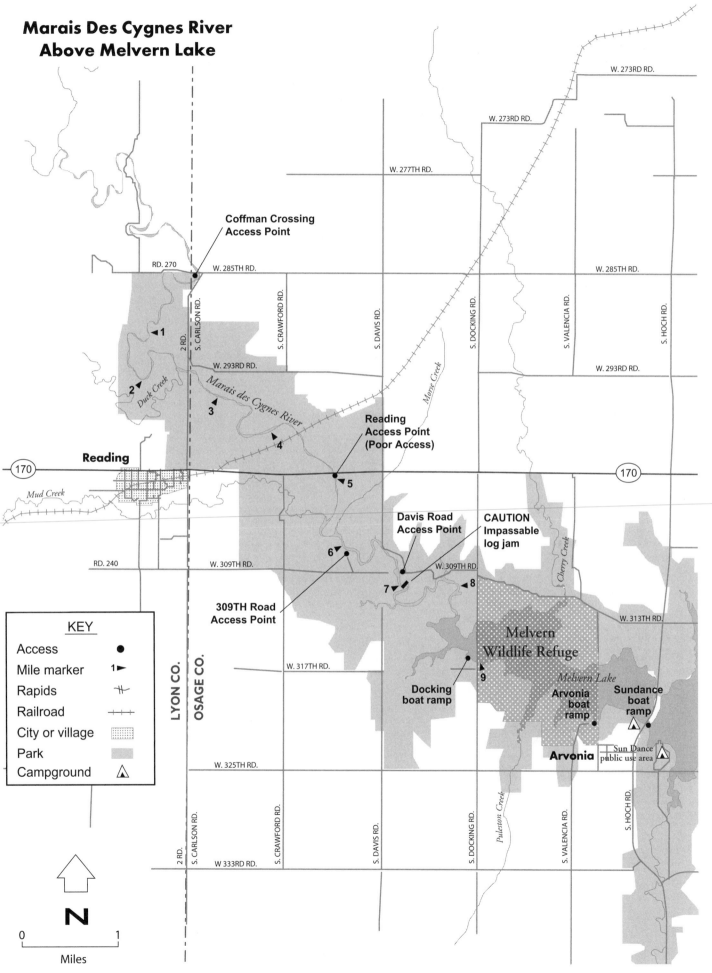

Marais Des Cygnes River
Above Melvern Lake

Coffman Crossing
Access Point

RD. 270
W. 285TH RD.
W. 285TH RD.

W. 273RD RD.
W. 273RD RD.
W. 277TH RD.

S. CARLSON RD.
2 RD.
S. CRAWFORD RD.
S. DAVIS RD.
S. DOCKING RD.
S. VALENCIA RD.
S. HOCH RD.

◄1

W. 293RD RD.
W. 293RD RD.

Duck Creek
◄2

Marais des Cygnes River
◄3

◄4

Morse Creek

Reading
Access Point
(Poor Access)

(170)   **Reading**   (170)

Mud Creek

◄5

Davis Road
Access Point

CAUTION
Impassable
log jam

Cherry Creek

RD. 240   W. 309TH RD.

6►

W. 309TH RD.

309TH Road
Access Point

7◄◀   ◄8

Melvern
Wildlife Refuge

W. 313TH RD.

KEY

Access	●
Mile marker	1►
Rapids	╫
Railroad	┼┼┼
City or village	▦
Park	▨
Campground	⛺

LYON CO.
OSAGE CO.

W. 317TH RD.

9◄

Melvern Lake

Docking
boat ramp

Arvonia
boat
ramp

Sundance
boat
ramp

Arvonia

Sun Dance
public use area

W. 325TH RD.

2 RD.
S. CARLSON RD.
W. 333RD RD.
S. CRAWFORD RD.
S. DAVIS RD.
Puleston Creek
S. DOCKING RD.
S. VALENCIA RD.
S. HOCH RD.

N

0 ___ 1
Miles

MARAIS DES CYGNES RIVER:
THROUGH THE MARAIS DES CYGNES WILDLIFE AREA ABOVE HIGHWAY 69

5.5 miles, intermediate access available, Class I difficulty
Unit G to Highway 69

SOUTHERN FLYING SQUIRRELS

At about 8 1/2 to 9 1/2 inches long, this is the smallest squirrel species in Kansas. It is a protected species with a population that only exists in oak-hickory forests of southeastern Kansas. The squirrels glide on broad flaps of skin on each side that stretch from their front to back legs, guiding themselves through the air with their broad tails.

The last 14.5 miles of the Marais des Cygnes River that flow through Kansas meander through the Marais des Cygnes National Wildlife Refuge and Marais des Cygnes State Wildlife Area. This long river segment is easily broken into two completely dissimilar parts. The first part is a 5.5-mile reach upstream of the U.S. Highway 69 bridge that is managed by the Kansas Department of Wildlife and Parks. The second reach is a 9-mile long segment that passes through the Marais des Cygnes National Wildlife Refuge and Wildlife Area, all the way from the Highway 69 bridge to the Missouri State Line.

These two segments can be combined to make one long day trip or two shorter day trips. The 5.5-mile segment that is upstream of Highway 69 is presented here. For the next river segment, please see the next section in this book.

A natural limestone dam, located downstream of the Highway 69 bridge, creates a deep pool that extends upstream, beyond the end of the wildlife area. The pool provides enough water for a good float anytime of the year, except when the river is frozen over. This calm piece of water is nice for paddlers, bird-watchers, photographers, anglers, and hunters. The river is well protected from the wind, easy to maneuver, and full of big catfish. By boat, hunters can access parts of the wildlife area that are otherwise more difficult to reach. Waterfowl hunters must register and obtain a permit at the wildlife area office. Although portions of Unit A are closed to all shooting during the dark goose season, the river is open for use all year.

Camping and building fires are not allowed anywhere in the refuge, but there are several designated sites in the wildlife area that allow these activities. These sites have a fire ring, a table, and an outhouse. No trashcans are available, so haul your trash out. Linn County Park, located 5 miles north of the refuge, has good camping facilities. The **gauging station** for this section is the Marais des Cygnes at La Cygne. The average **gradient** for this part of the creek is less than .5 foot per mile. There are no **canoe or kayak**

The Marais des Cygnes near Unit G

rentals in the area.

The **put-in** is at the **Unit G pump station**. After the new divided highway is completed the shuttle directions below may need adjustment. To get to the put-in at Unit G, from the intersection of U.S. Highway 69 and State Highway 52 (near Trading Post), go west to the frontage road (Old Highway 69) then turn north (right) one mile to 1700 Road (aka County Road 406), then turn west (left) on 1700 Road and go 2 miles west across the river to Queens Road. Turn north (right) on Queens and go 1.2 miles northwest to Unit G (the northernmost wetland). Take the first right turn (onto an unmarked road), staying close to the river for another seventh of a mile, to the second small camping area on the east side of the road. The 5-mile **round-trip shuttle** route to Unit A takes you back to Highway 69 the way you came in and then you turn south and follow Highway 69 until you cross the Marais des Cygnes River. Take the first right turn and make your way to the river. The banks are steep but there are a few good spots for a take-out.

Put in at the Unit G pump station. The public use area extends one mile upstream of the Unit G pump station and extends 5 miles downstream to Highway 69. In addition to its reputation for catfish, the refuge is a regular zoo of waterfowl and other wildlife. Keep your eyes peeled for critters like southern flying squirrels, otters, hooded mergansers, scissor-tailed flycatchers, paddlefish, foxes, deer, coyotes, bobcats, and over 30 species of warblers.

At river mile 2.7, the **Trego Road Boat Ramp**, the only boat ramp on this reach of the river, is on river left. There are two small campgrounds between the Trego Ramp and Highway 69, both on river right. Unless you intend to float all the way to State Line Road, do not venture downstream of the Highway 69 bridge. The deep pool that you have been paddling on extends about 75 yards downstream of the bridge; there, the limestone ledge that created the pool upstream also creates a rapid. Once you go over that drop, you will not be able to paddle back upstream.

Take out at either the Trego Road Boat Ramp or at a convenient spot along river right, upstream of **Highway 69**. Motorized boats should not go beyond the Highway 69 bridge. Once you drop over that first ledge, you will be unable to either return or go downstream. There are no boat ramps downstream, and it is a violation of federal regulations to have a motorized boat in the wildlife refuge, within 4.5 miles of state line access.

Local Contacts: Kansas Department of Wildlife and Parks, (913) 352-8956

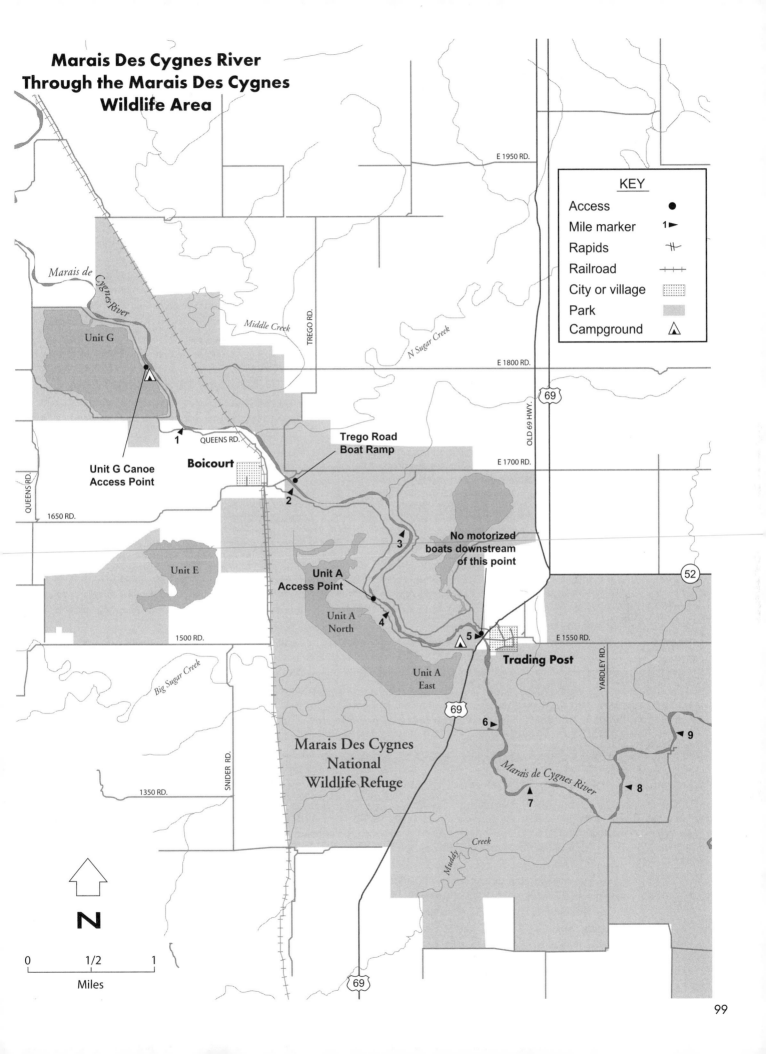

Marais Des Cygnes River
Through the Marais Des Cygnes
Wildlife Area

KEY

Access ●
Mile marker 1►
Rapids
Railroad
City or village
Park
Campground △

Marais de Cygnes River

Unit G

Middle Creek

N Sugar Creek

E 1950 RD.

E 1800 RD.

69

Unit G Canoe
Access Point

1
QUEENS RD.

Boicourt

TREGO RD.

OLD 69 HWY.

**Trego Road
Boat Ramp**

E 1700 RD.

2

QUEENS RD.

1650 RD.

Unit E

3

**No motorized
boats downstream
of this point**

52

Unit A
Access Point

1500 RD.

Unit A
North

4

5

E 1550 RD.

Unit A
East

Trading Post

YARDLEY RD.

Big Sugar Creek

**Marais Des Cygnes
National
Wildlife Refuge**

69

6

9

SNIDER RD.

1350 RD.

Marais de Cygnes River

7

8

Muddy Creek

N

0   1/2   1
Miles

69

99

MARAIS DES CYGNES RIVER:
THROUGH THE MARAIS DES CYGNES WILDLIFE AREA
9 miles, intermediate access available, Class II difficulty
State Highway 69 to State Line Road

The last 14.5 miles of the Marais des Cygnes River that flow through Kansas meander through the Marais des Cygnes National Wildlife Refuge and Marais des Cygnes State Wildlife Area. This long river segment is easily broken into two completely dissimilar parts. The first part is a 5.5-mile reach upstream of the U.S. Highway 69 bridge that is managed by the Kansas Department of Wildlife and Parks (See section above.) The second reach is a 9-mile long segment that passes through the Marais des Cygnes National Wildlife Refuge and Wildlife Area, all the way from the Highway 69 bridge to the Missouri State Line.

These two segments can be combined to make a long day or two shorter, multi-day trips. The segment downstream of Highway 69 is presented here.

Although both motorized and nonmotorized boats are allowed upstream of the Highway 69 bridge, motorized boats should not proceed downstream from there. A rock ledge spans the river. Once over that ledge you will not be able to motor back upstream. Further, there are no boat ramps downstream, federal regulations prevent motorized boats in the 4.5 miles upstream of State Line Road, and endangered mussels in this reach would be harmed by propellers, exhaust, oil, and gasoline.

The river downstream of Highway 69 is a Class II series of pools, riffles, and rapids. Surrounded by hills, bluffs, and mature trees, the river is well protected from the wind. Big catfish hang out in the deep pools. By boat, hunters can access other parts of the wildlife area that are otherwise more difficult to reach. Waterfowl hunters must register and obtain a permit at the wildlife area office. Although portions of Unit A are closed to all shooting during the dark goose season, the river is open for use all year.

Camping and building fires are not allowed along the river. Linn County Park, located 5 miles north of the refuge, has good camping facilities. There are no **canoe or kayak rentals** in the area.

The **minimum recommended flow is 300 CFS**, but at that level it is scratchy at the ledges, so an extra 100 CFS is very nice. Many people think the river is most beautiful when it is low and the rock and gravel beds are partly exposed, but whitewater enthusiasts will prefer the 800-1500 CFS range. The **gauging station** for this run is the Marais des Cygnes at La Cygne. You can gauge the river with your eye from the takeout. If there is plenty of water flowing over the riffle just upstream of the State Line Access, there will be enough to float the whole reach. The average **gradient** between Highway 69 and State Line is only 1.7 feet per mile but most of that comes in large drops. Depending on the usual factors, the 9-mile trip to State Line takes about three to five hours.

To get to the **put-in**, go south of the intersection of **Highway 69** and State Highway 52, take the first right turn (west) after you cross the bridge, and then find your way to a good spot along the river. The banks are generally steep and often muddy. The 14.6-mile **round-trip shuttle** route takes you back to the intersection of Highways 69 and 52, then 3.5 miles east to State Line Road, and then south 2.7 miles to the southwest edge of the bridge over the river. The path down to the river is overgrown with poison ivy, badly rutted, and muddy when wet.

Put in at a spot of your choosing just upstream of Highway 69. The action starts just below the bridge. An outcropping of Lenapah limestone forms a series of ledges that create fun, Class II rapids. Skilled boaters surf the waves and holes at levels between 800-1500 CFS. Once past those upper ledges, the rest of the river is a pleasant series of long pools, easy ledges, and gravel bars. Keep your eyes peeled for critters like southern flying squirrels, otters, hooded mergansers, scissor-tailed flycatchers, paddlefish, foxes, deer, coyotes, bobcats, and over 30 species of warblers.

The river meanders through mature oak and hickory forests and is also bordered by cottonwoods, sycamores, maples, and elms. During the fall, the adjacent wetlands attract many thousands of waterfowl. Parts of the river are bordered by high bluffs and cliffs. Gravel bars will invite you to rest, the deep pools will tempt you to take a swim, and the riffles will keep you wanting more. Big Sugar Creek enters from river right near river mile 6. Near river mile 6.8, Muddy Creek enters on river right. The **Jim Jones Access**, near river mile 8.5, is a steep climb from the river, but it can be useful if you would like to shorten your float. It is on a small dirt path on Vincent Lane west of the only private homes along the river. Please park on the road and carry your boat the short distance to the river. The access is steep and is especially unsuitable for wet weather or high water. Although the access is on federal land, both the land beside it and the shoreline are private property for a short distance downstream. Please do not disturb the peace or beauty of this setting.

Davis Creek enters on river left just less than one mile from State Line Road. **Take out** at **State Line Road**.

Local Contacts: Marais des Cygnes National Wildlife Area and Refuge, (913) 352-8956.

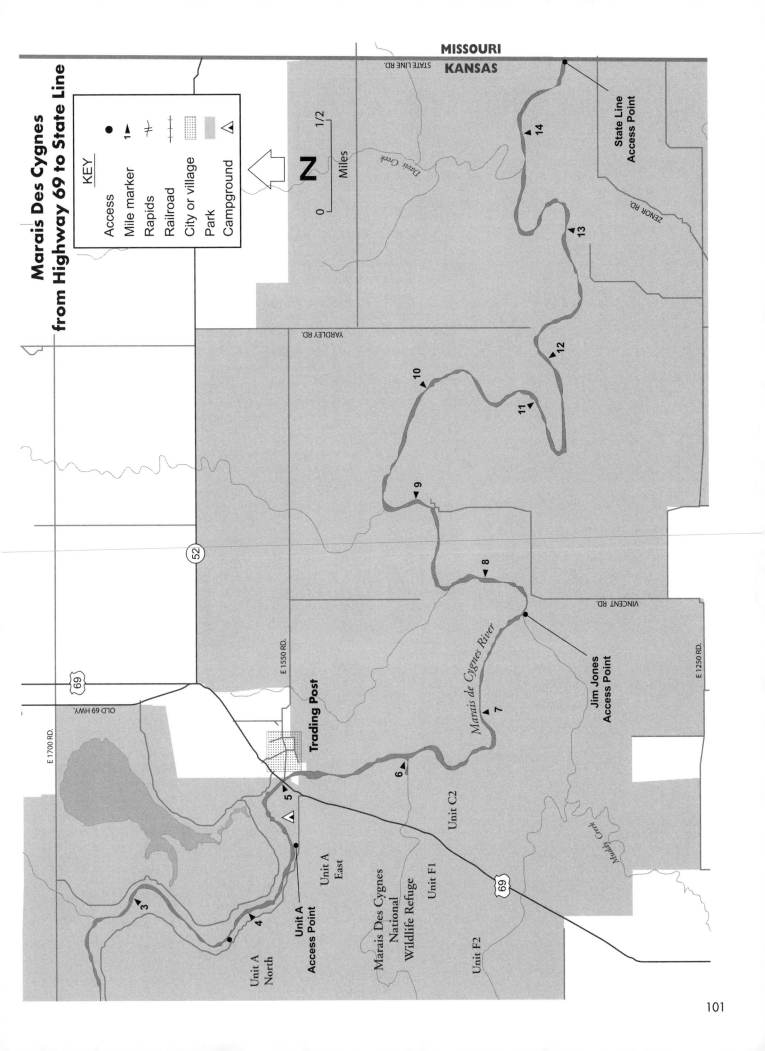

Marais Des Cygnes
from Highway 69 to State Line

KEY

- Access
- ▲ 1 Mile marker
- Rapids
- Railroad
- City or village
- Park
- ⌂ Campground

N

Miles

0   1/2

MISSOURI

KANSAS

Davis Creek

State Line
Access Point

ZENOR RD.

STATE LINE RD.

YARDLEY RD.

VINCENT RD.

E 1250 RD.

E 1550 RD.

E 1700 RD.

OLD 69 HWY.

Trading Post

Marais de Cygnes River

Jim Jones
Access Point

Unit C2

Unit F1

Unit F2

Unit A
East

Unit A
North

Unit A
Access Point

Marais Des Cygnes
National
Wildlife Refuge

Muddy Creek

52

69

69

3
4
5
6
7
8
9
10
11
12
13
14

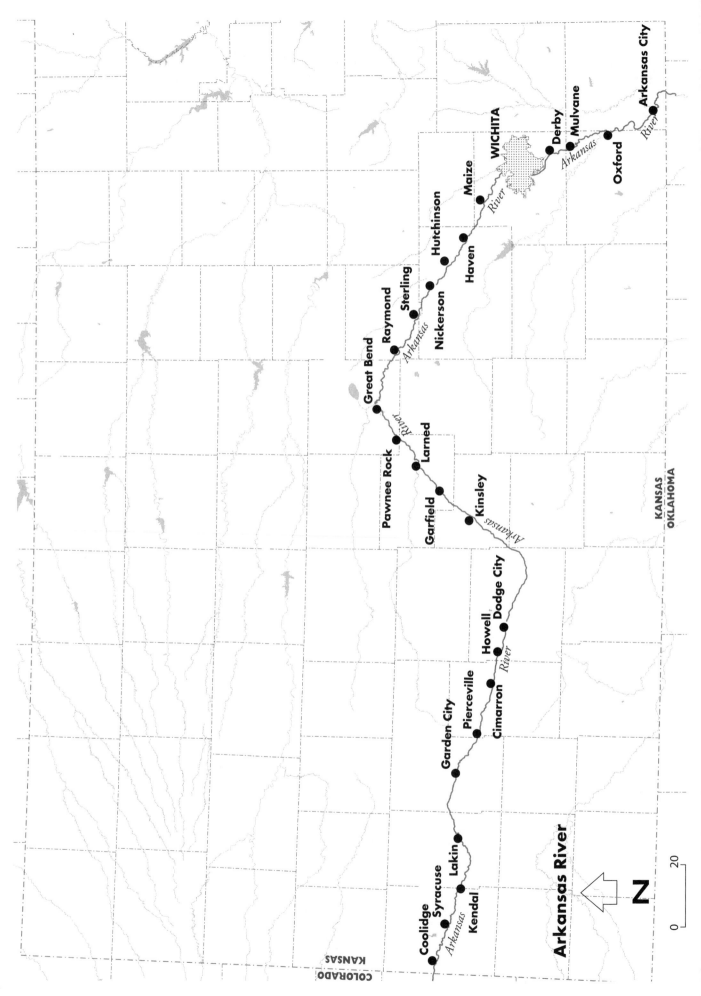

Arkansas River

N

0   20

WICHITA

Arkansas City
Mulvane
Derby
Oxford
Maize
Hutchinson
Haven
Sterling
Raymond
Nickerson
Great Bend
Larned
Pawnee Rock
Garfield
Kinsley
Dodge City
Howell
Cimarron
Pierceville
Garden City
Lakin
Syracuse
Coolidge
Kendal

Arkansas River
Arkansas River
Arkansas
Arkansas
Arkansas

KANSAS
OKLAHOMA

COLORADO
KANSAS

102

ARKANSAS RIVER AND WATERSHED

The fifth-longest river in the country, at 1,450 miles, the Ark springs to life from snow on 14,000-foot peaks in the Sawatch Mountains near Leadville, Colorado. Whitewater rafting companies, thrill seekers, and expert boaters from all over the world flock to Colorado towns like Buena Vista, Salida, and Cañon City to enjoy the Ark's roaring rapids and clean water.

The Spaniards first called this river "St. Paul" and "St. Peter." They changed it to what the Indians called it, "Ne Shuta," which means "red water." The French named it after the Indian tribe, the Arkana, who lived in the area. In 1806, the governor of the Louisiana Territories, James Wilkinson, called it the Arkansaw. The "official" Kansas pronunciation of Arkansas is "Ahr-Kan-Zuhs." In every place else in the world, it is called either the "Ar-kin-saw" or the more familiar "Ark."

From a paddler's perspective, the Arkansas River in Kansas is logically divided into four arbitrary, unequal, and dissimilar segments. The uppermost 130 miles, between Coolidge and Dodge City, rarely has enough water for a good float. The river at Dodge City is hardly more dependable, but over the 117-mile journey to Raymond the river becomes more reliable. The 83 miles between Raymond and Wichita enjoy a steady increase in flows and, thus, popularity with boaters. Within the 85 miles from Wichita to the Oklahoma border, the channel has much greater flows than the upper reaches, but it has become so broad that without at least **600-700 CFS** the river is not floatable.

Along its 415-mile Kansas length, the riverbed is mostly composed of shifting sand and fine gravel. With an average **gradient** over 5.5 feet per mile, the sandy riverbed creates elusive channels that run fast and rarely pool. A paddler can become expert at finding and staying in the main channel, yet still get stuck on a shallow sandbar while gawking.

Except during periods of heavy runoff, the water is fairly clear in the upper reaches. As the soils and land use change along the route, the water becomes more turbid. Water quality in the river fluctuates with rainfall and runoff from croplands, feedlots, and city streets. Overall, expect better water quality at medium flows and clearer water at low flows.

Between the Colorado border and the Oklahoma border, the Ark travels 418 miles, loses 2313 feet, and has an average gradient of over 5.5 feet per mile. This is more gradient than many of the popular Ozark streams in Missouri or Arkansas. There are many USGS **gauging stations** along the Ark and all are easily accessed by computer.

As the river passes larger towns, a paddler can usually pick up supplies and learn more about local history and culture. Most access points along the river are good, but parking is limited.

There are no **canoe or kayak rentals**, guides, or outfitters along or near the Arkansas River.

River maps, even mine, can be misleading with regard to the actual mileage you may paddle between one point and another on any river, but this is especially true on the Ark. At low flows, the river is no more than a small, shifting, creeklike channel that meanders like a snake within the larger river flood channel. Map mileage indicates the mileage of the larger channel, but does not account for the additional low-water meanders within the main channel. Even though the gradient would suggest a faster pace, initially plan on about 2.5 to 4 map-miles per hour and adjust your estimate to suit your paddling style and the water level.

Frequent flooding and the meandering nature of the river have kept development a respectful distance from the river. Agricultural over-pumping has decimated natural flows west of Great Bend. Yet heavy snows in the mountains combined with spring rains on the Great Plains can restore the river's life. When that happens, it is a great opportunity to experience the wide-open country of southwest and central Kansas in a way that few people have ever experienced.

Dropping 1,730 feet over the distance of 248 miles between Coolidge and Raymond, the average **gradient** is nearly 7 feet per mile, enough to get you where you're going with very little effort when there is enough water under your keel.

From the Colorado border to about 15 miles above Wichita, the **minimum recommended flow is about 100 CFS**. There are special considerations, however, that are discussed for each river segment to provide more detailed guidance.

The politics of water have done much to shape what you will see and experience from the river. Colorado and Kansas formed the Arkansas River

ABOUT THE ABBREVIATED NARRATIVE ON THE ARKANSAS RIVER

By the merits of its length, beauty, history, and condition, navigating the Arkansas River deserves a book of its own. Rather than including only the most popular segments and keeping the beauty of the western two-thirds of the river hidden from public knowledge (much as it is now), yet mindful of limited space in this volume, I chose to abbreviate the river narratives and change the scale of the maps for those upper reaches. This abbreviated format includes general watershed, access, and descriptive information, but without detailed shuttle routes and on-river narrative.

Compact in 1948 to be sure that the waters of the Arkansas would flow forever across the Great Western Desert. Under that compact, Colorado was required to limit the water taken from the river to that which was already being taken at that time. However, Colorado farmers cared not a whit for that agreement and began growing corn in the desert. Corn needs about 30 inches of water per year, but eastern Colorado gets only about 15 to 20 inches of rain; the difference is taken from the river and its underlying aquifer. Kansas sued. The courts ruled in favor of Kansas, but Colorado has, to a large extent, ignored the ruling. Consequently, the Arkansas River at the Colorado/Kansas border often looks like a dry arroyo.

Kansas farmers also seized upon cheap land prices and seemingly unlimited water and have used both with little restraint. Kansas finally began to limit new irrigators, but had already over-allocated the rapidly dwindling supply of water. Center pivot irrigation pumps sunk deep into the sandy soils drain water from the river; once that is gone, they drain the water from the sands beneath the river, then take even more water from the rapidly depleting Ogallala Aquifer. You'll generally find more water in the Ark between Coolidge and Kendall than you will between Kendall and Great Bend. By the time the "river" reaches Garden City, nothing is left except during the wettest years.

Although western Kansas would sometimes seem better suited to a trail ride than a float trip, there are those special years when warm winds melt an extremely heavy snow pack high in the Sawatch Mountains and rains bless the prairie. When that happens, few things can compare to a trip across Kansas by canoe.

A spring or early summer float would be ideal, but the most likely time of the year to find water between Coolidge and Lakin is late October through April, after the center pivot irrigation systems have been switched off and the diversion canals have been closed for several months. Once you pass Lakin, the most dependable window for water decreases to December through March. Controlled more by irrigation withdrawal than by rainfall, the river can rise or fall rapidly without warning. Below Dodge City, more regular flows occur from November through March, with a peak in February and March that provides the best window. Near Larned, the chances of finding water shrink again, but as the Ark nears Great Bend, it is not unusual to find adequate flows for a float trip at any time of the year, with the most promising discharges statistically from February through June. Within the 47 miles between Great Bend and Nickerson, the river's average annual discharge doubles and seasonal flows become much more dependable.

Western Kansas is still the place of song and legend, where porcupines can be seen perched in trees, kestrels hunt overhead, and mule deer and antelope stand in disbelief as you float by. In the evening, coyotes will sing you to sleep and, of course, "the skies are not cloudy all day." You can camp on sandbars, cool your feet in the river, and eat your beans surrounded by the moods, sounds, and colors of this unusual place. In all, when the Ark is flowing, a paddler will find the river to be one of the most beautiful, interesting, and soulful ways to experience the wide-open, high plains country of southwest Kansas.

THE FATE OF THE COMMONS

Near a small village, a king saw how hard and wisely the farmers worked on their little plots of land. He admired the self-reliance, work ethic, and determination that produced the bountiful crops that had always sustained this area. In an act of generosity, he announced that the people could use 10,000 hectares of his land to raise their livestock in any way they desired. The land was just downstream of the village, so it didn't take long for the people to take out small, manageable loans to purchase animals and equipment. Soon all of the farmers had a few animals and things were going well.

Some of the more industrious farmers figured out that they could profit more if they had more animals. As those herds grew, the other farmers saw the profit potential and did the same. Soon the grass was gone, the soil was eroding, and the streams were trampled and polluted. The damaged soil could no longer support the livestock, so they either died or were sold at a loss. The fish, forests, wildlife, and small farms that had sustained the people for thousands of years were gone. The people were broken under a burden of debt and the small farms were left behind in ruin.

This is "the fate of the commons." When a shared resource is used without adequate restriction, each user will take as much and as fast as possible until it is all gone or ruined. This is what is happening to western Kansas water. What we do now to protect our children's future will define our love or our disdain, our wisdom or our foolishness.

For the Arkansas River, water and politics are inseparably connected. I hope that readers come away with an appreciation for the river, our history, and some of the challenges that lay ahead.

ARKANSAS RIVER: COOLIDGE TO LAKIN

52 miles, intermediate access available, Class I difficulty
Coolidge Access at river mile 1,100 to Highway 25 at river mile 1,048

Check the USGS **gauging station** for the Arkansas River near Granada, Colorado, and at both Syracuse and Deerfield, Kansas. Despite the healthy **gradient** in this reach, 6.6 feet per mile, expect to make only 2.5 to 4 miles per hour, point to point, due to the tightly meandering inner channel within the larger flood channel. Although a **minimum desirable stream flow of 100 CFS** is sufficient to carry a loaded canoe, it is best to have 200 CFS or more at the put-in. Be sure to check all of the river gauges, both upstream and down, plus the gauges on all of the diversion canals. The last thing you want is to find the river disappearing down an irrigation canal.

Coolidge, *river mile 1,100*—Take Main Street south out of Coolidge, then make a jog west on Road 17 to C (aka County Road 308) and go south to the river. Thomas Jefferson Coolidge, former president of the Atchison, Topeka and Santa Fe Railroad, left his name on this town.

U.S. Highway 50/400 is never more than 1.5 miles from the river, with irrigated cornfields in between. To the south, sagebrush, yucca, and sand dunes covered with native grasses dominate the view at the beginning, but corn fields sometimes displace them where the floodplain is wide enough. The river channel is fairly wide at your put-in just south of Coolidge, but it will gradually narrow over the next 10 miles. By the time you get to Syracuse, the river's channel will be noticeably narrower and there may be a loss of water as irrigation canals deplete the river. The river's floodplain near Coolidge is 1.5 to 2 miles wide, gradually becoming somewhat narrower near Syracuse.

All of the canals in this section are on the north side of the river. The first irrigation canal you will come upon is the Frontier Ditch. It comes out of the river at about river mile 1095, where a long, northward mean-der brings you within a quarter mile of Highway 50. At about river mile 1094, East Bridge Creek and the Alamo Ditch enter and exit at the same spot. At about river mile 1088 the Fort Aubrey Ditch begins pulling water. From the air and to the north you would see a lot of center pivot irrigations systems and their big circles of corn along the river. To the south, scenic hills and dunes cover the landscape. From the river, there is plenty to see and enjoy that is nearer at hand. You will know you are two miles from Syracuse when you come to the overhead power lines near river mile 1083. River Road is now a few hundred yards to the south

Syracuse Access, *river mile 1,081*—From Syracuse, go south past the fairgrounds on State Highway 87. If you peek over the edge of the river channel, the corn fields have disappeared almost entirely, only to return just above Lakin, about 40 miles downstream. Sandy Creek comes in at about river mile 1075 from the north and Shirley Creek comes in just before the Kendall Bridge. Both creeks have been dewatered by over-pumping.

Kendall Access, *river mile 1,067*—From Kendall, take County Road Y south to the river. At about river mile 1060, the Amazon Ditch gulps more water out of the already depleted Ark. The river channel remains about the same, but near river mile 1056 the river valley widens from an average of one mile to more than three miles in width. Above the river's main channel, farm fields often straddle both sides of the river. This agricultural scenery will continue on and off for most of the next 200 miles, changed only by the backdrop of either flatlands or rolling hills all the way to Raymond. Watch for the pipeline that crosses the river at about river mile 1051.

Lakin Access, *river mile 1,048*—Take Kansas Highway 25 south from Lakin.

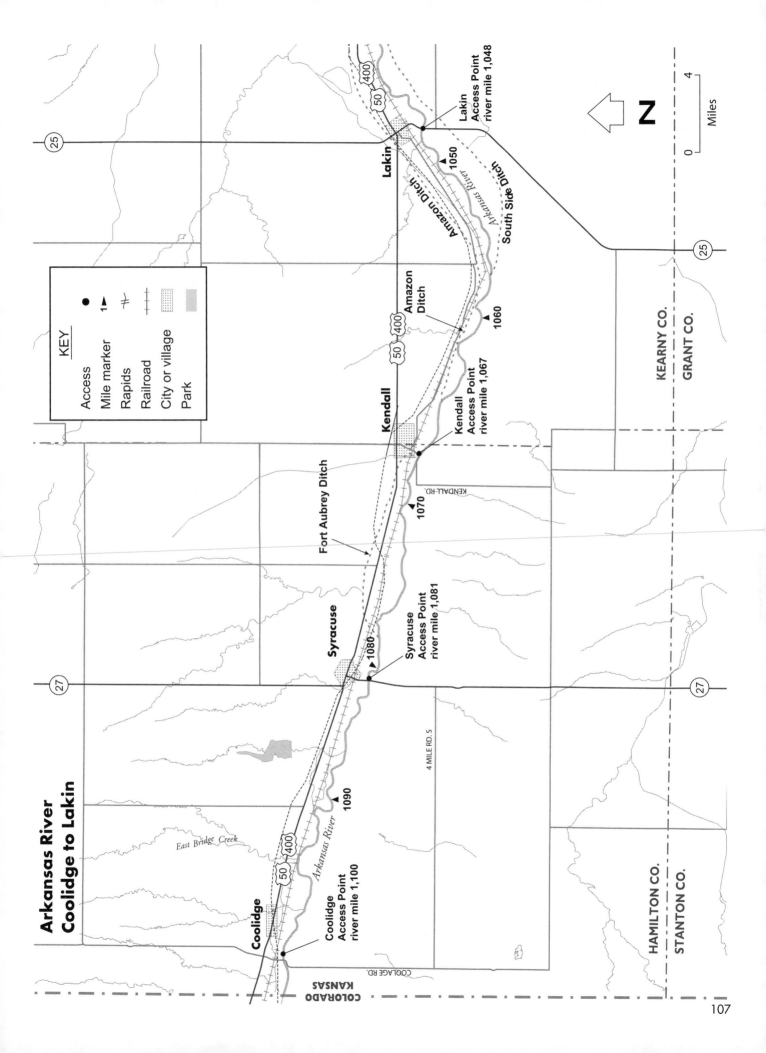

Arkansas River
Coolidge to Lakin

KEY

Access
Mile marker
Rapids
Railroad
City or village
Park

Lakin Access Point river mile 1,048

Lakin

Amazon Ditch

1050

Arkansas River

South Side Ditch

Amazon Ditch

1060

400

50 400

Kendall Access Point river mile 1,067

Kendall

KENDALL RD.

1070

Fort Aubrey Ditch

Syracuse

1080

Syracuse Access Point river mile 1,081

4 MILE RD. S

1090

East Bridge Creek

Arkansas River

50 400

Coolidge Access Point river mile 1,100

Coolidge

COOLIGE RD.

COLORADO
KANSAS

KEARNY CO.
GRANT CO.

HAMILTON CO.
STANTON CO.

N

0   4
Miles

ARKANSAS RIVER: LAKIN TO CIMARRON

58 miles, with intermittent accesses available, Class I difficulty
Lakin Access at river mile 1,048 to Highway 23 at river mile 990

Check the USGS **gauging stations** at Kendall, Deerfield, Garden City, and Dodge City. Be aware that flash floods can rise very quickly on this segment. This reach is typified by undependable flows and remote settings. Roads rarely approach the river and the riverbanks are well traveled by mule deer and other wildlife. Except during rare times of high water, this wonderful river can go from looking like a beautiful little creek to a dry arroyo within the course of a few miles.

The **minimum recommended flow** of 70-100 CFS is enough to carry a moderately loaded canoe, but be aware that those minimum flows can disappear into the sand or an irrigation canal very quickly. Be sure to check the USGS Arkansas River gauging stations both upstream and downstream. The average **gradient** between Lakin and Cimarron is 6.6 feet per mile. Expect to make speeds of about 2.5 to 4 miles per hour, point to point.

Lakin Access, *river mile 1,048*—Take State Highway 25 south from Lakin. At river level, the scenery is what you would expect of a small stream in western Kansas, but now the valley, visible only from above the river's shoulders, is nearly four miles wide. From the air, it looks like a checkerboard of corn with green or brown checkers on almost every square. For the next 26 miles, the low, rolling hills to the north disappear from view as the river enters a vast, open area that would be characterized by shortgrass prairie if not for the impact of forced agriculture in this Great American Desert.

Deerfield Access, *river mile 1,040*—From Deerfield, take Main Street (County Road 243) south. By this time, the river really struggles to maintain its flow. In a growing sea of corn, the river channel continues to hug the north side of the valley, meandering near the railroad tracks, then far away. The floodplain gradually narrows on its way to Holcomb. At about river mile 1038, the Farmers Ditch takes more water, if there is any, northward. Another branch of the same ditch has its mouth near river mile 1037. A dirt track crosses the river near river mile 1031, about 1.5 miles upstream of Holcomb.

Holcomb Access, *river mile 1,033*—Take South Main Street (aka River Road or Holcomb Lane) south of town. According to *1001 Kansas Place Names*, "A Holcomb native known as Mother Truitt described the naming of Holcomb to novelist Truman Capote: 'Them days, we called this place Sherlock. Then along (came) this stranger by the name Holcomb. A hog-raiser, he was. Made money, and decided the town ought to be called after him. Soon as it was, what did he do? Sold out. Moved to California.'"

Near river mile 1031, you'll go under a railroad bridge. The center pivot irrigation systems disappear as you approach Garden City. The river is now most commonly a large, dry scar across the prairie that awaits the return of water and common sense. Above river mile 1025, about a mile upstream of Garden City, you'll pass under power lines. Here, Sagebrush Road begins to parallel the river on the south side.

Garden City Access, *river mile 1,024*—Take U.S. Highway 83 Business Route (Main Street) south out of town. Garden City was given its name in 1878 by a vagabond who told Mrs. William D. Fulton that, although there weren't any trees around the place, the buffalo grass was so green and pretty they should call the town "Garden City." The town lies directly on the Mountain Branch of the Santa Fe Trail that went along the Arkansas River between Dodge City and La Junta, Colorado. Finnup Park, conveniently located south of town and just north of the river, is a convenient place to rendezvous. A river gauging station is located under the northeast corner of the Main Street bridge, at the put-in. As the river heads east out of town, rolling hills return to the northern horizon and the river valley narrows a bit. Almost two miles downstream, the river passes under Highway 83. Near river mile 1018, the river crosses under an unnamed road. One mile later, it crosses under some power lines.

Pierceville Access, *river mile 1,013*—Take Pierceville Road south out of town.

Charleston Access, *river mile 1,005*—From Charleston, take 6 Road (County Road 285) south to the river. There is a sand pit about a quarter mile upstream of Ingalls on river left.

Ingalls Access, *river mile 998*—Take Main Street (Monte Ingalls Road) south out of town. The town was named after Kansas Senator John James Ingalls who chose the Kansas Motto: *Ad astra per aspera* (To the stars through difficulty).

Just downstream from river mile 997, the city has a low-head dam that should be portaged.

Cimarron Access, *river mile 990*—Take State Highway 23, Main Street, south out of town. The location of the town is near the crossing of the Santa Fe Trail, where one branch of the trail went south to the Cimarron River.

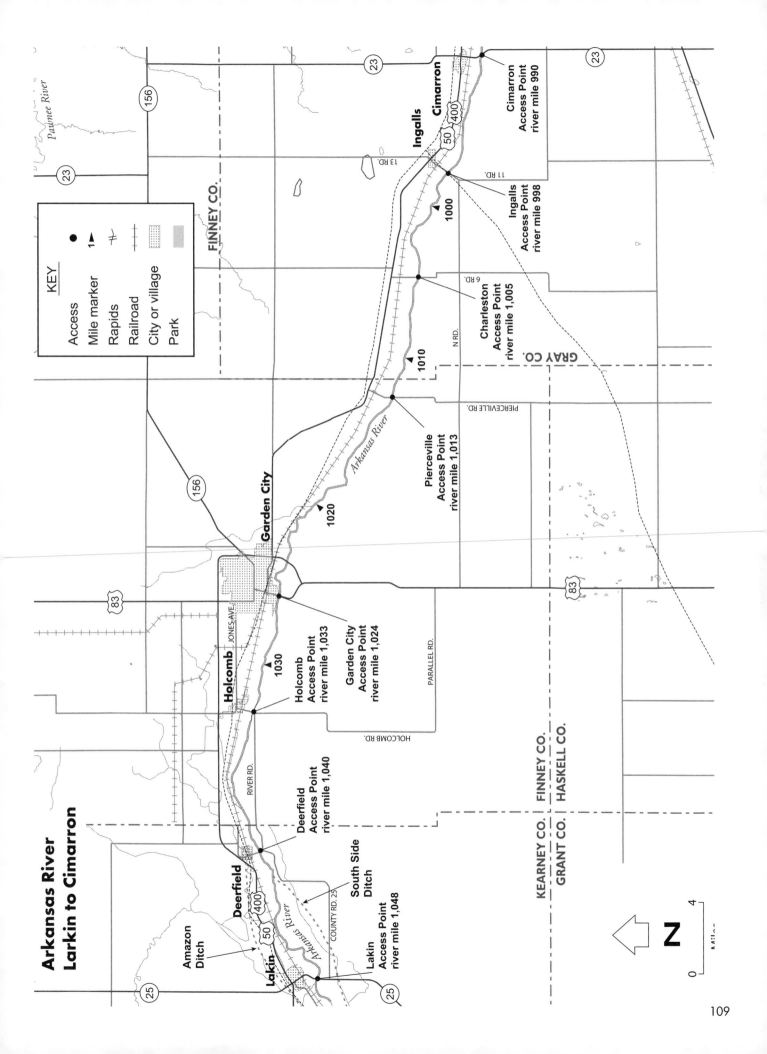

Arkansas River
Larkin to Cimarron

KEY

- • Access
- ▲ Mile marker
- ⌗ Rapids
- Railroad
- City or village
- Park

FINNEY CO.

Pawnee River

Cimarron Access Point
river mile 990

Ingalls Access Point
river mile 998

Charleston Access Point
river mile 1,005

Pierceville Access Point
river mile 1,013

Arkansas River

Garden City Access Point
river mile 1,024

Holcomb Access Point
river mile 1,033

Deerfield Access Point
river mile 1,040

South Side Ditch

Lakin Access Point
river mile 1,048

Amazon Ditch

Cimarron

Ingalls

Garden City

Holcomb

Deerfield

Lakin

GRAY CO.

KEARNEY CO. FINNEY CO.
GRANT CO. HASKELL CO.

JONES AVE.

RIVER RD.

PARALLEL RD.

HOLCOMB RD.

PIERCEVILLE RD.

N RD.

6 RD.

11 RD.

13 RD.

COUNTY RD. 25

1000
1010
1020
1030

N

0   4
Miles

ARKANSAS RIVER FROM CIMARRON TO BUCKLIN ROAD

42 miles, with intermediate access available, Class I difficulty
Cimarron Access at river mile 990 to Bucklin Road at river mile 948

THE COWBOY CAPITAL

Dodge City was originally named Buffalo City because of the estimated 25 million buffalo in the surrounding area. Between 1875 and 1885, cattlemen drove longhorns up from Texas and New Mexico to the railway station. Dodge City has retained its cowboy notoriety longer than most cow towns of the old railroad frontier. According to a historical marker near Highway 50, "For ten years this was the largest cattle market in the world and for fifteen it was the wildest town on the American frontier. Established with the coming of the Santa Fe Railroad in 1872, Dodge City became the shipping center of the Southwest.... By 1875 most cattle trails led to Dodge; in 1884 Texas drovers alone brought 106 herds numbering 300,000 head.... Near Dodge City are sites of old Fort Mann and Fort Atkinson. The Santa Fe Trail, which they were established to protect, may still be traced on the near-by prairie."

From Cimarron to Bucklin Road, east of Dodge City, the river continues to be typified by beauty and undependable water. The general NW-to-SE direction and a larger riparian forest in some areas provide some wind protection. Small dirt farm roads often approach the river from the south, but do not cross. The riverbanks are well traveled by mule deer, and the river retains the character of a sandy-bottomed creek. The **minimum recommended flow of 70-100 CFS** is enough to carry a moderately loaded canoe, but be aware that this flow can disappear into the sand. Be sure to check the USGS Arkansas River **gauging stations** both upstream and downstream at Garden City, Dodge City, and Kinsley. The average **gradient** between Cimarron and Bucklin Road is almost 6.9 feet per mile. The inner channel meanders dramatically within the larger flood channel so, despite the favorable gradient, expect to make speeds of about 2.5 to 4 miles per hour, point to point.

Cimarron Access, *river mile 990*—Take State Highway 23 (Main Street) south out of town. The location of the town is near the crossing of the Santa Fe Trail, where one branch of the trail went south to the Cimarron River. A sand and gravel quarry is located on the south bank at about river mile 989, and there is a pipeline at river mile 988. A farm road crosses the river near river mile 982 and could serve as a convenient alternate take-out, since U.S. Highway 50/400 is just a stone's throw to the north.

Howell Access, *river mile 980*—From Howell, take Howell Road (102nd Road) south. There is a sand and gravel plant near river mile 972. At that point, you are on the outskirts of Dodge City. As you approach the city, you can expect to see where the locals use the

riverbed for an ATV and motorcycle playground. The first city bridge you come to will be 14th Avenue, just below river mile 971. Next is a railroad bridge, where the tracks switch to the south side of the river, and remain until Ford, where the tracks leave the river.

Dodge City Access, *river mile 970*—Go south out of town on U.S. Highway 283/56 (aka 2nd Avenue). Wright Park is conveniently located at the northwest edge of the bridge.

Note that flash floods roaring out of Dodge City can bring the river up quickly. Through town and all the way to Ford, the corn fields and center pivot systems maintain a greater distance from the river and the low, rolling hills disappear. Near river mile 968 you'll cross 113 Road (Highway 56 Bypass) and near river mile 967 you'll cross 114 Road. At about river mile 966, you'll go under some large power lines. Fort Dodge is along the north bank near river mile 965, where an intermittent stream enters. At about river mile 964 you'll cross under Coronado Road (aka 117 Road). At about river mile 957, you'll see a pipeline. Mulberry Creek enters from the south, about a half mile upstream of the U.S. Highway 154 bridge.

Ford Access, *river mile 954*—From Ford, go north on Highway 400 (Main Street). More of the natural, wild Kansas resumes as the railroad heads southeast and the river begins a giant meander toward Great Bend. One of the last traces of civilization that you will see is a power line at river mile 952. By now, the mean annual rainfall has increased to 20-25 inches. During the late winter and early spring, the river has fairly dependable flows until the irrigation pumps kick on again. Even so, by now you may notice a change in and along the river. Trees are a little more common and they grow a little taller.

Bucklin Road Access, *river mile 948*—From the town of Bucklin, take Seacat Road north and then jog left (west) on Bollinger Road (aka Wilburn Road) and then right (north) on Bucklin Road. At Highway 400/154 jog left for about 1,000 feet and then right to continue on Bucklin Road.

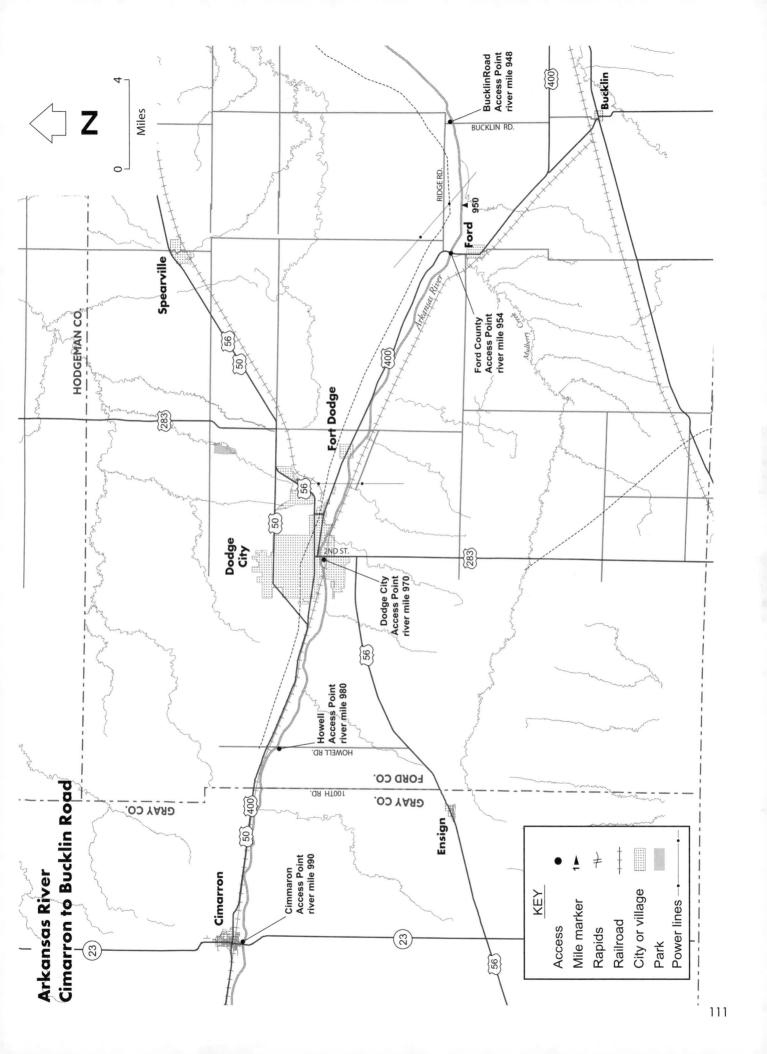

Arkansas River
Cimarron to Bucklin Road

N

Miles
0   4

BucklinRoad
Access Point
river mile 948

Bucklin

400

BUCKLIN RD.

RIDGE RD.

950

Ford

Ford County
Access Point
river mile 954

Arkansas River

Mulberry Creek

Spearville

56

50

400

Fort Dodge

56

283

Dodge City

50

2ND ST.

Dodge City
Access Point
river mile 970

283

56

Howell
Access Point
river mile 980

HOWELL RD.

FORD CO.
GRAY CO.

100TH RD.

Ensign

56

HODGEMAN CO.

283

GRAY CO.

400
50

Cimarron

Cimarron
Access Point
river mile 990

23

23

56

KEY

- ●   Access
- ▲   Mile marker
- ≠   Rapids
- ╫   Railroad
- ▦   City or village
- ▨   Park
- ·—·— Power lines

ARKANSAS RIVER: BUCKLIN ROAD TO LARNED

51 miles, intermediate access available, Class I difficulty
Bucklin Road Access at river mile 948 to Highway 19 at river mile 897

From Bucklin Road to Larned, the river enters an area that is greener and wetter than the reaches upstream. With the river now matching the direction of the prevailing southwest wind, it can feel like you're being pushed forward through a wind tunnel. A dirt road, sometimes named but most often not, roughly parallels the river along the south side as it meanders across Ford, Kiowa, and Edwards Counties. A few very small dirt farm roads intermittently approach or parallel the river along the north shore. The riverbanks are well traveled by mule deer and other wildlife. The riparian forest of cottonwoods and willows grows thicker and taller, but the river continues to retain the character of a sandy-bottomed creek near the **minimum recommended flow of 70-100 CFS**. The average **gradient** between Bucklin Road and Larned is almost 6.4 feet per mile. The inner channel meanders dramatically within the larger flood channel, so although the current moves fairly quickly, you can only make speeds of 2.5 to 4 miles per hour point to point. Use the **gauging stations** for the Arkansas River at

The Ark between Garfield and Larned with 100 CFS

Kinsley and Larned and keep in mind that this "creek" can flash flood very quickly.

Bucklin Road Access, *river mile 948*—From the town of Ford, take U.S. Highway 154 (U.S. Highway 400) four-tenths of a mile north of the river, then go east 6 miles on Ridge Road to Bucklin Road. Turn south to the river. This is one of the river's longest and wildest segments. You will never see it from the river, but near mile 927 the river approaches a cluster of center pivot systems along river right and they continue along the river's edge for just a few miles until sand dunes and rolling hills begin to grow again to the south.

Kinsley West Access, *river mile 923*—Take U.S. Highway 183 south out of town. You'll cross under one bridge upstream of mile 921.

Kinsley East Access, *river mile 920*—Take U.S. Highway 50 east out of town. Kinsley to Garfield is, perhaps, the most remote and relatively wildest part of the reach that runs northeast toward Great Bend. Near river mile 915, the channel widens and only a few roads approach. Here, the paddler is confronted by complex, braided channels. As you approach Garfield, irrigated fields reappear along the southern horizon, but the foreground is almost all rolling sand dunes coved with sagebrush and yuccas. Just before the Garfield Bridge (County Road 225), Coon Creek, a substantial creek for these parts, enters from the north.

Garfield Access, *river mile 908*—From Garfield, go south on Pawnee Street (County Road 225). The town was named in 1886 after President James A. Garfield. Above the riverbanks and beyond the shelter of the riparian forest, the view leaving Garfield is largely of sandy hills. Approaching Larned, this view transitions completely to cultivated farms.

The **take-out** is at the southeast edge of the bridge south of Larned on the State Highway 19 spur.

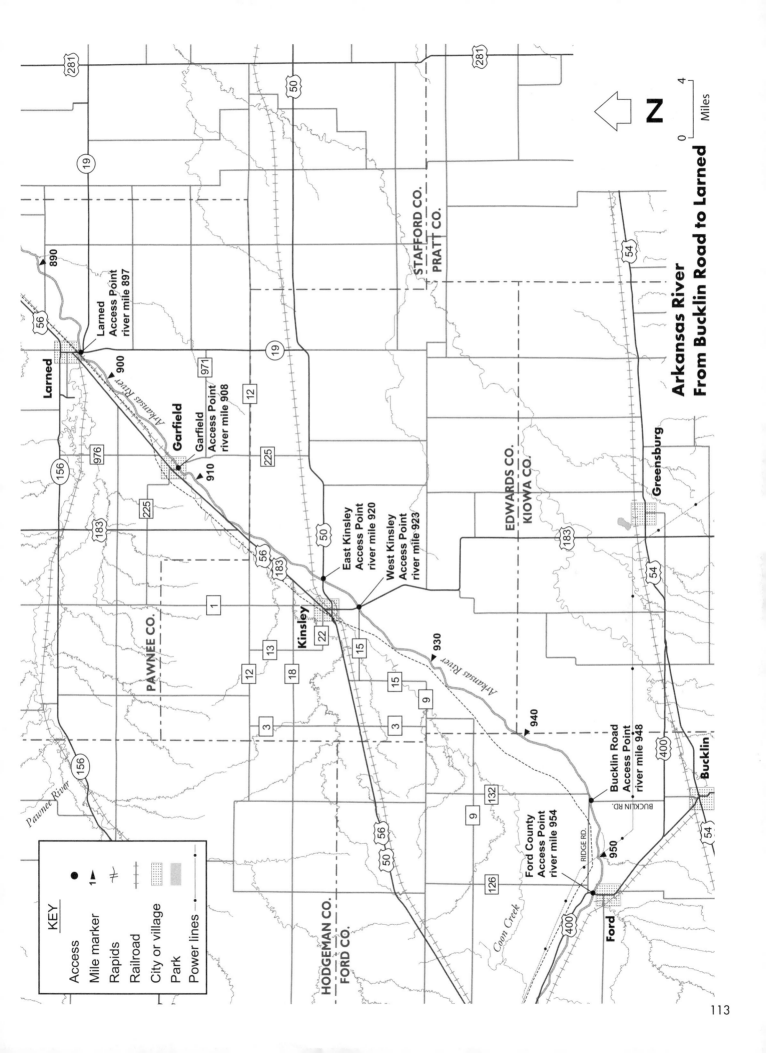

Arkansas River
From Bucklin Road to Larned

N

4

0 Miles

KEY

Access
Mile marker
Rapids
Railroad
City or village
Park
Power lines

Larned Access Point river mile 897

Garfield Access Point river mile 908

East Kinsley Access Point river mile 920

West Kinsley Access Point river mile 923

Bucklin Road Access Point river mile 948

Ford County Access Point river mile 954

Larned
Garfield
Kinsley
Greensburg
Bucklin
Ford

PAWNEE CO.

STAFFORD CO.
PRATT CO.

EDWARDS CO.
KIOWA CO.

HODGEMAN CO.
FORD CO.

Arkansas River
Pawnee River
Coon Creek

BUCKLIN RD.
RIDGE RD.

890
900
910
930
940
950

113

ARKANSAS RIVER: LARNED TO THE RAYMOND WEST ACCESS

46 miles, with intermediate access available, Class I difficulty
Larned Access at river mile 897 to Avenue Q at river mile 851

FROM THE HISTORIC MONUMENT IN LARNED, KANSAS

"Near the end of Lewis and Clark's journey to the Northwest and return to St. Louis, Lt. Zebulon Pike was dispatched to explore the Southwest. In short, what Lewis and Clark meant to the Northwest, Pike meant to the Southwest. What the Missouri River meant to Lewis and Clark, the Arkansas River meant to Pike. On October 29, 1806, Pike and his men crossed the Pawnee River near the south edge of present Larned. Pike's maps and notes were used by William Becknell in 1821 when he opened what we now call the Santa Fe Trail."

This segment has an average **gradient** of over 5.7 feet per mile and is easily run with only 70-100 CFS, depending on boat loading and skill. Check the USGS **gauging stations** for the Arkansas River at Larned and at Great Bend. Figure 2 to 4.5 miles per hour depending on river levels, dawdling time, and paddling skills. This segment has a few easy riffles, long runs, and very few pools. Typical of a small river that has a large flood channel, the inner channel makes tight meanders within the larger flood channel. Thus, at low to medium flows, the paddler will travel more miles than are indicated by river-mile designations at the put-ins and take-outs.

Larned Access, *river mile 897*— From Larned, take the State Highway 19 spur south to the river and put in near the southeast edge of the bridge. In addition to the gauge listed above, check the Pawnee River at Rozel. The Pawnee River is downstream of the Ark's gauge at Larned and immediately downstream of the Larned put-in.

Fort Larned has been given high praise for one of the best-preserved Indian War-era forts anywhere. The fort was built to protect the wagon trains that moved through this area along the Santa Fe Trail. Check out the **Santa Fe Trail Center and History Museum** at the National Historic Site on State Highway 156 six miles west of Larned.

The Pawnee River runs through Larned. The Ark is typically crystal clear, but if the Pawnee River is up, chances are that it will be extremely turbid and the Ark will become turbid from there to its confluence with the Mississippi River. From the Pawnee River's confluence with the Ark, it is evident that people have been very unkind to the river. The shoreline is now trashed with garbage from homes, businesses, and industry for miles out of town.

Near river mile 894 the pilings of an old bridge have created a logjam that must be portaged. An iron bridge at river mile 890.5 makes a good midway access.

Pawnee Rock Access, *river mile 887*—From the west edge of Pawnee Rock, go 1.5 miles south on Pawnee Rock Road, then east another 1.75 miles to the river. North of town, there is a road that leads to a shelter house on top of the Dakota sandstone bluffs above town. The monument there describes the history and geology

of the area. The spot was once a common meeting place for various tribes of Pawnee—hence the town's name. Here, the river intermittently gets a little more shoulder room from plowed ground. You won't see another road until you come to the Dundee Bridge.

Dundee Access, *river mile 880*—Go northeast on U.S. Highway 56 to Southwest 50th Avenue, then south to the river. (Note that Southwest 50th Avenue is just south of the Great Bend Municipal Airport.) You'll pass under a power line near river mile 877 and will soon see Great Bend ahead.

Great Bend Access, *river mile 873*— From Great Bend, go south on U.S. Highway 281 to the river. The town is located at the apex of a giant bend that takes the river south and east toward Wichita. The Santa Fe Trail ran through the point where Great Bend is now located, bringing Indians and settlers together for trade. Note that after a hard rain the runoff from Great Bend can flash flood the river. So consider this when planning your trip and when picking your campsite. Walnut Creek, near river mile 867, can add significant flow. In addition to the Ark River gauges listed above, check the Walnut Creek gauge below the Cheyenne Bottoms Diversion near Great Bend. Walnut Creek enters the Ark about halfway to Dartmouth and can pump up the flow dramatically.

Dartmouth Access, *river mile 866*—From Dartmouth, go west one mile on Highway 56 to 60th Avenue, then go south a half mile to the river. The river crosses under a road about a half mile above the Ellinwood Bridge. Although the inner channel remains fairly small during times of low to medium flow, the larger flood channel is noticeably wider due to flash floods from Great Bend.

Ellinwood Access, *river mile 859*—From Ellinwood, go south a half mile on Main Street (aka 105th Avenue) to the river. In the early years, most of the residents were of German descent, which explains the German names on many of the north and south streets. Watch for a pipeline less than a half mile downstream from the Ellinwood Access. A second pipeline is located between river miles 857 and 858. As the river approaches the Raymond West Access, the channel becomes braided. At low flows the main channel becomes harder to follow as it divides and redivides through an interlaced web of paths around and through small willows, cottonwoods, and horsetails.

Raymond West Access, *river mile 851*—From Raymond, go north on 4th Road to Avenue Q, then go west 2.5 miles to the southwest side of the bridge.

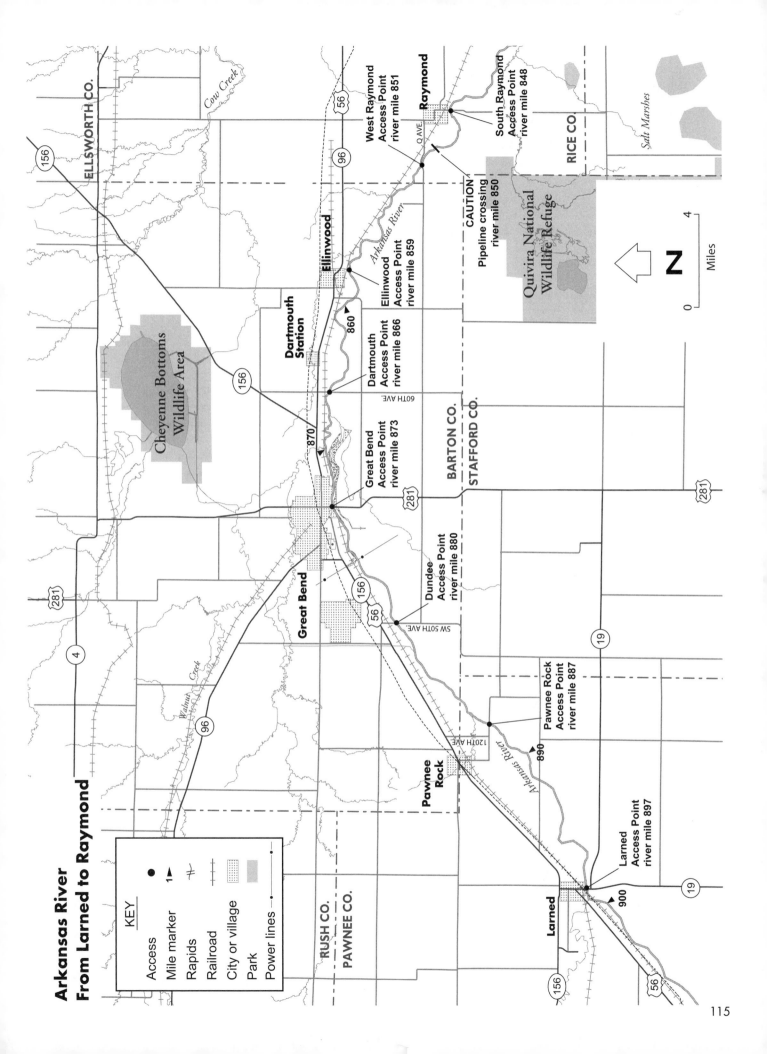

Arkansas River
From Larned to Raymond

KEY
- ● Access
- ▲ Mile marker
- ╪ Rapids
- ┼┼┼┼ Railroad
- ▦ City or village
- ▨ Park
- •━━• Power lines

ELLSWORTH CO.

Cow Creek

156

56

96

West Raymond
Access Point
river mile 851

Raymond

Q AVE.

South Raymond
Access Point
river mile 848

RICE CO.

Salt Marshes

Ellinwood

Arkansas River

Ellinwood
Access Point
river mile 859

860

CAUTION
Pipeline crossing
river mile 850

Quivira National
Wildlife Refuge

N

0 4
Miles

Dartmouth Station

Dartmouth
Access Point
river mile 866

870

60TH AVE.

Great Bend
Access Point
river mile 873

Cheyenne Bottoms
Wildlife Area

156

BARTON CO.
STAFFORD CO.

281

Great Bend

156

56

Dundee
Access Point
river mile 880

SW 50TH AVE.

281

Walnut Creek

96

Pawnee Rock
Access Point
river mile 887

19

120TH AVE.

890

Pawnee Rock

Arkansas River

4

281

RUSH CO.
PAWNEE CO.

Larned
Access Point
river mile 897

19

900

Larned

156

56

ARKANSAS RIVER: RAYMOND TO HUTCHINSON

35 miles, many intermediate access points available, Class I difficulty
West Raymond Access at river mile 851 to South Hutchinson Access at river mile 812

The 84-mile segment of the Ark between Raymond and Wichita is one of the most enjoyable floats in the state. The 35-mile run from Raymond to Hutchinson is the perfect length for an extended weekend trip. Depending on the typical factors, this reach can be paddled in two or three days, yet there are enough well-spaced intermediate access points to create many single-day or half-day floats. Figure paddling time at about 2.5 to 4 miles per hour, depending on flow, skill, and dawdling time. Expect only a few nice riffles, a lot of long, fast runs, and very few pools. Though parking is limited, the rustic access points are some of the best in the state. The banks are neither steep nor muddy. This part of the river is protected from the prevailing southwest wind by a tall canopy of trees and its general southeast direction of flow. Except during times of high flows, the river is rarely more than a few feet deep and often only wide enough to maneuver a canoe. Every turn brings a new view, and the turns, meanders, and doglegs are constant, maintaining your interest every foot of the way.

The river's average **gradient** here is 6 feet per mile. The **minimum recommended flow is 100 CFS**. Use the USGS **gauging stations** for the Arkansas River at Great Bend, near Nickerson, and near Hutchinson. Except after a hard rain, the water is fairly clear and flows are usually sufficient for good paddling except during times of extreme drought. So beautiful is this river and so pleasant is the riverbed that I recommend it for backpacking or day hikes, when you can find it low enough. You can fish the holes, frog the banks, and camp along the thousands of sandbars and islands.

The river now meanders within a broad valley of rich farmland. The river is a hub for wildlife. With plenty of food and water available, white-tailed and mule deer are common and large. In these remote settings, views of beavers, foxes, coyotes, bobcats, raccoons, opossums, squirrels, hawks, owls, mergansers, and other wild critters are common. Small channels meander back and forth within a much larger flood channel so, like elsewhere on the Ark, unless the river is high, you can expect to paddle more miles than the map shows. Swept clear of most obstructions with each high-water event, this creek of a river dances sprightly. The channel is usually fairly uncomplicated, but on occasion it can become braided with islands of horsetails, willows, and cottonwoods. The shoulders of the riverbed and larger islands are well forested by cottonwoods, but the forest is now becoming more diversified with trees such as elms, pecans, and mulberries. Tamarisk has found a foothold, but has not completely taken over yet. Although high-water conditions keep the channels fairly clear, some low-hanging tree limbs and river-wide blockades should be expected.

Raymond West Access, *river mile 851*—From Raymond, go north on 4th Road to Avenue Q, then go west 2.5 miles to the southwest side of the bridge. Except during high-water events, the Ark looks like a creek here and through the next several sections. For the first few miles the channel is braided, but it soon consolidates. In those first miles, shifting channels and sandbars will keep you guessing for the best route. A pipeline near river mile 849.5 is marked with yellow signs on both banks.

The Raymond South Access, *at river mile 848*, is a half mile south of Raymond on 4th Road. The first tamarisk trees appear at about river mile 846. From there on down these invasive, water-thirsty plants have begun displacing our native trees.

The Alden West Access, *at river mile 843*, is south of Alden on Pioneer Street (9th Road) to Avenue U, then west on Avenue U. The river adds water fairly fast in this section, but the river channel doesn't change much. About a half mile downstream of this access, the larger channel divides to form a three-quarter-mile-long island. Halfway around the south side of that island, Salt Creek enters near river mile 842 on river right. Salt Creek drains a large area to the south and west that contains salt deposits. A pipeline crosses the river just upstream of the South Alden Access.

The South Alden Access, *at river mile 840*, is south of Alden on Pioneer Street (9th Road) to Avenue U, then west one block to 9th Road, then south (with a jog west on Avenue V) to the river. Power lines cross the river downstream of river mile 838.

The West Sterling Access, *at river mile 837*, is 3.5 miles west of Sterling on Avenue W, then south on 12th Road to the southeast edge of the bridge. Peace Creek enters on river right near river mile 834.

The South Sterling Access, *at river mile 832*, is south of Sterling on State Highway 96/14 at the northwest side of the bridge.

The West Nickerson Access, *at river mile 826*, is west of Nickerson on Highway 96 (West 82nd Avenue) at the northwest side of the bridge.

The Nickerson South Access, *at river mile 824*, is south of town on Nickerson Street (aka South Morgan Street) to the northwest edge of the bridge. You will cross under some large power lines near river mile 822.5 and over a pipeline near river mile 818.

Take out at the **West Hutchinson Access**, *at river mile 816*. To get there, go west from Hutchinson on West 4th Avenue about a quarter mile past Highway 96.

The Arkansas River from just east of Raymond. This part of the river, normally not much more than a creek in size, is protected from the prevailing southwest wind by the larger flood channel and a substantial riparian forest.

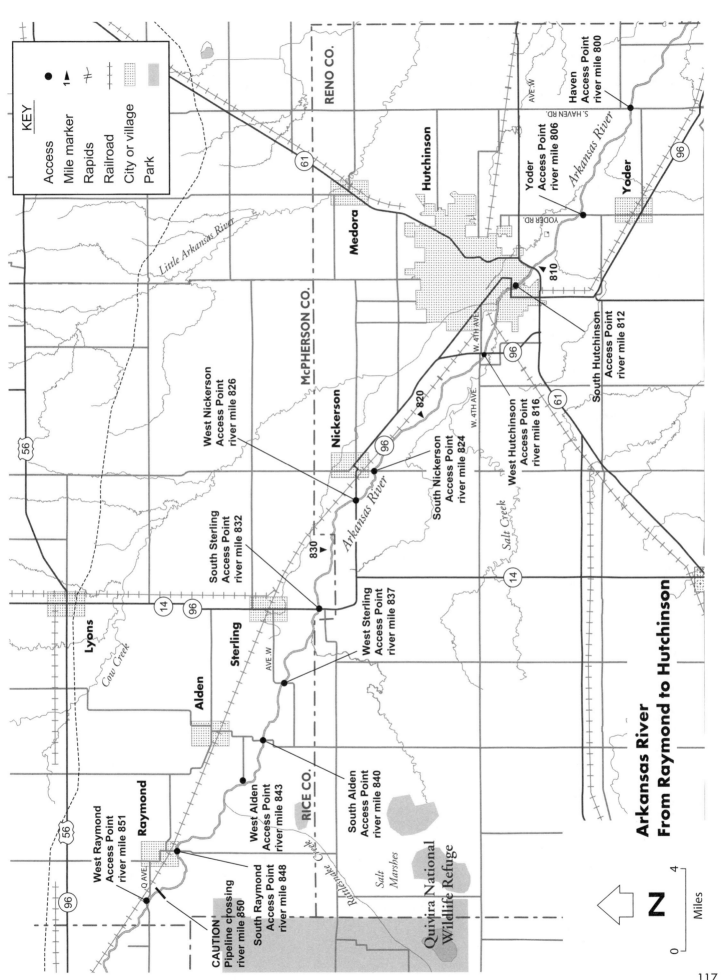

KEY

- **●** Access
- **1▲** Mile marker
- **⊬** Rapids
- **┼┼┼** Railroad
- City or village
- Park

Arkansas River
From Raymond to Hutchinson

N

Miles
0 — 4

RENO CO.

McPHERSON CO.

RICE CO.

Little Arkansas River

Arkansas River

Salt Creek

Cow Creek

Rattlesnake Creek

Salt Marshes

Quivira National Wildlife Refuge

Hutchinson

Medora

Nickerson

Lyons

Alden

Sterling

Raymond

Yoder

S. HAVEN RD.

AVE. W

YODER RD.

W. 4TH AVE.

W. 4TH AVE.

AVE. W

Q AVE.

61

56

56

14

96

96

96

96

61

14

96

810

820

830

Haven Access Point river mile 800

Yoder Access Point river mile 806

South Hutchinson Access Point river mile 812

West Hutchinson Access Point river mile 816

South Nickerson Access Point river mile 824

West Nickerson Access Point river mile 826

South Sterling Access Point river mile 832

West Sterling Access Point river mile 837

South Alden Access Point river mile 840

West Alden Access Point river mile 843

South Raymond Access Point river mile 848

CAUTION! Pipeline crossing river mile 850

West Raymond Access Point river mile 851

117

ARKANSAS RIVER: HUTCHINSON TO BENTLEY

33 miles, many intermediate access points available, Class I difficulty
West Hutchinson Access at river mile 876 to 151st Street at river mile 783

THE HUTCHINSON AREA

While you're here, visit the Dillon Nature Center, a 130-acre National Urban Wildlife Sanctuary. The park includes butterfly and hummingbird gardens, birdhouses and feeders, and special displays. An interpretive trail will help you learn more about local plants and animals prior to your float. Take State Highway 61 north to East 30th Avenue and turn east.

Sand Hills State Park is a rolling sand prairie located north of Hutchinson on Highway 61. The dunes were formed by wind-deposited sands from the Arkansas River at the end of the Ice Age. The dunes have been stabilized by the roots of the sand prairie grasses. An interpretive trail will introduce you to this unique habitat. Camping is not available.

Hutchinson is reputed to have one of the richest salt deposits in the world and salt is still being mined there today. Its nickname is The Salt City.

Depending on the typical factors, this entire reach can be paddled in two or three days, yet there are enough well-spaced intermediate access points to create as many as four separate day floats.

The **minimum recommended flow from here to Maize is 100 CFS**. The USGS **gauging station** for this segment is the Arkansas River at Hutchinson and the average **gradient** is 4.8 feet per mile.

There are three good access points in the greater Hutchinson area. The westernmost access is our put-in for the purpose of this narrative.

The **Hutchinson West Access** is at *river mile 816*. To get there from State Highway 96 in Hutchinson, go west on West 4th Avenue. It is about a quarter mile to the northeast edge of the bridge. A diversion canal that carries floodwater from Cow Creek enters on river left upstream of river mile 814. Salt Creek enters on river right near river mile 814. One-half mile later, you will pass under the first of three railroad tracks in quick succession. Downstream of the last railroad track, the Harsha Canal enters on river left, carrying more overflow from Cow Creek. This is about one-half mile upstream of the South Hutchinson Access.

The **South Hutchinson Access**, at *river mile 812*, is in a motorcycle park that borders on the river. The carry from the parking lot to the river is about 100 yards, but it is a nice parking lot and the shoreline is like a public beach. From U.S. Highway 50, go north on Main Street about 1.5 miles through South Hutchinson to East 6th Avenue, then go east to the park.

The **Carey Park Access** in Hutchinson is *near river mile 811*. To get there from Highway 50, go north on Main Street through South Hutchinson. Cross the river then turn east on F Avenue (your first right turn). A few blocks later make another right (south) on Main Street. Main Street becomes Carey Park Boulevard. Follow this until you pass under a railroad bridge, then turn into the first parking lot on the right (west) side, next to the river, the railroad tracks, and the baseball field. Carry your boat over the levy and a short distance

to the river. Of all the Hutchinson area access points, this is probably the most secure.

The river is wider here than near Raymond and Sterling. Flood waters off of the city streets can bring the river up very quickly. There seem to be more and bigger sandbars, especially on your way out of town. When the river's not full of water, the locals run up and down the streambed with their motorcycles and four-wheelers. Aside from that, the river is absolutely beautiful as it meanders back and forth in its wide channel.

If you put in at the **South Hutchinson Access**, you'll cross under three bridges before you leave town. The first is Kansas Avenue just a half mile from your launch site, the next is a railroad bridge near river mile 811, and the last is Highway 50/State Highway 61 near mile 810. For the next four miles, the river is bordered by a narrow band of wetlands.

The **Yoder Access** is at *river mile 806*, north of town on Yoder Road. A lot of seasonal creeks enter on both sides of the river through this section. The only one of significance is Cow Creek that is downstream of river mile 805 on river left. This is the same Cow Creek that had diversion canals upstream of Hutchinson. **Caution**—There is an electric fence wire located on a bridge and another fence wire 1 mile farther downstream. (Watch for the warning signs.)

The **Haven Access** is at *river mile 800*. It is 3 miles north of town on South Haven Road. You'll pass under Worthington Road shortly after river mile 797 and Gar Creek enters on river right above river mile 794.

Mount Hope Access, *river mile 793*—Go north from town on North 279th Street W past Highway 96. There are no "mounts" or even hills near this little town, but "Mount Hope" was a popular name for cemeteries, including the one near here. Visitors will admire the beautiful cottonwood and maple trees that line Main Street. From river mile 793 to river mile 760, the river flows within the levees of the Wichita-Valley Center Floodway. The average height from riverbed to the top of the levee is about 19 feet, about 9.5 feet higher than the top of the normal banks. Near river mile 786, Greenfield Creek enters from river left. There is a power line near river mile 783.4.

The **take-out** is at the **Bentley Access** at *river mile 783*. To get there from Highway 96, go north on North 151st Street W toward Bentley to the river.

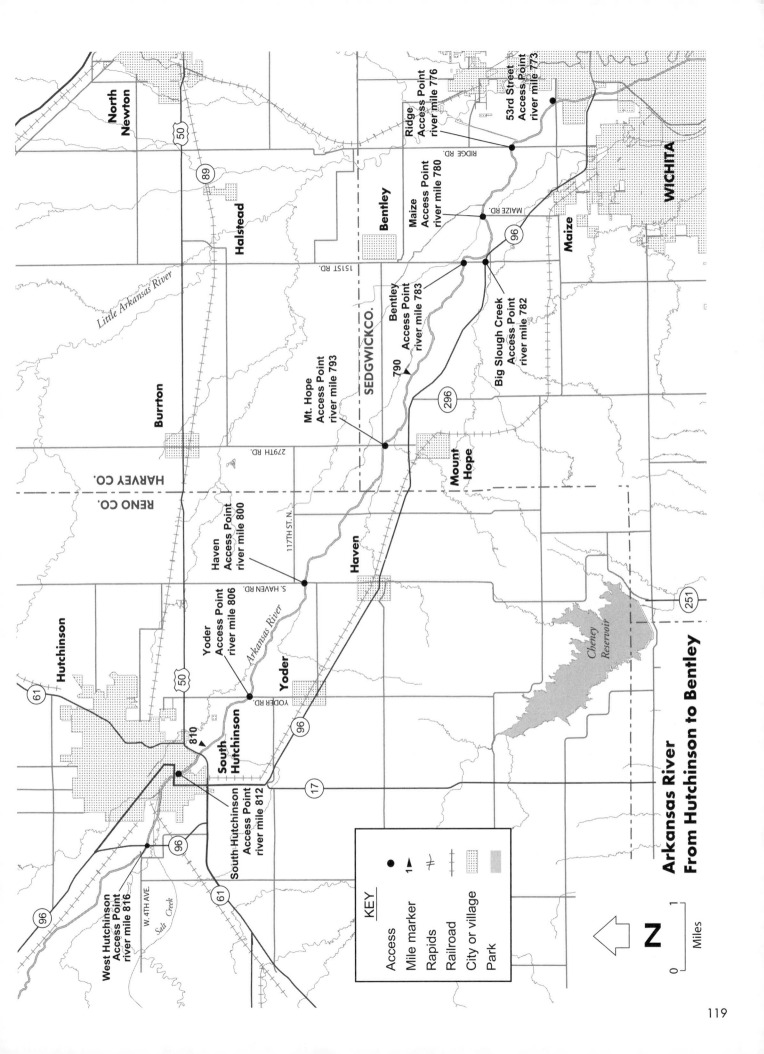

Arkansas River
From Hutchinson to Bentley

North Newton

Halstead

Burrton

Bentley

WICHITA

Maize

Mount Hope

Haven

Hutchinson

South Hutchinson

Yoder

Little Arkansas River

Arkansas River

Salt Creek

Cheney Reservoir

SEDGWICK CO.

HARVEY CO.

RENO CO.

53rd Street Access Point river mile 773

Ridge Access Point river mile 776

Maize Access Point river mile 780

Big Slough Creek Access Point river mile 782

Bentley Access Point river mile 783

Mt. Hope Access Point river mile 793

Haven Access Point river mile 800

Yoder Access Point river mile 806

South Hutchinson Access Point river mile 812

West Hutchinson Access Point river mile 816

790

810

RIDGE RD.

MAIZE RD.

151ST RD.

279TH RD.

117TH ST. N.

S. HAVEN RD.

YODER RD.

W. 4TH AVE.

50

89

96

96

96

96

61

61

17

251

296

KEY
- ● Access
- ▲ Mile marker
- ≠ Rapids
- Railroad
- City or village
- Park

N

0   1
Miles

119

ARKANSAS RIVER: BENTLEY TO WICHITA

16 miles, many intermediate access points available, Class I difficulty
Bentley Access at river mile 783 to 53rd Street Access at river mile 773

WICHITA-VALLEY CENTER FLOODWAY

From about river mile 760 to river mile 793, this project consists of levees, floodways, improved channels, and control structures. Runoff from the intercepted areas is contained in 50 areas that are reserved for high-water ponding. The project provides protection to approximately 49,000 acres of urban and rural lands, in and adjacent to the cities of Valley Center and Wichita, against floods from the Little Arkansas River, the Arkansas River, Big Slough, Cowskin Creek, and Chisholm Creek and its west-, middle-, and east-branch tributaries.

The combined flows of Chisholm Creek, the Little Arkansas River, and the Arkansas River that exceed the channel capacity of the Arkansas River are diverted to the west of Wichita by a leveed floodway. From there, the flows are diverted to the Arkansas River at a point south of Wichita by improved channels, levees, and canals.

The character of the Arkansas River makes a dramatic change as it gains flow and comes within the influence of the Wichita-Valley Center Floodway. Because the channel widens rapidly, the **minimum recommended flow** for this river segment changes from **100 CFS at the top to 200 CFS** at the bottom. The average **gradient** also flattens to 3.1 feet per mile. Use the **gauging stations** on the Arkansas River at Hutchinson and at Maize.

The **Bentley Access,** *at river mile 783,* is north of State Highway 96 on N 151st Street W toward Bentley. Here, the **minimum recommended flow is 100 CFS.** Over the next 10 miles, this intimate little river will grow much wider.

Big Slough Creek enters *at river mile 782.* There is an access about one quarter mile up this canal. To drive there from Maize, go northwest on Highway 96 to North 151st Street W (Bentley Road). Go north 100 feet, then east along the canal about a half mile. This straightened and diked canal is part of the Wichita-Valley Center Floodway. Be sure you have more than enough water before proceeding downstream from Big Slough Creek. As the river continues to widen, you will need at least **150 CFS** to paddle to Maize. Check **gauging stations** for the Arkansas River at Hutchinson and at Maize.

The **Maize Access,** *at river mile 780,* is northwest of town on N 119th Street W, about 2 miles north of Highway 96, on the south side of the burned-out twin bridges. This is a long carry and there is limited parking. From here to Ridge Road, the **minimum recommended flow is 175 CFS** or more to clear the ever-broadening sandbars and shallow channels. The largest Osage orange tree in Kansas is located in a fencerow on the west side of the road.

At river mile 776, **Ridge Road Access** is at the southeast edge of the bridge. This access is located 3.5 miles north of Highway 96. Parking is limited. Do not proceed below 53rd Street without reading the warnings in the next section. About a quarter mile downstream, a canal from the Little Arkansas River enters on river left. The occasional addition of this floodwater and the breadth of the floodway have further widened the channel. Most canoes will need **175-200 CFS** for this section.

53rd Street Access, *river mile 773*—Located 4 miles east of Maize on West 53rd Street N, at the southeast edge of the bridge, this is an easy access and the last access before you enter the even broader riverbed of the Wichita area and beyond. The city skyline and the width of the river both grow as you approach town. **Two Hundred-Fifty CFS** is barely adequate as you approach town. This is a good section to take a light boat, since you'll have a long portage ahead.

Caution—As you approach *river mile 768,* stay to river left. You will come to what first appears to be the end of the river. As you approach you will see that the river goes through a set of large **Tubes** (with a capital "T") to your left and into a flood diversion canal (during high water) on your right. Do not approach the Tubes at any level and do not approach the diversion channel if water is flowing over that spillway.

Portage on river left (east side), upstream of the Tubes. These tunnels take the river under the large berm in front of you. At flood stage, only part of the river flows through the Tubes and the rest of the river flows over the spillway that you see to the south and into a diversion ditch that takes the excess water around the west side of town. Follow the grassy path that goes southeast under the I-235 bridge to the outflow of the Tubes. You can continue to carry your boat to the Big Arkansas River Park just beyond I-235 or you can launch your boat and float about 150 yards closer. If you proceed farther downstream than the parking lot, you must portage the ledge under the 21st Street bridge (the second bridge) at the edge of the park, plus two other dangerous low-head dams downstream.

The Ark is usually clear except during high water. The color variation in the riverbed is where fresh sand was just washed over the older, algae-stained riverbed.

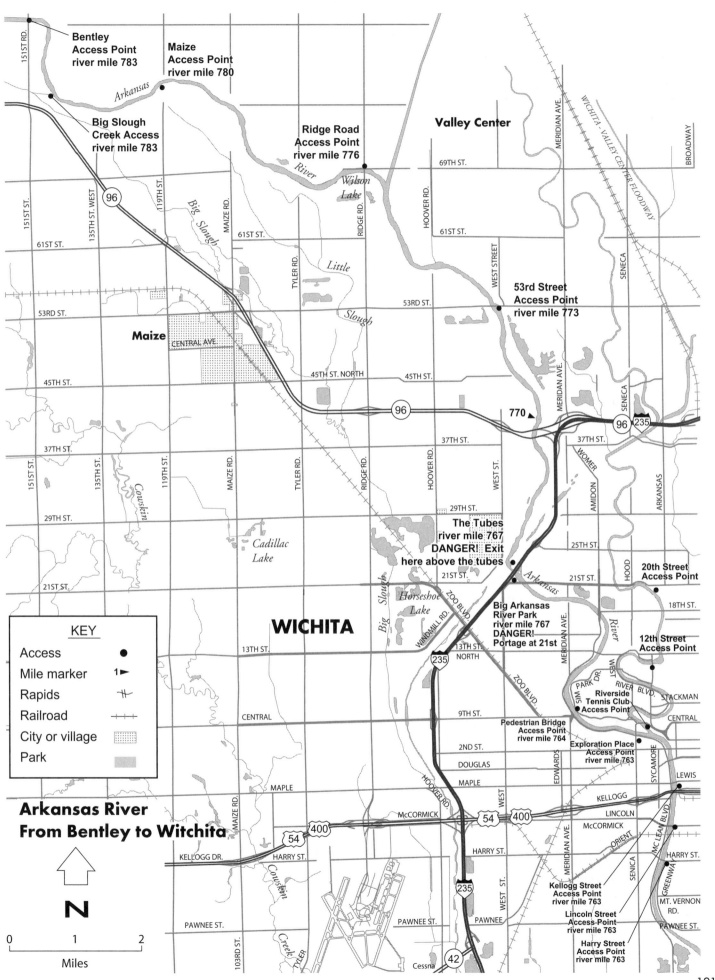

Bentley Access Point river mile 783

Maize Access Point river mile 780

Big Slough Creek Access river mile 783

Ridge Road Access Point river mile 776

Valley Center

Arkansas River

Wilson Lake

53rd Street Access Point river mile 773

Little Slough

Maize

CENTRAL AVE.

770 ▶

The Tubes river mile 767 **DANGER! Exit here above the tubes**

20th Street Access Point

Cadillac Lake

WICHITA

Horseshoe Lake

Arkansas River

Big Slough

Big Arkansas River Park river mile 767 **DANGER! Portage at 21st**

12th Street Access Point

Riverside Tennis Club Access Point

Pedestrian Bridge Access Point river mile 764

Exploration Place Access Point river mile 763

KEY

Access	●
Mile marker	1 ▶
Rapids	‡
Railroad	+++
City or village	⣿
Park	▨

Arkansas River From Bentley to Witchita

N ↑

Kellogg Street Access Point river mile 763

Lincoln Street Access Point river mile 763

Harry Street Access Point river mile 763

0   1   2
Miles

ARKANSAS RIVER: WICHITA TO DERBY

17 miles, many intermediate access points available, Class I difficulty, plus manmade hazards
Big Arkansas River Park at river mile 767 to Derby Access at river mile 750

On any weekend, you may see enthusiasts honing their whitewater skills just below the Tubes that carry the river under I-235. Use the gauging station on the Arkansas River at Maize. The upper holes are surfable from 300–1,000 CFS. The lower ledge becomes surfable from 1,500 up. These holes can be powerful and should be attempted only by experienced boaters with skilled paddling partners ready to help in case you get into trouble. Danger—There is a dangerous low-head dam about 300 yards downstream of the Tubes that is most easily portaged along the trail on river right.

The minimum recommended flow for paddling downstream from the Tubes to the confluence with the Little Arkansas River is 300 CFS.

Below Wichita, the Arkansas River turns south and the river channel becomes very broad. From the 21st Street Access to Derby, the river travels 17 miles, drops about 82 feet, and has an average **gradient** of 4 feet per mile. Yet, due to a series of **low-head dams**, the effective gradient is somewhat less, particularly through town where long pools are divided by mandatory portages around manmade river hazards. City ordinances require boaters to portage and to maintain specified distances from the low-head dams under the 21st Street bridge, the confluence with the Little Arkansas, and the Lincoln Street Dam.

The **minimum recommended flow** increases as the river widens, starting with **300 CFS** at the Tubes and then **500-600 CFS** leaving town. Several **gauging stations** will be useful to you on this section of the river. Above the confluence with the Little Arkansas River, check the USGS gauging station on the Arkansas River at Hutchinson. If you are paddling below the confluence with the Little Arkansas, add the flow from the Little Arkansas River at Valley Center.

The **Big Arkansas River Park**, *at river mile 767*, is in Wichita at the intersection of North West Street and West 21st Street N. Use the large parking lot next to the river.

The next bridge will be Amidon Street, and then comes W 13th Street N, *near river mile 765*. The **Pedestrian Bridge Access**, *at river mile 764*, is on river left (the east side of the river). The access is west of "Cowtown" on Sim Park Drive, under the pedestrian

bridge. Another bridge crosses the river about a mile downstream, North Seneca Street.

From the **Access behind Exploration Place**, on river right at *river mile 763*, to below river mile 760, the river has **many manmade hazards** that must be portaged or paddled with caution. The confluence with the Little Arkansas River is immediately downstream of Exploration Place at river mile 763. It is unlawful and **dangerous** to paddle within 50 feet of the falls. Start your portage from behind the Exploration Place parking lot.

The **minimum recommended flow** below the confluence with the Little Ark is **400 CFS**. The river is crossed by several bridges in this section—W 1st Street N, Douglas Avenue, and Maple Street/Lewis Street. The Kellogg Bridge Boat Ramp is at river mile 763 on the east side of the river, immediately underneath the Kellogg Bridge (U.S. Highway 400/54).

Use caution as you approach river mile 762. The **dangerous** low-head dam under Lincoln Street bridge must be portaged. City ordinance prohibits you from boating within 150 feet upstream or downstream of the dam. About 600 feet downstream is a railroad bridge. The next bridge, at river mile 761.5, is the Harry Street bridge. Old bridge pilings and rebar here can be **hazardous** at low-water levels. Portage, as necessary, on the east side. At river mile 760, there is a sewer pipe across the channel that can also be dangerous at some water levels.

The riverbed will be over 100 yards wide by the time it gets to Derby, so the **minimum recommended flow is 600 CFS**. You will pass under six more bridges on your way to Derby—I-135, South Hydraulic Street, I-35 (Kansas Turnpike), MacArthur Road, 47th Street, and 63rd Street.

The **South Arkansas River Greenway Access**, at *river mile 751*, is located off 71st Street. To get there from the intersection of S Broadway Street and E 63rd Street S, go east to S Grove Street, then south on Grove to E Cider Street, then southeast on Cider to E 71st Street S, and then east on 71st Street to the new access. Near river mile 750, the Wichita-Valley Center Floodway enters on river right. If the floodway is discharging a high volume of water, you might consider giving it some clearance as you pass.

The **take-out** is at the **Derby Access**, at *river mile 750*, located west of Derby on W Market Street (E 83rd Street S) at the northeast side of the bridge.

Jim Johnson and Roger Norton surf at "the Tubes" in Wichita (photos by T.J. Hittle)

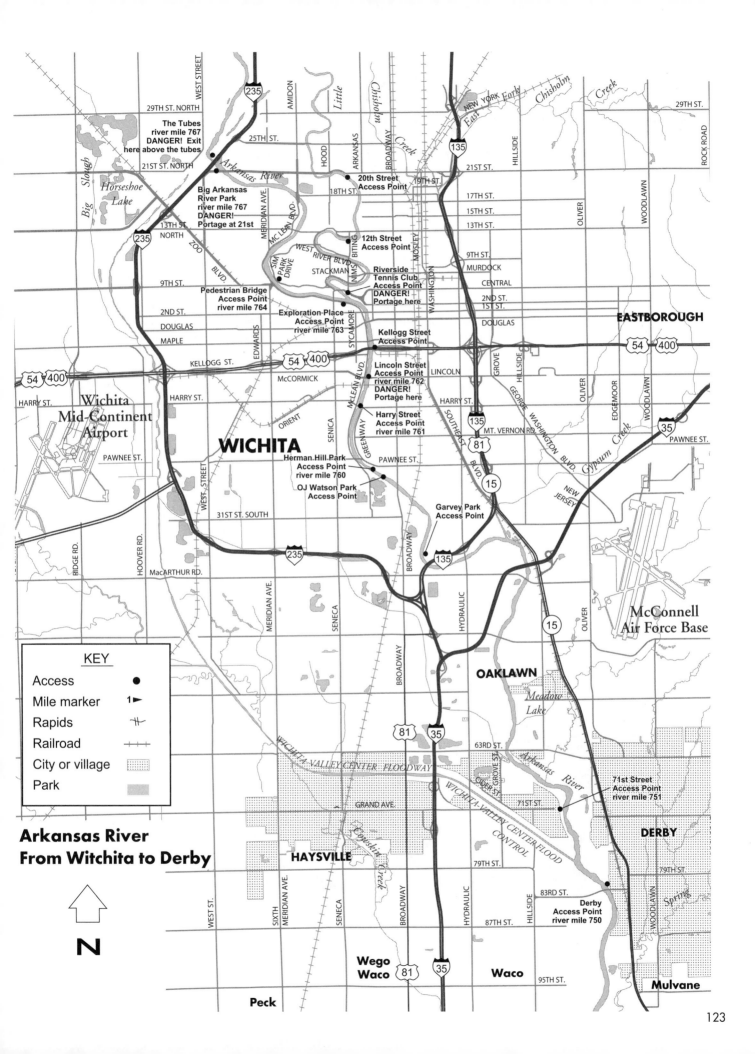

The Tubes
river mile 767
DANGER! Exit
here above the tubes

Big Arkansas River Park
river mile 767
DANGER!
Portage at 21st

20th Street Access Point

12th Street Access Point

Riverside Tennis Club Access Point
DANGER! Portage here

Pedestrian Bridge Access Point
river mile 764

Exploration Place Access Point
river mile 763

Kellogg Street Access Point

Lincoln Street Access Point
river mile 762
DANGER! Portage here

Harry Street Access Point
river mile 761

Herman Hill Park Access Point
river mile 760

OJ Watson Park Access Point

Garvey Park Access Point

71st Street Access Point
river mile 751

Derby Access Point
river mile 750

Horseshoe Lake

Big Slough

Wichita Mid-Continent Airport

WICHITA

EASTBOROUGH

OAKLAWN

Meadow Lake

McConnell Air Force Base

DERBY

HAYSVILLE

Wego Waco

Waco

Peck

Mulvane

KEY

Access	●
Mile marker	1▶
Rapids	⤬
Railroad	+++
City or village	
Park	

Arkansas River From Witchita to Derby

N

123

ARKANSAS RIVER: DERBY TO OXFORD

26 miles, many intermediate access points available, Class I difficulty
Derby Access at river mile 750 to Highway 160 at river mile 724

There are hardly any apples-to-apples comparisons you can make between the Arkansas River at Derby and the river that it was just 30 miles upstream. The little river has turned into a gentle giant, with shoulders 300-600 feet across. Most of the year, the relatively flat, sandy riverbed is a playful challenge for paddlers reading their way along the elusive main channel. The huge sandbars and remote setting can provide a wonderful multi-day river wilderness experience.

Flathead catfish grow big in the deep pools. Deer, coyotes, foxes, beaver, eagles, hawks, great blue herons, and many other kinds of wildlife are common along the river. Cottonwoods, sycamores, willows, elms, and silver maples make up the bulk of the riparian forest.

Easy intermediate access points make either single- or multi-day trips easy. Popular two-day floats include the stretches from Mulvane to Oxford, from Oxford to Geuda Springs, from Geuda Springs to Traders Bend, Oklahoma, or a float down Grouse Creek from Silverdale and then down the Ark to Traders Bend, Oklahoma. The average **gradient** is just over 4 feet per mile. The **minimum recommended flow for this reach is 600-700 CFS** and the **gauging station** is on the Arkansas River at Derby.

Frequent meanders to the southwest can pit you directly against the prevailing Kansas wind; the boat of choice is a low-profile canoe or kayak. Discounting the effects of wind, dawdling, and frequent stops, you can plan to make roughly 2-3 miles per hour depending on flows.

The Ark between Wichita and Oxford is easy to paddle and the sandbars make great campsites.

The **Derby Access**, at *river mile 750*, is west of Derby on West Market Street (East 83rd Street S) at the northeast side of the bridge. The primo campsite is a giant sandbar at river mile 748, along the inside (river left) of the bend. There are also two smaller sandbars above and below the big one, on the opposite side of the river. Spring Creek enters the river near *river mile 747*.

The **Mulvane Access**, at *river mile 743*, is west of Mulvane on State Highway 53 to the southeast edge of the bridge. Don't launch from or pass by Mulvane without planning either a very difficult climb out of the river at Belle Plaine/Udall or paddling all the way to Oxford.

There are a lot of great campsites along this segment and you probably need one of them unless you plan a marathon (26 miles) trip to Oxford. The largest sandbars are on the inside curves near river miles 743, 740, and 738. About one-third mile downstream of Mulvane are the remnants of two old bridges. The Cowskin Creek cutoff enters on river right at about *river mile 741.7*. Then a railroad bridge crosses the river at about river mile 741.3. Another bridge remnant is at about river mile 740. Dog Creek enters at about river mile 736. Power lines cross the river at about river mile 734.4.

The 55 Highway bridge, at *river mile 733*, between the towns of **Belle Plaine and Udall**, should be considered as an access for emergency use only. The banks are too steep, the poison ivy is too thick, and the parking is too poor. Yet in an emergency, you take what you can get. The beautiful **Ninnescah River** enters the Ark on river right, at river mile 727. Just downstream of the confluence there is an old rock dam that spans the river. **Caution**—At some water levels you should land on the island on the river right (west) side to scout the dam. You can usually run the dam through the breaches, but check it out for yourself. There are several medium-size sandbars along the tighter river bends; none are huge, but you can find good campsites if you look.

The **take-out** is at the **Oxford Access**, at *river mile 724*, in the city park at the northwest edge of the U.S. Highway 160 bridge. There is a nice concrete ramp and good parking.

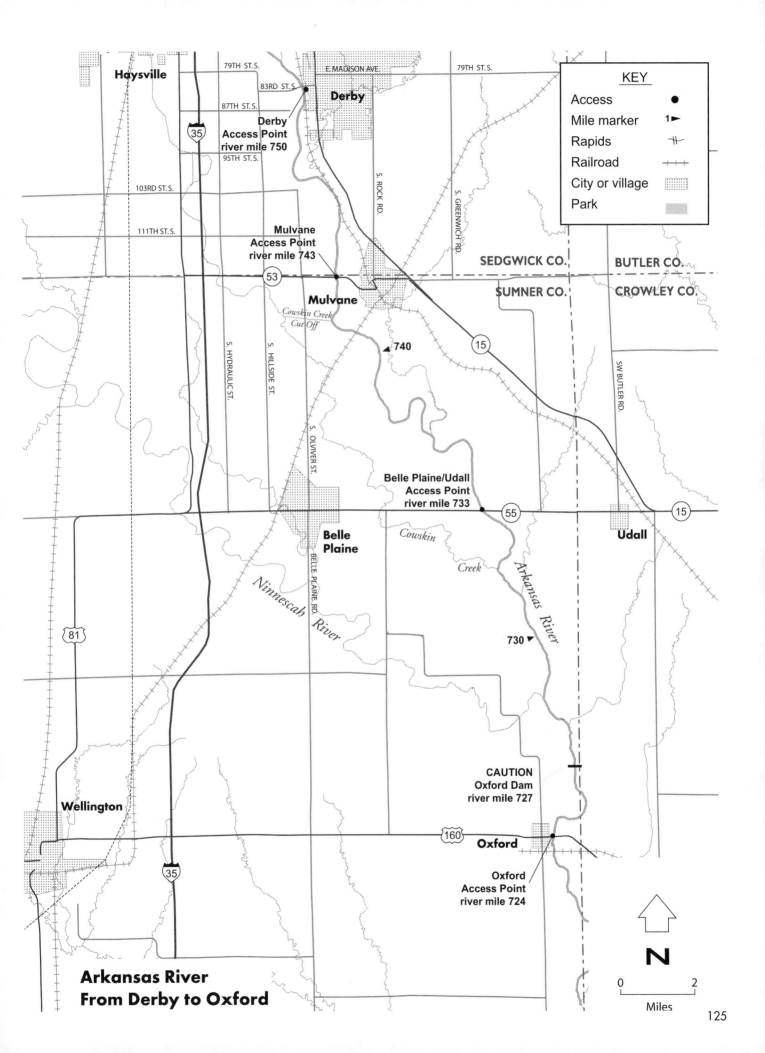

Haysville

79TH ST. S.

E MADISON AVE

79TH ST. S.

Derby

83RD ST. S.

87TH ST. S.

Derby
Access Point
river mile 750

95TH ST. S.

103RD ST. S.

111TH ST. S.

S. ROCK RD.

S. GREENWICH RD.

Mulvane
Access Point
river mile 743

53

SEDGWICK CO.   BUTLER CO.

SUMNER CO.   CROWLEY CO.

Mulvane

Cowskin Creek
Cut Off

▲ 740

15

S. HYDRAULIC ST.

S. HILLSIDE ST.

S. OLIVER ST.

SW BUTLER RD.

Belle Plaine/Udall
Access Point
river mile 733

55

15

Udall

**Belle
Plaine**

Cowskin

Creek

Arkansas River

BELLE PLAINE RD.

Ninnescah River

730 ▼

81

CAUTION
Oxford Dam
river mile 727

Wellington

160   **Oxford**

35

Oxford
Access Point
river mile 724

Arkansas River
From Derby to Oxford

N

0   2

Miles

KEY

Access	●
Mile marker	1▶
Rapids	┼┼
Railroad	+++++
City or village	▦
Park	▨

ARKANSAS RIVER: OXFORD TO ARKANSAS CITY

23 miles, intermediate access points available, Class I difficulty
Oxford Access at river mile 724 to Cottonwood Park at river mile 701

This reach of the river enjoys more water and more green scenery than anywhere else on the river. Leaving Derby, the river channel is already very broad and exposed. It spreads out even more as it moves into and through the beautiful **Kaw Wildlife Area**. Frequent meanders into the southwest wind can pit you directly against the prevailing Kansas gale. To keep the effects of wind on your boat to a minimum, the boat of choice is a low-profile canoe or a kayak. Discounting the effects of wind, dawdling, and frequent stops, you can roughly plan to make about three miles per hour with a reasonable effort.

The **minimum recommended flow for this reach is 600-700 CFS**, depending on your boat, its load, the weather, and your paddling skills. The **gauging station** is for the Arkansas River at Derby. The average **gradient** is 3.3 feet per mile.

The Arkansas River with the minimum recommended flow of roughly 600 CFS. At this level, sandbars and campsites are plentiful, so pick a good one. The sandbar shown here is too low to be safe. Always pick campsites that are high enough that an overnight rise in the river will not reach your camp. Pull boats high on the shore and/or tie them to something that will not float away.

The **put-in** is at the **Oxford Access**, at *river mile 724*, in the city park at the northwest edge of the U.S. Highway 160 bridge. There is a nice concrete ramp and good parking.

The best campsites are at the bend near river mile 722. The first is on the west side and the second is immediately downstream on the other side. The first sandbar is probably the better of the two. The next two access points are difficult carries, so this segment is usually enjoyed as an overnight float.

The **Rainbow Bend Access**, at *river mile 716*, is on County Road 4 at the northwest edge of the bridge. It is a steep path to the river. At river mile 714, a long sandbar hugs the inside curve of Rainbow Bend. The **Geuda Springs Access**, at *river mile 708*, is east of Geuda Springs on County Road 10, at the northwest edge of the bridge. This steep "access" should be considered for emergency use only. A great camp spot can be found on river left (east side) a few hundreds yards downstream. Spring Creek enters a mile farther downstream, on river left, just below *river mile 707*.

Arkansas City has two access points and both work well. The **Arkansas City North Access**, at *river mile 702*, is at the site of an old bridge. From the junction of U.S. Highways 166 and 77, go a few blocks north to Chestnut Street, then go west on Chestnut (State Highway 16) to the closed bridge. Park here and walk (about 200 yards) to the park on the south side of the old bridge. The park has a concrete boat ramp, but you cannot drive to it.

The preferred **take-out** is in the **Arkansas City Cottonwood Park Access**, on river left, just after you cross under the Highway 166 bridge at *river mile 701*. The access is southeast of the bridge, on Madison Avenue.

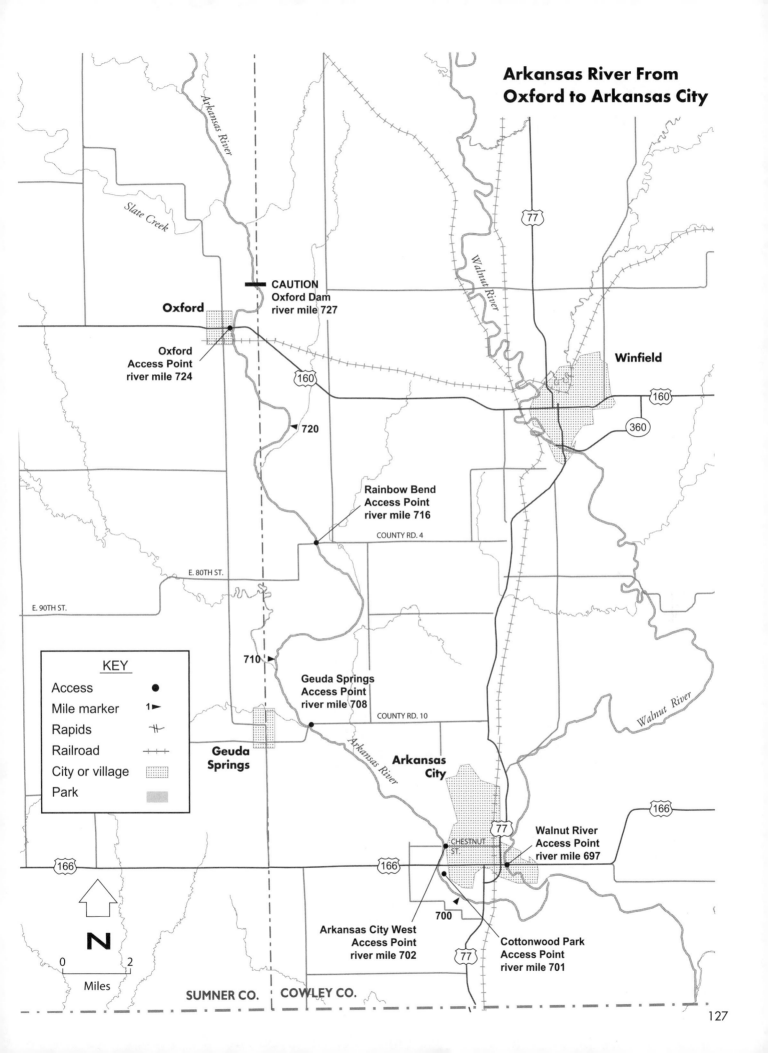

Arkansas River From Oxford to Arkansas City

Arkansas River

Slate Creek

Walnut River

CAUTION
Oxford Dam
river mile 727

Oxford

Winfield

Oxford
Access Point
river mile 724

160

720

Rainbow Bend
Access Point
river mile 716

COUNTY RD. 4

E. 80TH ST.

E. 90TH ST.

710

Geuda Springs
Access Point
river mile 708

COUNTY RD. 10

Walnut River

**Geuda
Springs**

Arkansas River

**Arkansas
City**

KEY

Access	●
Mile marker	1 ►
Rapids	+H
Railroad	+++
City or village	
Park	

166

166

Walnut River
Access Point
river mile 697

CHESTNUT
ST.

77

700

N

0   2

Miles

Arkansas City West
Access Point
river mile 702

Cottonwood Park
Access Point
river mile 701

77

SUMNER CO.   **COWLEY CO.**

127

ARKANSAS RIVER: ARKANSAS CITY TO TRADERS BEND

19 miles, intermediate access points available, Class I difficulty
Cottonwood Park at river mile 701 to Traders Bend Boat Ramp at river mile 129

THE KAW WILDLIFE AREA

The Kaw Wildlife Area upstream of Kaw Lake covers 20,595 acres, of which 4,341 are in Kansas and the rest in Oklahoma (where it becomes the Kaw Wildlife Management Area). The WMA adjoins the upper two-thirds of Kaw Lake in north-central Oklahoma and extends up the Arkansas River to Arkansas City, Kansas.

The Kaw WMA is a mixture of upland and bottomland forest, tallgrass prairie, old fields, and cropland. Bluestem grasses and post/blackjack oak forests predominate on upland sites, which are interspersed with sand plum thickets and agricultural fields. Bottomland forests consist of burr oak, hackberry, sycamore, sand plum, and other species. The average annual precipitation for the area is 30 inches.

The entire 4,341-acre area within Kansas, including this river segment, is well above the conservation pool of Kaw Lake. Within Kansas, about a quarter of the land area is under cultivation through leases to local farmers. A portion of the crop is left standing to provide food and cover for wildlife. The rest of the area is grasslands and riparian timber. There are approximately 20 to 25 acres of pumped wetlands on the west side of the river.

The WMA is managed for hunters, but provides benefits that range well beyond hunting. If you are tramping through the fields during the hunting season, expect to see plenty of quail and an occasional pheasant. White-tailed deer are abundant, as are Rio Grande turkeys, rabbits, squirrels, coyotes, bobcats, raccoons, and doves. Ducks, geese, herons, and egrets are common along the river. Osprey and bald eagles are present year-round, but migrate here in large numbers during the winter months.

Kaw Lake and the Arkansas River have long been known for producing large catfish. Flathead, blue, and channel catfish all reside in the lake and move up into the river. The river and lake also offer crappie, sand bass, black bass, and walleye fishing. The lake covers 17,000 surface acres and has 168 miles of shoreline.

At Arkansas City the river channel is already very broad and exposed. It spreads out even more as it moves into and through the beautiful **Kaw Wildlife Area**. **Wind** can be a significant factor as the river turns to the south near Grouse Creek. From only a mile downstream of the put-in, this reach is within the beautiful Kaw Wildlife Area. Keep an eye peeled for bald eagles, osprey, and other wildlife along the river.

The **put-in** at the **Arkansas City Cottonwood Park Access** is at *river mile 701* and at the southeast edge of the U.S. Highway 166 bridge on Madison Avenue. On the river, you will cross under two bridges on your way toward the confluence with Walnut Creek. The first is the U.S. Highway 77 bridge. The second is a railroad

This limestone post stands at the western end of a survey that was done in 1871 along the 37th Parallel. It marks the boundary between the Cherokee Nation and the State of Kansas. The marker is located on a path immediately downstream of the Ark's confluence with Grouse Creek (photo by Kurt Grimm).

bridge. Just downstream of the railroad bridge, the river enters the Kaw Wildlife Area.

The confluence with the **Walnut River** is at *river mile 697*. Two miles up the Walnut, the **Walnut River Boat Ramp** in Arkansas City is located on the east side of town, next to the Highway 166 bridge. This segment of the Walnut is within the Kaw Wildlife Area. Unless the Ark is low, the river backs up to this access. When it does, or when Walnut Creek is high enough, you can use this access as a put-in or take-out. Either way, you'll have a two-mile float to or from the Arkansas River. A logjam on the Walnut is passable at this writing, but may require portaging in the future if it is not blown out soon. The nearest **gauging station** is on the Walnut River at Winfield. The average **gradient** is 2.8 feet per mile.

The confluence with Grouse Creek is at *river mile 690*, on river left. The **Grouse Creek Access** is immediately downstream of the confluence, also on river left (east side) and immediately upstream of the Kansas/Oklahoma border. The road and boat ramp can be very muddy. To get there from Newkirk, Oklahoma, go east on River Road (aka East 0090 Road) to North 3400 Road (the first road east of the river) and turn north. This gravel road becomes North Silverdale Lane and is paved on the Kansas side.

One of the most popular and scenic floats in the area is a one-day float on Grouse Creek combined with a day on the Ark on the way to Traders Bend. See the Grouse Creek chapter for more details.

Near *river mile 686* **Chilocco Creek** enters on river right.

The **take-out** at the **Traders Bend Boat Ramp** is on river right, at *river mile 682*. Go four miles east of Newkirk, Oklahoma, on River Road to Traders Bend Road (aka N 3380 Road) and then go north one mile to East 0080 Road; this is a dirt road that goes east. Follow that road (unmarked at this writing) about 1.6 miles, through two turns (north onto North 3385 Road and then east onto East Fork Road/E 0070 Road, all unmarked) and watch for the small access road on the right side before you come to the third turn. Without road signs, you should count your turns and check your odometer carefully. If you are paddling farther downstream, your next river stop is Newkirk, Oklahoma. Then there is another 73 miles of river between Kaw and Keystone Reservoirs.

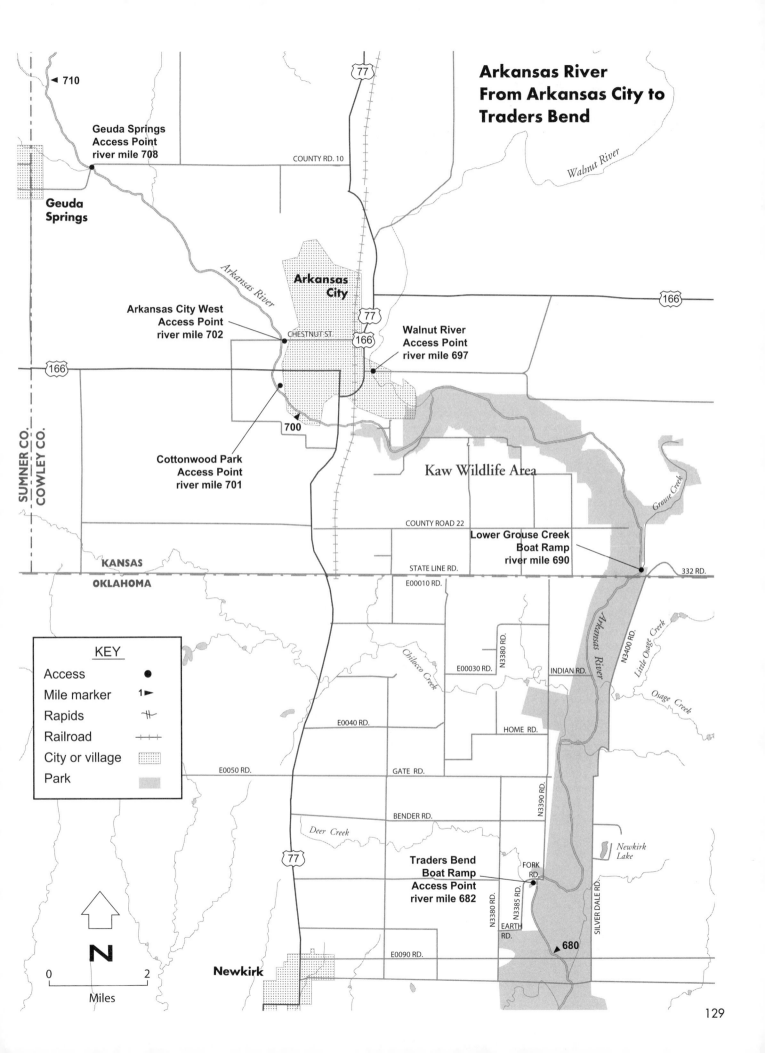

Arkansas River From Arkansas City to Traders Bend

◄ 710

Geuda Springs
Access Point
river mile 708

Geuda Springs

COUNTY RD. 10

77

Walnut River

166

Arkansas River

Arkansas City

Arkansas City West
Access Point
river mile 702

CHESTNUT ST.

77

166

Walnut River
Access Point
river mile 697

166

700

Cottonwood Park
Access Point
river mile 701

Kaw Wildlife Area

Grouse Creek

COUNTY ROAD 22

Lower Grouse Creek
Boat Ramp
river mile 690

SUMNER CO.
COWLEY CO.

KANSAS

OKLAHOMA

STATE LINE RD.

E00010 RD.

332 RD.

Chilocco Creek

N3380 RD.

E00030 RD.

INDIAN RD.

Little Osage Creek

N3400 RD.

Arkansas River

Osage Creek

KEY

Access	●
Mile marker	1►
Rapids	
Railroad	
City or village	
Park	

E0040 RD.

HOME RD.

E0050 RD.

GATE RD.

BENDER RD.

N3390 RD.

Deer Creek

Newkirk
Lake

77

Traders Bend
Boat Ramp
Access Point
river mile 682

FORK
RD.

N3380 RD.

N3385 RD.

EARTH
RD.

SILVER DALE RD.

680

N
0 2
Miles

Newkirk

E0090 RD.

LITTLE ARKANSAS RIVER
**8.3 miles round-trip, intermediate access points available,
Class I difficulty, plus manmade hazards (see below)**

The Little Ark, "paddle central" for many Wichita locals, flows through a pleasant streamway park in the north central part of Wichita. The park lines the river from 21st Street to its confluence with the "Big" Arkansas River. A low-head dam near the downtown area, at about the intersection of North Seneca Street and West Central Avenue, creates a shallow, sandy-bottomed pool that is normally deep enough to paddle, regardless of flow. It takes three to four hours for a round-trip tour during **low-medium flows**. You can **put-in** anywhere that you find convenient, but you should not approach the **hazardous low-head dam** that is about an eighth of a mile downstream from the West Central Avenue bridge at the confluence with the "Big" Arkansas River. You can check the **gauging station** on the Little Arkansas River near Sedgwick for the most accurate flow report. The average **gradient** for this segment is less than .5 feet per mile.

Most paddlers tour the park by starting at their preferred put-in and then return to that same access, thus avoiding the need for running a **shuttle**. The following access points are most convenient.

The northern end of the streamway park is at 21st Street, but the uppermost public access is seven-tenths of a mile downstream on the east side of the river, three

**The Little Arkansas River in the Wichita Area,
upstream of the 20th Street Access**

blocks west of North Waco Street on West 20th Street N. There is a small parking lot and a concrete storm drain that makes it easy to get in and out of your boat. The banks are wide and the paddling can be as easy or hard as you want your workout to be. If you head upstream, you will come to the end of the park as you cross under the 21st Street bridge. Beyond that, the bank is lined with private residences. If you paddle downstream, you will discover a beautiful recreational corridor of trees, grass, and walking trails that are pleasantly divided by nicely done bridges.

At about river mile 1.7, you will pass North High School on river left. Then you will pass under two closely spaced bridges (West 13th Street N and North Bitting Avenue). Just downstream of the second of these bridges, at *river mile 1.9*, you will find a good concrete landing on river left. This access is in the Oak Park area at the intersection of West 12th Street N and North Bitting Avenue, a little upstream of Oak Park. Continuing downstream, you will pass under four bridges—West 11th Street N, North Bitting Avenue, West Murdock Street, and North Nims Street—before reaching the **Riverside Tennis Center Access** at *river mile 3.9*. There, you will find a floating dock on river left. The tennis center, located at West Central Avenue and Nims, has nice parking and restrooms. You can paddle roughly 400 yards downstream past the Tennis Center, until you come to a series of warning signs for a low-head dam. Do not proceed beyond the warning signs. The low-head dam is very dangerous and it is against a city ordinance and common sense to paddle in this area.

Other cool stuff: If you would like to continue downstream on the "Big" Arkansas River, you can take out on river right, at the low-head dam warning signs, and portage your boat a quarter mile south to the Big Ark.

Local Contacts: City of Wichita Parks Department, (316) 268-4361.

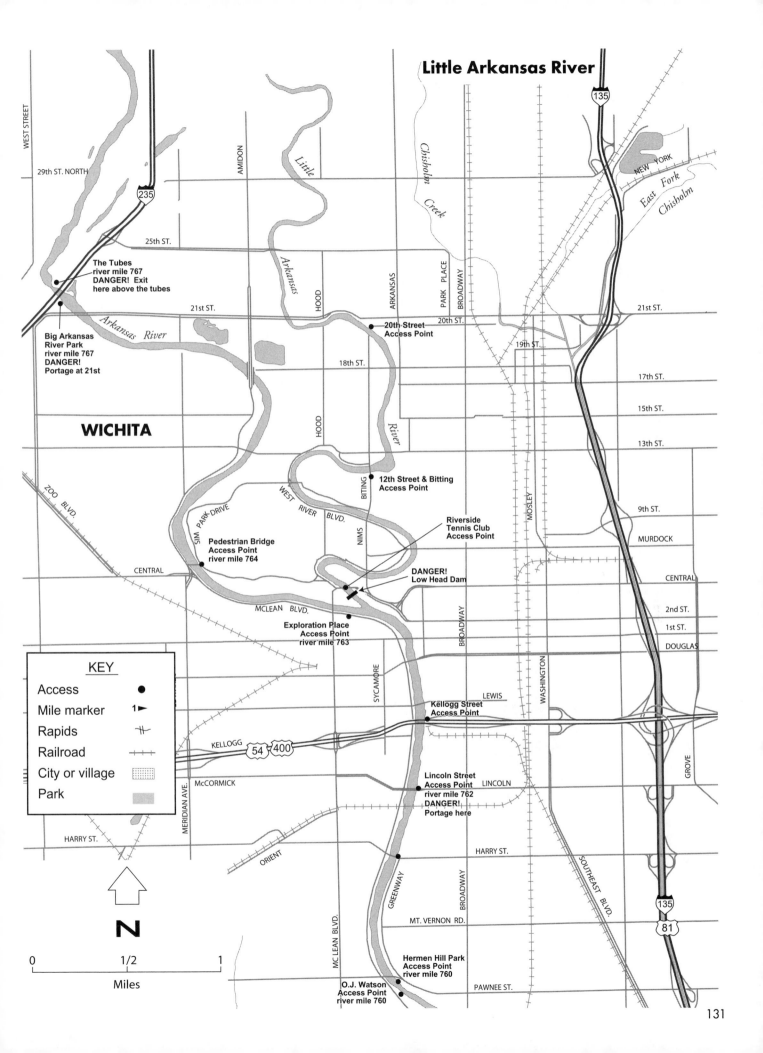

Little Arkansas River

WEST STREET

Chisholm Creek

East Fork Chisholm

NEW YORK

135

29th ST. NORTH

AMIDON

Little

25th ST.

Arkansas

HOOD

ARKANSAS

PARK PLACE

BROADWAY

21st ST.

21st ST.

235

The Tubes
river mile 767
DANGER! Exit
here above the tubes

Arkansas River

20th ST.

19th ST.

17th ST.

20th Street
Access Point

**Big Arkansas
River Park**
river mile 767
DANGER!
Portage at 21st

18th ST.

15th ST.

13th ST.

WICHITA

HOOD

River

9th ST.

MOSLEY

12th Street & Bitting
Access Point

WEST RIVER BLVD.

BITTING

MURDOCK

ZOO BLVD.

SIM PARK DRIVE

NIMS

Riverside
Tennis Club
Access Point

CENTRAL

CENTRAL

Pedestrian Bridge
Access Point
river mile 764

DANGER!
Low Head Dam

2nd ST.

MCLEAN BLVD.

1st ST.

Exploration Place
Access Point
river mile 763

BROADWAY

DOUGLAS

SYCAMORE

WASHINGTON

LEWIS

GROVE

Kellogg Street
Access Point

KEY

Access ●

Mile marker 1▶

Rapids

Railroad

City or village

Park

KELLOGG

54 400

MERIDIAN AVE.

McCORMICK

Lincoln Street
Access Point
river mile 762
DANGER!
Portage here

LINCOLN

HARRY ST.

HARRY ST.

ORIENT

GREENWAY

BROADWAY

SOUTHEAST BLVD.

135

N

MC LEAN BLVD.

MT. VERNON RD.

81

0   1/2   1

Miles

Hermen Hill Park
Access Point
river mile 760

PAWNEE ST.

O.J. Watson
Access Point
river mile 760

WALNUT RIVER ABOVE EL DORADO RESERVOIR

6 miles round-trip, intermediate access points available, Class I difficulty
From Chelsea Boat Ramp

DURECHEN CREEK ABOVE EL DORADO RESERVOIR

4 miles round-trip, Class I difficulty

Touring paddlers, birders, hunters, and anglers enjoy this one-hour round trip. The creek's east-to-west valley and large trees offer welcome protection from the south wind. Launch at and return to the turnout at the northeast or northwest sides of the Highway 177 bridge. There used to be a boat ramp on the east side, but it has long been buried in dirt and rock.

The creek is floatable to near the end of the public use area anytime the lake is at or above 1,337 feet, but the upper reach is more passable with a few more feet of water. Log jams can block the channel, especially at the lower levels. Check the El Dorado Lake levels at www.swt.usace.army.mil/recreat/recreat.htm. There are no gauges upstream to find out what kind of flows might be coming down the river, but you can look at the inflow and precipitation gauges at the El Dorado Web site listed above.

The Walnut River had been running much higher just a few days before, but was calm and quiet this day.

The Walnut River, through the upper reaches of the El Dorado Reservoir, is an easy, flatwater stream. Its only challenges are downed trees and log jams that can make passage difficult, particularly near the upper end of the public use area.

Flowing from the western edge of the Flint Hills into and through the El Dorado Wildlife Area, the Walnut River is a good destination for touring paddlers, anglers, hunters, and bird-watchers. As you paddle upstream from the lake, the channel closes in until you find yourself on a very small stream, surrounded by trees and, finally, blockaded by logjams. Although it is possible to drag your boat down the bank at Northeast 90th Street, logjams will prevent easy passage to the lake.

Normal pool (1,339 feet) should provide enough water for small motorboats, but you can work your way upstream by canoe with two feet less. The round-trip distance, assuming that you can make your way nearly to the end of the public use area, is 6 miles. Crappie, white bass, and flatheads are the ticket, but largemouth bass can be found lurking around old snags.

It takes two and a half to four hours for a round-trip canoe tour. This section above the lake is floatable anytime the lake is at or above 1,337 feet but is better with a few more feet of water. Check the El Dorado Reservoir levels at the Corps' Tulsa District Information Web site, www.swt.usace.army.mil/recreat/recreat.htm. There are no gauges up-stream, but you can read the water level from the 90th Street bridge. You can also look at the inflow and precipitation gauges at the El Dorado Web site above and check the **gauging stations** on the White-

water River at Towanda and on the Walnut River at Winfield to get some idea of what other rivers in the area are doing. **Camping** is not allowed along the river, but there are good campsites around El Dorado Lake. (See map.) There are no **canoe rentals** in the area.

The return half of this tour is likely to be into a headwind, so a careful check on the weather, prior to launch, is advised.

The **put-in** and **take-out** for the Walnut River above El Dorado Reservoir are at the **Chelsea Boat Ramp**. To get there from the east side of El Dorado Lake, take State Highway 177 to NE 75th Street, then west (toward the lake), following the curves to the southwest until the road becomes NE 70th Street. Continue on 70th Street until just before the bridge. At the northeast edge of the bridge, take the gravel road down to the Chelsea Boat Ramp. Drop off your boats and then leave your vehicle in the gravel parking lot.

As you leave the boat ramp, paddle north under the I-35 bridge, then follow along the east side of the lake, staying in the old river's meandering easternmost channel. When the lake is high enough, you can meander around in this arm of the lake wherever you like, but when the lake is low you can find it difficult to regain the old channel once you leave it. At the mouth of the lake, there are two channels that can be followed. The western (left) channel was recently cut by the river, but the eastern (right) channel is still the larger and better of the two. The river is fairly broad here. Fallen trees have accumulated brush and other trees, making it an increasing challenge to work your way upstream. The river grows narrower over the course of the next few miles until it is blockaded by an impassible logjam.

Other cool stuff: Also branching upstream from El Dorado Lake, Cole Creek is a theoretical 8-mile round-trip tour. Durechen Creek (see details below) is a round-trip tour of 4 miles, Satchel Creek is 2 miles, and Bemis Creek is 1.5 miles. All four of these creeks need at least normal pool to be worth floating and all except Cole Creek have useable canoe access at their respective bridges on Highway 177. All offer good crappie and white bass fishing, but Bemis Creek, due to its more turbid water, is favored for flathead catfish.

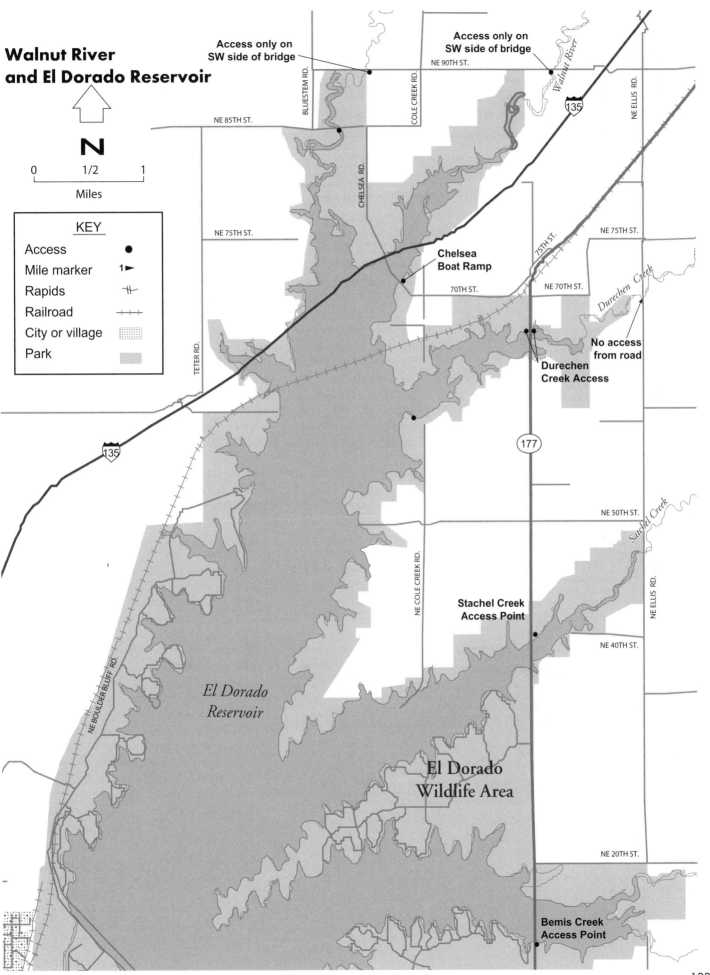

Walnut River
and El Dorado Reservoir

N

0   1/2   1

Miles

KEY

Access	●
Mile marker	1▶
Rapids	
Railroad	
City or village	
Park	

Access only on
SW side of bridge

Access only on
SW side of bridge

NE 90TH ST.

Walnut River

BLUESTEM RD.

COLE CREEK RD.

NE ELLIS RD.

135

NE 85TH ST.

CHELSEA RD.

NE 75TH ST.

NE 75TH ST.

75TH ST.

**Chelsea
Boat Ramp**

Durechen Creek

70TH ST.

NE 70TH ST.

TETER RD.

**No access
from road**

**Durechen
Creek Access**

135

177

NE 50TH ST.

Satchel Creek

NE COLE CREEK RD.

NE ELLIS RD.

NE BOULDER BLUFF RD.

**Stachel Creek
Access Point**

NE 40TH ST.

*El Dorado
Reservoir*

**El Dorado
Wildlife Area**

NE 20TH ST.

**Bemis Creek
Access Point**

GROUSE CREEK FROM SILVERDALE TO TRADERS BEND

**4.5 miles, combinable with a float on the Arkansas River to make
13.5 miles, intermediate access points available, Class I difficulty**

Grouse Creek is a paddler's delight. Its small size, gravel bars, rocky ledges, cliffs, bluffs, shaded canopy, and abundance of wildlife would be enough to make this a local favorite. Combine this with good accesses and a 9-mile float on the beautiful Arkansas River through the Kaw Wildlife Area and you have a spectacular one- or two-day paddling, fishing, camping, hunting, and bird-watching scenic expedition.

It takes only two to four hours to paddle to the Lower Grouse Creek Access and another three to four hours down to Traders Bend. The **minimum recommended flow** on Grouse Creek is **200 CFS**, but there are no gauges upstream. The nearest **gauging station** for determining nearby weather and stream flows is on the Walnut River at Winfield. The average **gradient** is 7 feet per mile.

The **Silverdale Boat Ramp** is at the northwest edge of the first bridge south of the town of

Grouse Creek is characterized by long, narrow, deep, clear pools that are accentuated by rocky ledges, gravel bars, good fishing, and plenty of wildlife.

Grouse Creek at Silverdale Access

Silverdale. The 8.2-mile **round-trip shuttle** takes you 3 miles south from Silverdale on 141st Road (County Road 1), then west seven-tenths of a mile on County Road 332. The turnoff is on the right side of the road in the middle of a hairpin turn.

Put in at the **Silverdale Boat Ramp**. The ramp is at an easy riffle. Depending on levels in Kaw Lake and the flows in Grouse Creek, there may be a few similar riffles farther downstream. From the put-in, it is 4.5 miles to the confluence with the Arkansas River. That float can be combined with a 9-mile float on the Arkansas River that will take you to the Traders Bend Boat Ramp in Oklahoma (13.5 miles total). The channel is wide, but there is always the threat of downed trees to create strainers. The backwater from Kaw Reservoir may extend all the way up to this access when the Kaw Reservoir and the Arkansas River are high.

The next bridge you see has an access at its northeast edge. It is simply called the **2nd Bridge Access**. From there it is three miles to the confluence with the Ark. You can usually see deep into the normally clear pools.

The third bridge also has an access and it is naturally called the **3rd Bridge Boat Ramp**. The access here is on the northwest side of the bridge. From here, it is 2 miles to the confluence with the Ark.

Take out at the **Lower Grouse Creek Boat Ramp**. The ramp is on river left, just downstream of the mouth of Grouse Creek. The road and boat ramp can be rutted and muddy. If you're coming from Newkirk, go east across the river, then north on N 3400 Road. This becomes N Silverdale Lane and is paved once you get to the Kansas State Line.

Other cool stuff: If you are continuing downstream on the Ark, see the last section on the Arkansas River for details of that float and driving directions to that take-out at the **Traders Bend Boat Ramp**, nine miles downstream on the Ark from the Lower Grouse Creek Boat Ramp.

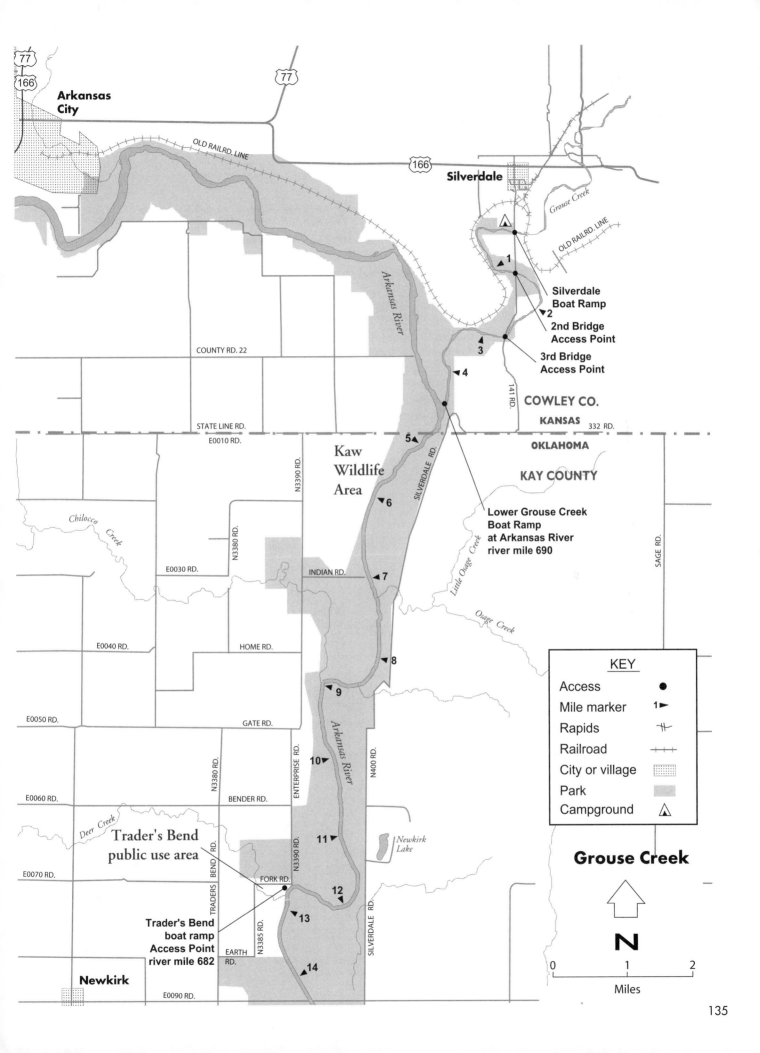

Arkansas City

Arkansas River

OLD RAILRD. LINE

Silverdale

Grouse Creek

OLD RAILRD. LINE

▲ 1
Silverdale
Boat Ramp

▼ 2
2nd Bridge
Access Point

▲ 3
3rd Bridge
Access Point

▼ 4

141 RD.

COUNTY RD. 22

STATE LINE RD.

E0010 RD.

COWLEY CO.

KANSAS   332 RD.

OKLAHOMA

KAY COUNTY

Kaw
Wildlife
Area

5 ▲

Silverdale Rd.

Little Osage Creek

Lower Grouse Creek
Boat Ramp
at Arkansas River
river mile 690

N3390 RD.

▼ 6

Chilocco Creek

N3380 RD.

E0030 RD.

INDIAN RD.

▼ 7

Osage Creek

SAGE RD.

E0040 RD.

HOME RD.

▼ 8

E0050 RD.

GATE RD.

◄ 9

Arkansas River

N3380 RD.

ENTERPRISE RD.

10 ▼

N400 RD.

E0060 RD.

BENDER RD.

Deer Creek

Trader's Bend
public use area

TRADERS BEND RD.

N3390 RD.

11 ▼

Newkirk
Lake

E0070 RD.

FORK RD.

12 ▼

Trader's Bend
boat ramp
Access Point
river mile 682

N3385 RD.

EARTH
RD.

◄ 13

SILVERDALE RD.

Newkirk

◄ 14

E0090 RD.

KEY

Access ●
Mile marker 1 ►
Rapids ‡‡
Railroad ┼┼┼
City or village ▦
Park ▨
Campground ⛺

Grouse Creek

N

0   1   2
Miles

135

NEOSHO RIVER ABOVE COUNCIL GROVE LAKE

6 miles, intermediate access points available, Class I difficulty
From Canning Creek Grove Boat Ramp

THE NEOSHO RIVER WATERSHED

The northern part of the Neosho Watershed runs through the tallgrass prairies of the Flint Hills. The river changes character as it cuts a diagonal from the prairie near Junction City to the bottomlands of the southeast corner of the state. Thanks to rich soil and adequate rainfall, wildlife thrives along the river corridors that meander through hills, prairies, and then farmland.

The river flows from its headwaters in Morris County to the Arkansas River in northeastern Oklahoma near Muskogee. Some of the Neosho's tributaries also drain portions of Missouri and Arkansas. The river is about 460 miles long and is ultimately part of the Mississippi River watershed.

Three large reservoirs—Council Grove Lake, John Redmond Reservoir, and Marion Lake—were built by the Corps of Engineers to aid in flood control. Above each of these lakes, national wildlife refuges provide wonderful habitats for local and migratory wildlife.

The fishing is good, especially above the reservoirs, where the white bass collect during their spawn. Mussel shells, once important to the button makers, are easily found on gravel bars throughout most of the area.

The watershed is largely agricultural and some of the less thoughtful farming practices, combined with the growth of some of the larger communities, have impacted the quality of the water in the lower reaches.

The Neosho River is also known as the Grand River, particularly in its lower reaches. You will often see it called the Grand on Corps of Engineers maps, even in Kansas. The Osage Indians called it the Neosho, which means "stream with water in it." The Indians described it as "water like the skin of a summer cow wapiti (elk)." It has more recently been called the "No Show" because of low stream flows.

This part of the river is nestled in the northern part of the Flint Hills and flows through the 2,638-acre Council Grove Wildlife Area. It is equally enjoyed by touring boaters, hunters, anglers, and birders. The abundance of wildlife and good fishing makes this a worthy float. The river boasts a good population of channel and flathead catfish, white bass, and crappie.

Camping is not allowed along the river, but there are nice campgrounds in the park areas around the lake. The Canning Creek campground is conveniently close to the river and more out of the wind than most of the other campgrounds. (See map.) There are no **canoe rentals** available in the area.

If the lake elevation is at or above 1,275 feet, power and touring boats can motor upstream from the lake to Kelso Road. If the lake is low, **100 CFS or more is recommended** for paddlers. There are **no gauges** upstream, but you can use the inflow and precipitation gauge on Council Grove Lake at www.swt-wc.usace.army.mil/coun.lakepage.html. The average **gradient** is only about .8 feet per mile between Kelso Road and the Neosho Boat Ramp.

This river segment can be paddled in a number of ways. For a 6-mile round trip to the upper end of the public use area, a launch and return to the Neosho Boat Ramp provides an easy trip with **no shuttle** needed. That tour can be combined with a 2.5-mile float downstream to the Canning Creek Cove Boat Ramp and Campground. An alternate route, the one used in the narrative below, is a 11-mile round-trip tour from the lake to the end of the public use area and back.

The **put-in** and **take-out** are at the **Canning Creek Cove Boat Ramp**. The Canning Creek Cove Area is west of the Council Grove Lake Dam. The first leg of this trip takes you roughly 1.5 miles up the west arm of the lake. This arm tends to be better protected from wind than the rest of the lake, but since open water and wind are always problematic, check the wind forecast before launching.

Follow the deep water to stay in the old river channel. The arm of the lake soon narrows and the trees begin to close in around you. Gilmore Creek will be on your left as you paddle upstream. If you have time for a side trip, paddle or hike the creek. The **Neosho River Boat Ramp** is on the left as you go upstream, 2.5 miles from the Canning Creek Cove Boat Ramp. This ramp and parking area can be very muddy in wet weather.

Still heading upstream, it is 3.8 more miles upstream to the end of the public use area. Prolonged periods of submersion, caused by the lake, have caused the riverbanks to slough off, leaving them rather steep in most areas, but in the upper reaches you can still find good places to stretch your legs. Rock ledges add to the scenery of cottonwoods and sycamores that prevail along the river.

It is possible to climb out at the Kelso Bridge, but the banks are steep and covered with poison ivy. You will come to a fork where Lairds Creek comes in from the right and the river comes in from the left. Take the left fork. The end of the public use area and the wildlife area are one mile upstream of that confluence.

If you're continuing downstream and looking for a diversion, after you pass the Neosho Boat Ramp, watch on river right for Gilmore Creek. The water is fairly clear and the bed is gravelly once you get past the backwater area of the lake. Another diversion is up Slough Creek, farther downstream, on river left.

Other cool stuff: Paddle Munkers Creek on the north arm of the lake. See the next section for more details.

Local contacts: Kansas Department of Wildlife and Parks, (620) 767-5900; U.S. Army Corps of Engineers, (620) 767-5195.

Rocky ledges on the Neosho above the Neosho River Boat Ramp (photo by Susan Kysela)

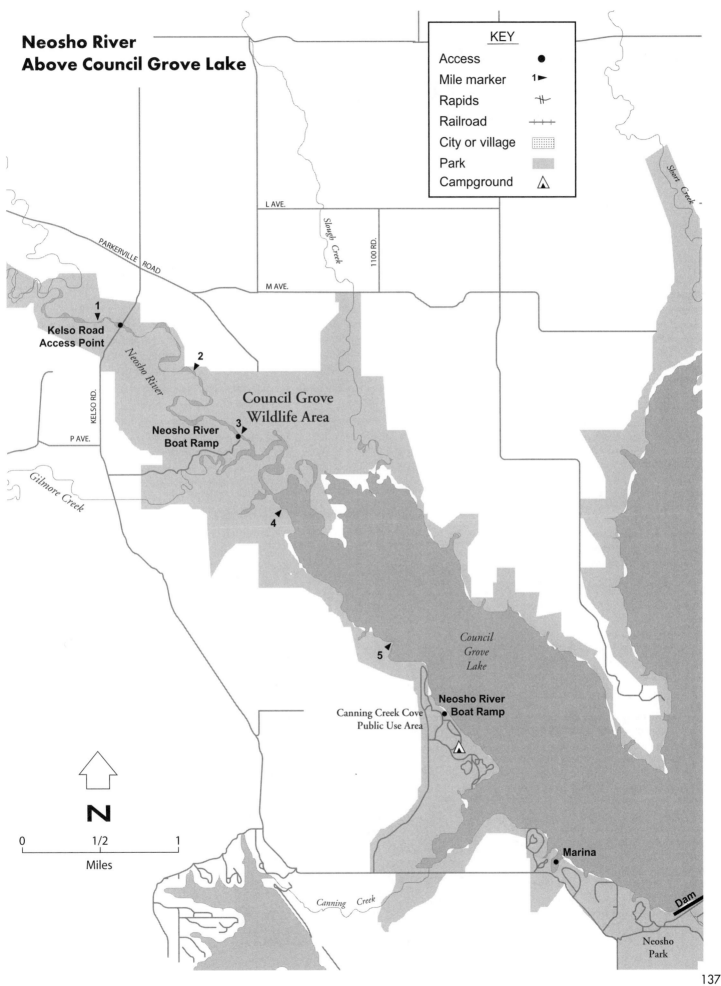

Neosho River
Above Council Grove Lake

KEY

Access ●

Mile marker 1▶

Rapids

Railroad ++++

City or village

Park

Campground ⛺

L AVE.

Slough Creek

1100 RD.

Short Creek

PARKERVILLE ROAD

M AVE.

1
Kelso Road
Access Point

Neosho River

KELSO RD.

P AVE.

2

Council Grove
Wildlife Area

3
Neosho River
Boat Ramp

Gilmore Creek

4

5

Council
Grove
Lake

Canning Creek Cove
Public Use Area

Neosho River
Boat Ramp

N

0   1/2   1
Miles

Canning Creek

Marina

Dam

Neosho
Park

MUNKERS CREEK ABOVE COUNCIL GROVE LAKE

5 miles round-trip, intermediate access points available, Class I difficulty
From Munkers Creek Boat Ramp

THE FIRST KANSANS

In preparation for the construction of Council Grove Lake in the early 1960s, excavations were made to investigate several prehistoric sites that would soon be flooded. One of the main investigations was on property owned by William Young of Council Grove. At that site, two ceramic artifacts were recovered. Both were modeled clay human effigy heads. The effigies were created by inhabitants, classified by archeologists as "Munkers Creek People," who lived in the Flint Hills region from 3550 to 3050 B.C. They had large campsites covering several acres. Munkers Creek People returned time and again to this area, where they chipped chert from nearby hills into tools. Aside from the fact that the Munkers Creek ceramic effigies are our earliest surviving portraits of humans in Kansas, these finds were unexpected because previous archeological research indicated that pottery making did not become a common practice in Kansas until sometime around A.D. 1. This may be an example of a technology that enjoyed brief popularity, was forgotten, and then was resurrected at a later date.

TOWN OF COUNCIL GROVE

Council Grove is full of history. The marked stump of the Council Oak is still visible on the north side of Main Street. Post Office Oak, where letters were left for caravans passing through the area between 1825 and 1847, still stands on the same side of the street. The Santa Fe Trail's peak traffic year was 1860, when a government survey reported that 3,000 wagons, 7,000 men, and 60,000 mules used the route. The heavy traffic continued until after the Civil War. Other historic sites include the Old Hays Tavern, built in 1857, and the Custer Elm, where General George Armstrong Custer camped in 1867.

Reminiscent of an Ozark stream that is surrounded by wooded hills and rocky ledges, Munkers Creek is one of the local paddling hot spots. Expect to take two to four hours for a round-trip tour, plus as much time as you choose to paddle into the lake area. There are two good access points, but of the two the Munkers Creek Boat Ramp is preferred, especially under wet weather conditions.

There are **no gauges** on Munkers Creek, but you can use the inflow and precipitation chart on Council Grove Lake to get some idea about the lake level, weather history, and other stream flows in the area. Go to www.swt-wc. usace.army.mil/coun.lakepage.html. A lake elevation of 1,275 feet or more is sufficient for a good float with or without any water coming down the creek. The average **gradient** of this section is 2.6 feet per mile, though; when the lake is high, it is all flatwater.

Munkers Creek near the upper end of the public use area (photo by Susan Kysela)

Camping is not allowed along the creek, but there are nice campgrounds in the park areas around the lake. The Canning Creek Campground is at the far south side of the lake, but is less exposed to the prevailing southwest wind than most of the other campgrounds. (See the Neosho River map.) There are no **canoe rentals** in the area. There is no need for a **shuttle**, since you will likely want to return to the spot from which you launched.

Put-in and **take-out** are at the **Munkers Creek Boat Ramp**, located at the north end of the lake off State Highway 177. From the lake, go north 0.9 mile past the bridge over Munkers Creek to the first road (unnamed) that goes east (right). The Kansas Department of Wildlife and Parks has a kiosk at the corner. Turn east (right) at the kiosk, then take the next turn to the south (right). The boat ramp is at the end of the road.

From the ramp, paddle upstream along low limestone bluffs and meander with the creek through hardwood forests in the headwaters of the most scenic arm of Council Grove Lake. About one mile upstream, the Upper Munkers Creek Access is on the left as you paddle upstream.

The creek gradually closes in on you over the next 1.5 miles. Depending on the lake level and the flow in the creek, you may not have enough water to paddle to the end of the public use area. No worries. The channel becomes narrower and more interesting the farther up you go and is worth hiking or wading. The gravelly creek bed provides good footing and there are plenty of stones and pools for rock skipping. The public use area extends almost, but not quite, to the confluence with Wildcat Creek.

The return trip can be extended past the Munkers Creek Boat Ramp, beyond the creek and down to the lake. Combine this float on Munkers Creek with a tour of the lake and you can have a full day of paddling.

The **Upper Munkers Creek Access** is north of the Munkers Creek Boat Ramp. Just go north and then take a jog to the east, then north again to the end of the road.

Local Contacts: Kansas Department of Wildlife and Parks, Wildlife Area Manager, (620) 767-5900.

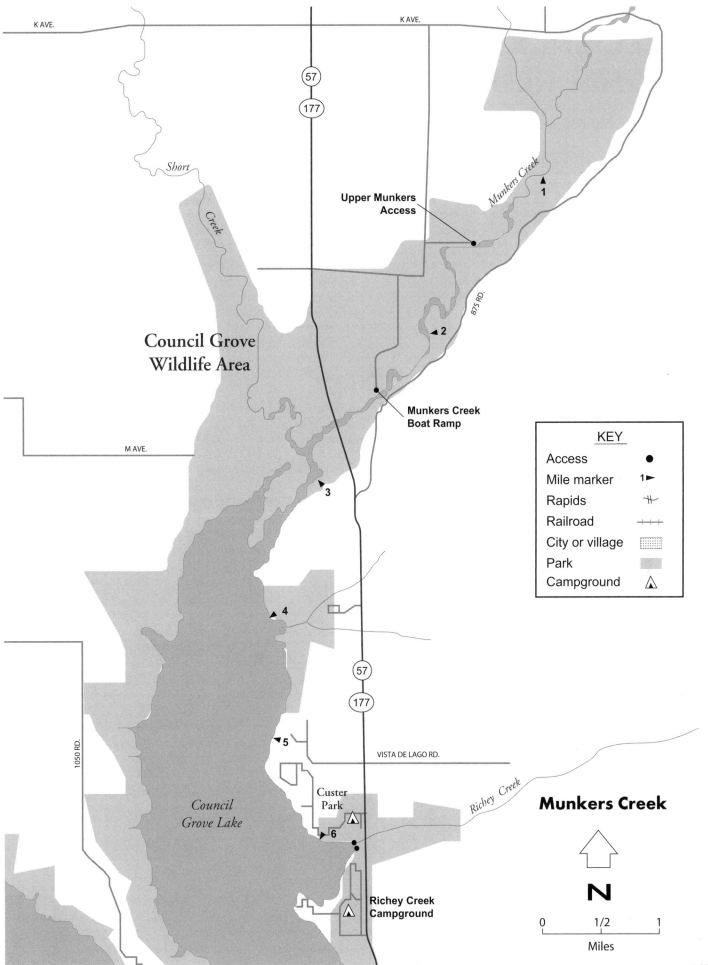

K AVE. K AVE.

(57)
(177)

Short

Creek

Munkers Creek

**Upper Munkers
Access**

1

875 RD.

2

**Council Grove
Wildlife Area**

**Munkers Creek
Boat Ramp**

KEY

Access	●
Mile marker	1►
Rapids	╫
Railroad	┼┼┼
City or village	▦
Park	▨
Campground	⛺

M AVE.

3

4

1050 RD.

(57)
(177)

5

VISTA DE LAGO RD.

Richey Creek

*Council
Grove Lake*

**Custer
Park**

6

Munkers Creek

⬆
N

**Richey Creek
Campground**

0   1/2   1
Miles

NEOSHO RIVER ABOVE JOHN REDMOND RESERVOIR

8.5 miles, intermediate access points available, Class I difficulty
Maxwell Pump Site to Katy Pump Site

From the put-in at the Maxwell Pump Site, it is 2.6 miles upstream to the end of the public use area, 5 miles to the Hartford Ramp, and 8.5 miles to the Katy Pump Station. The full trip to the Katy Pump makes a full day for most paddlers, but the Hartford Boat Ramp, at river mile 3, makes a perfect half-day float from either the top or the middle. It is a wonderful destination, particularly for birders, anglers, hunters, and touring boaters when the accesses are not too muddy. Otherwise, the boat ramp east of Hartford is the only option. In that case you will put in and take out at the Hartford Ramp.

Because of the backwater from John Redmond Reservoir, there is always enough water to paddle through the Flint Hills National Wildlife Refuge, except during the worst droughts. If the lake is low, the **minimum recommended flow is 150 CFS** for a lightly loaded canoe. There is no single **gauging station**, but you can calculate the flow on this part of the Neosho by adding the flows from the Cottonwood near Plymouth and the flows from the Neosho River near Americus. To determine the lake level, go to the Corps of Engineers Web site for John Redmond Reservoir, at www.swt-wc.usace.army.mil/john.lakepage.html. The average **gradient** for this section is 1.5 feet per mile, but the water can back up from the logjams and lake downstream, making most of it flatwater.

This logjam and mud delta has formed below the mouth of Eagle Creek and has already blocked access to Eagle Creek and Jacobs Landing.

Catfish are the mainstay for river angers upstream of the logjams, while white bass and crappie are good below the logjam. **Camping** is not allowed along the river, but good campsites are available around the lake. (See the John Redmond Reservoir map in the Appendix.)

The **put-in** is at the **Maxwell Pump Site**. To get there from the refuge office in Hartford (located on West Maple Avenue three-eighths of a mile west of State Highway 130), go north on Highway 130, zigzagging west as necessary along the river for 2.7 miles. Use the small parking area on the left (south) side of the road, opposite the undeveloped access on the north side. The 14.6-mile **round-trip shuttle** route from the Maxwell Pump Site Access to the take-out at the Katy Pump Site and back goes back to the Kansas Department of Wildlife and Parks office in Hartford, then east on Maple Avenue one block to Mechanic Street, and south on Mechanic. As you leave town, Mechanic turns to County Road Y5. Turn east (left) on Road 95, which becomes 18th Lane when you cross the county line. As you are heading east, you will pass through a set of gates. Take the first road to the left and follow it to the river. This unmarked muddy cut in the riverbank is the Katy Pump Site Access. If the area is flooded, the gates will be closed. In that case you can use the next pump site to the west (go west from the closed gates to the first turnoff). Whichever access you chose, **memorize** that spot so that you can find it when paddling from upstream.

From the Maxwell Pump, the river flows through both farmland and remote waterfowl marshes. The abundant wildlife of the 18,500-acre Flint Hills National Wildlife Refuge is most apparent during the migratory season, but you can spot herons, egrets, palliated woodpeckers, kingfishers, and wood ducks all year long. The refuge includes wetlands, croplands, old fields, tallgrass prairie, and the 14-mile Hickory Creek Trail. The river is lined with ash, black walnut, cedar, cottonwood, elm, hackberry, and hickory.

Prior to the fall migratory season, pumps are used to flood the surrounding wetlands. Except during high flows, the only perceptible moving water you will see is in a one-mile-long section called "The Riffles," just upstream of Highway 130, where you'll find a rocky riverbed. The ledge is shallow, so motorized boats are unable to travel very far above the bridge except with very high water conditions. The **Hartford Boat Ramp**, the only serviceable boat ramp on this part of the river, is at river mile 3. It is located east of the town of Hartford, on Plumb Avenue (aka 19th Lane).

Keep a sharp eye out for the **take-out** at the **Katy Pump Site**. It's easy to miss the spot and there are no other useable access points farther downstream at this time, unless the lake is high enough to float a boat past the mud delta that normally blockades the boat ramp on Eagle Creek.

Other cool stuff: Check out the Coffey County Museum in Burlington (1101 Neosho Street, seven blocks east of State Highway 75, aka 4th Street). See the map for seasonal access limitations.

Local Contacts: U.S. Fish and Wildlife Service, (620) 392-5553; U.S. Army Corps of Engineers at John Redmond Reservoir, (620) 364-8613; Kansas Department of Wildlife and Parks, (620) 431-0380.

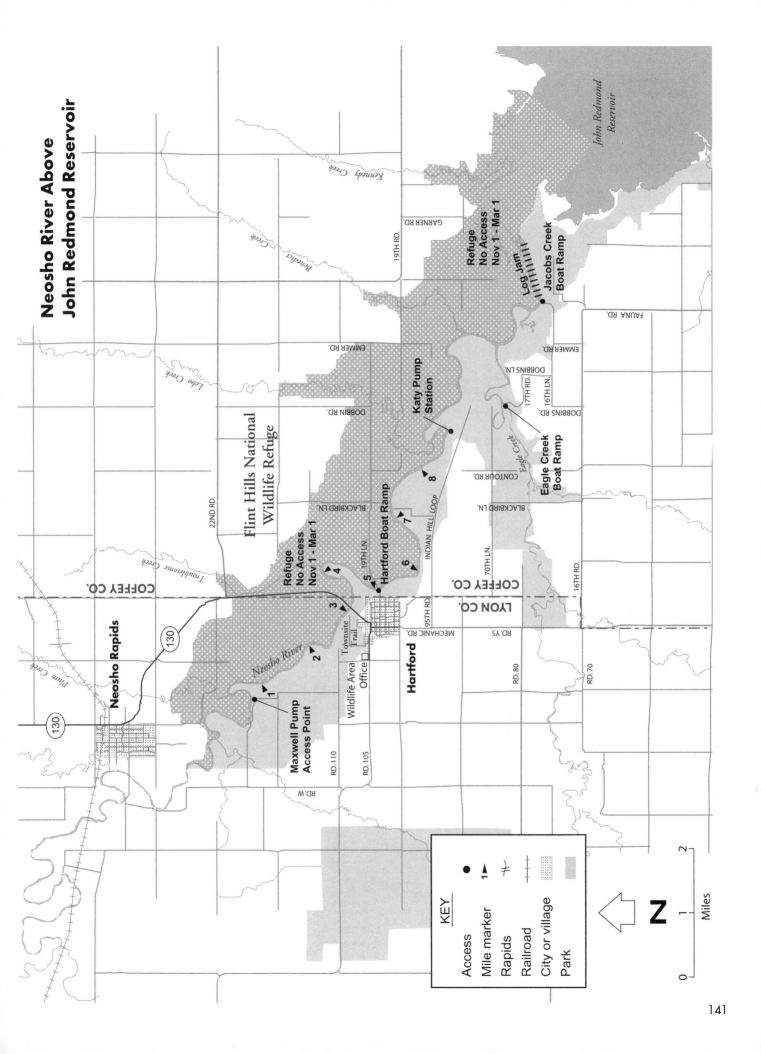

Neosho River Above John Redmond Reservoir

John Redmond Reservoir

Kennedy Creek

Benedict Creek

Lebo Creek

19TH RD.

GARNER RD.

Refuge
No Access
Nov 1 - Mar 1

Log Jam

Jacobs Creek
Boat Ramp

FAUNA RD.

EMMER RD.

EMMER RD.

DOBBINS LN.

17TH RD.

16TH LN.

DOBBINS RD.

Katy Pump
Station

Eagle Creek

Eagle Creek
Boat Ramp

Flint Hills National
Wildlife Refuge

DOBBIN RD.

22ND RD.

Troublesome Creek

CONTOUR RD.

BLACKBIRD LN.

BLACKBIRD LN.

8

INDIAN HILL LOOP

70TH LN.

7

Hartford Boat Ramp

19TH LN.

6

Refuge
No Access
Nov 1 - Mar 1

4

5

COFFEY CO.

LYON CO.

COFFEY CO.

16TH RD.

3

95TH RD.

RD. Y5

RD. 80

RD. 70

Neosho Rapids

130

Neosho River

2

Townsite Trail

Wildlife Area
Office

MECHANIC RD.

Hartford

1

Plum Creek

130

Maxwell Pump
Access Point

RD. 110

RD. 105

RD. W

KEY

●	Access
1 ▲	Mile marker
≠	Rapids
┼┼┼	Railroad
▦	City or village
▨	Park

N

0   1   2

Miles

COTTONWOOD RIVER ABOVE MARION LAKE

3-plus miles, Class I difficulty
Highway 15 Access to Broken Bridge Boat Ramp

THE NEOSHO WATERSHED

The Cottonwood River is the westernmost part of the Neosho River Watershed and at the eastern edge of the Western Plains, where millions of buffalo once roamed. For two decades after the Civil War, the Chisholm Trail was used to drive large herds of cattle from Texas north to railheads in Kansas. The Kaw Indian Trail crossed the county from northeast to southwest; it was the route used by the Kaw (Kanza) Indians for their annual hunting expeditions. The Santa Fe Trail crossed the northern portion of the country from east to west. First used in 1821 by William Becknell, it served as a commercial and military highway between Missouri and Santa Fe, New Mexico, until the railroad arrived in Santa Fe in 1880. The Santa Fe Trail crossed the Cottonwood River about a mile and a half west of Durham, at Cottonwood Crossing. The ruts of the old trail may still be seen today, though they are only barely visible through the tallgrass and prairie flowers.

The Cottonwood River is the westernmost reach of the Neosho River Watershed. Canopied by cottonwoods, sycamores, and willows, this float passes through the Marion Wildlife Area at the west end of Marion Lake. Having a relatively small watershed, the upper part of this segment is hard to catch with enough water unless the lake is high enough to back up to the State Highway 15 bridge. In that upper reach, the river looks more like a creek, but it soon fans out. "Marion" took its name from the nearby town that is named for General Francis Marion, the "Swamp Fox" of the American Revolution. The lake and river provide some of the best white bass fishing in Kansas, plus good populations of crappie, walleye, and catfish. Wipers (hybrid cross between the white bass and the striped bass) have also been stocked.

KDWP operates about 4,100 acres of project lands in the upper reaches of the lake for wildlife management and hunting. The designated hunting areas sport bobwhite quail, ducks, geese, mourning dove, cottontail rabbits, pheasants, squirrels, deer, and turkeys. These areas also support many species of birds and plants that naturalists and bird-watchers will enjoy.

The normal conservation pool in the lake will provide enough water for a good float. If the lake is low, the **minimum recommended flow is 100 CFS**. There are **no gauging stations** on this part of the river, but you can check the inflow and precipitation charts for Marion Lake at www.swt-wc.usace.army.mil/mari.lakepage.html. The average **gradient** for this river segment is 3 feet per mile but, when the lake is high, the river becomes mostly flatwater.

Camping is not allowed along the river, but good camping is available at designated sites around the lake. (See the Marion Lake map in the Appendix.) There are no **canoe rentals** in the area.

The **put-in** at the **State Highway 15 Access** is 0.8 mile south of Durham on Kansas Highway 15, about a quarter mile south of 280th Street at the northwest edge of the bridge. Park on the roadside and carry your boat down the banks. It is a bit of a steep carry. If you don't like the looks of it, a good **alternative** is to put in at the **Broken Bridge Boat Ramp** and paddle upstream. The 8-mile **round-trip shuttle** route from the Highway 15 Access to the Broken Bridge Boat Ramp goes one mile south on Highway 15, then east on 260th Road. Follow the signs for about 2.8 miles to the Broken Bridge Boat Ramp.

If you put in at the Highway 15 Access, it is three miles by boat to the Broken Bridge Boat Ramp. If the lake is high enough, you can paddle another half mile upstream to the end of the public use area. The narrow channel in the upper reach is susceptible to downed trees and strainers, but at this writing a small boat can slip through. Your float downstream to the Broken Bridge Boat Ramp should include some fishing gear and binoculars to take advantage of what the river has to offer as it meanders through the wildlife area. There are plenty of places to get out for a stretch, hike, or picnic.

The **take-out** is at the **Broken Bridge Boat Ramp**. If you prefer, you can paddle farther downstream and then return to the take-out or even paddle back upstream to the put-in, depending on flows.

Other cool stuff: French Creek enters the reservoir at its southwest edge. Follow the signs to French Creek Cove and then paddle up French Creek. You can go upstream about 3 miles at normal pool. (See the map of Marion Lake in the Appendix.)

Local Contacts: U.S. Army Corps of Engineers, (620) 382-2101.

Looking more like a creek where it crosses under Highway 15, the North Cottonwood will soon spread out as it meets the waters of Marion Lake.

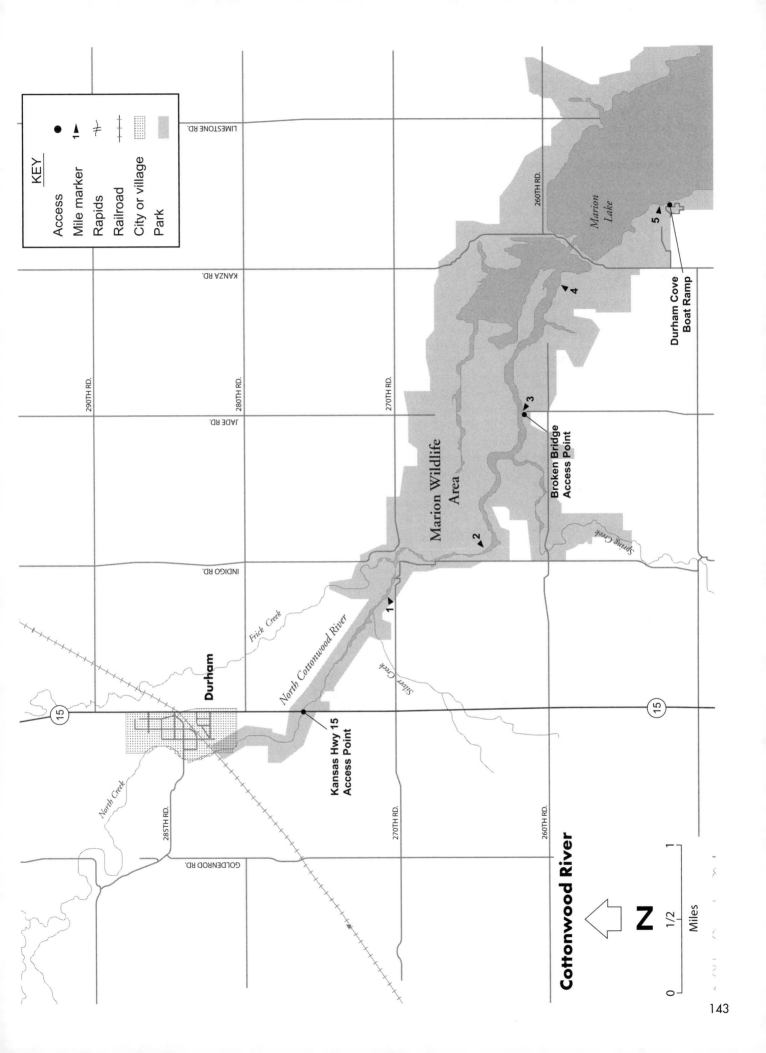

KEY

Access
Mile marker
Rapids
Railroad
City or village
Park

Marion Wildlife Area

Marion Lake

Durham Cove Boat Ramp

Broken Bridge Access Point

North Cottonwood River

Kansas Hwy 15 Access Point

Durham

Frick Creek

Silver Creek

Spring Creek

North Creek

LIMESTONE RD.

KANZA RD.

JADE RD.

INDIGO RD.

290TH RD.

280TH RD.

270TH RD.

260TH RD.

285TH RD.

GOLDENROD RD.

270TH RD.

260TH RD.

Cottonwood River

N

0   1/2   1

Miles

143

DEER TRACE CANOE TRAIL AND THE MINED LAND

Many trip and mileage choices, Class I difficulty
From Unit 21 Access Points

Unit 44 was the last working mine in the area and is the final resting place of Big Brutus, Bucyrus Erie Model 1850B, the second-largest electric shovel in the world. It is 16 stories tall (160 feet), weighs 11 million pounds, and has a boom 150 feet long and a dipper capacity of 90 cubic yards (150 tons), enough to fill three railroad cars with a single scoop. Its maximum speed was .22 mph and it cost $6.5 million in 1962. Big Brutus is on display near West Mineral, 6 miles west of the junction of State Highways 7 and 102 and a quarter mile south. The visitors' center has primitive camping, space for self-contained RVs, water/electrical hook-ups, a dump station, and hot-water showers.

The **Mined Land Wildlife Area** consists of 14,500 acres—1,500 acres of water and 13,000 acres of land. All but 2,000 acres of the property was surface-mined for coal from the 1920s through 1974. All of the mines in the area were closed due to the high sulfur content of the coal and are now flooded.

You can camp, paddle, hunt, and fish any of the strip-mined lakes in the Mined Land Wildlife Area. Most of the pits are surrounded by steep cliffs and dense forest. A few, such as Unit 41, are set in rolling native prairie grasses. From the lakes you can expect to see otters, beavers, bobcats, deer, and many other kinds of wildlife.

All of these lakes are Class I difficulty and are deep, clean, and cool. Though the paddling is easy, in some areas the walls of the quarries are steep and high and the water can be very deep and always cold. On windy days it is wise to stay on the smaller, better protected lakes, since getting yourself and your boat out of the water after a spill could be difficult.

The Deer Trace Canoe Trail—Cool, clear, clean water, plus great fishing.

Although these converted pit mines are neither rivers nor streams, their narrow channels and the high, rocky walls give some of them the feel of a clear, wide Ozark river. Swimming is not allowed, but I am told that as long as you have a fishing pole in your hand you can wade in as deep as you want.

This is rugged country, dotted with over 1,000 strip-mine lakes, steep-sided hills, and dense vegetation. The unmined areas consist of mature forested bottomland and small crop fields. The strip-mine lakes vary in size from a quarter acre to 50 acres, with depths to 60 feet. Native grass and some cool-season grasses dominate 4,000 acres of the property. The remaining 9,000 acres of land comprise bur oak, pin oak, walnut, hickory, and hackberry with a thick understory of dogwood, greenbrier, honeysuckle, poison ivy, and blackberry. The lakes are used primarily for fishing and the land for hunting, hiking, camping, viewing wildlife, and picking mushrooms and berries.

Except for the large lake in Unit 21, you need to have a valid hunting or fishing license in your possession to use these lakes. That lake was designated as the Deer Trace Canoe Trail and is the only lake that is open for public use without a hunting or fishing license. Camping is not permited near boat ramps.

The **Dear Trace Canoe Trail (Unit 21)** is 1.66 miles long, round-trip. To get there from Sherwin, go west on Old Highway 96 (aka State Highway 160) three-quarters of a mile to Northwest 70th Street. Then go north to Northwest Belleview Road. Turn west on Belleview Road and go one mile to Northwest 80th Street. (You can stop by the park office on Belleview Road.) Turn north and go one-quarter mile to the Deer Trace Canoe Trail on the east side of the road.

Take out and put in at almost, but not quite the same spot. The trail consists of two side-by-side lakes. Each lake has its own boat ramp; they are located almost across the parking lot from one another. You can leave from either ramp and return to the other by dragging your boat over a steep landmass that is located about two-thirds of a mile northeast from the boat ramps. Improvements on this passage were planned but have never been completed. You can paddle another mile or so farther northeast on either lake, but then return to the land bridge for your portage.

Again, be careful when paddling these lakes. The water is deep and cold and the sides are mostly vertical. Without skilled paddling buddies to help, in the event of a flip, you could find yourself in desperate trouble.

A good campsite would be hard to find on either of these two adjoining lakes. The walls are too steep to climb. Better choices for primitive camping sites near the water are found around the larger lakes in Units 23, 33, and 41.

Other cool stuff: A state record catfish was pulled out of one of these pits in 2003.

Local Contacts: Kansas Department of Wildlife and Parks, (620) 231-3173.

Deer Trace Canoe Trail

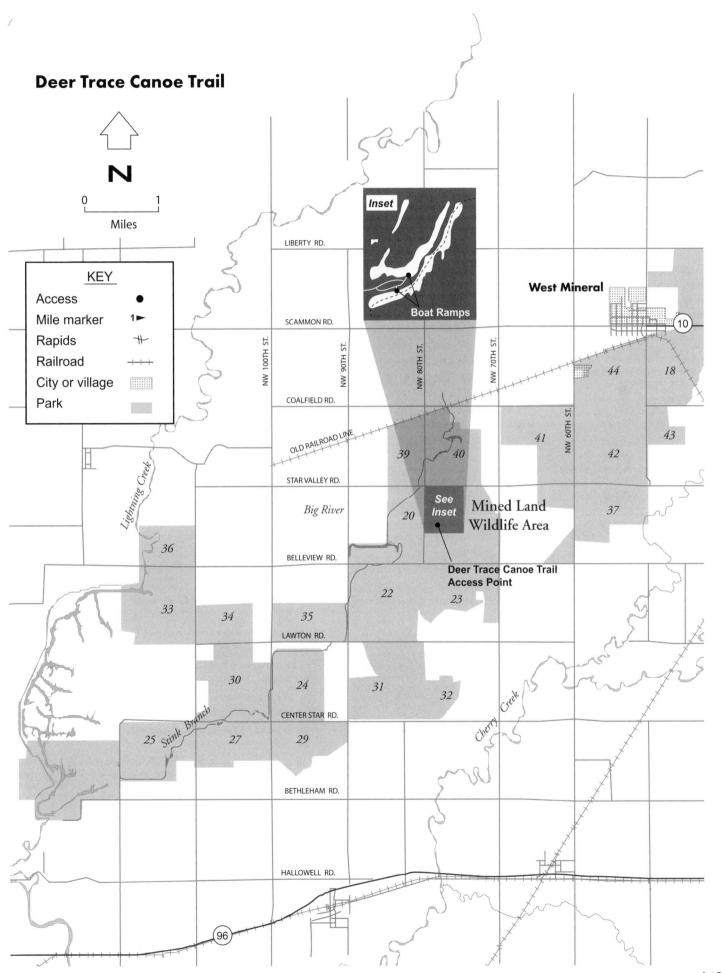

N

0   1
Miles

KEY

Access   •
Mile marker   1▶
Rapids   ╫
Railroad   ┼┼┼┼
City or village   ▦
Park   ▨

Inset

Boat Ramps

West Mineral

LIBERTY RD.

SCAMMON RD.

COALFIELD RD.

OLD RAILROAD LINE

STAR VALLEY RD.

Big River

BELLEVIEW RD.

LAWTON RD.

CENTER STAR RD.

BETHLEHAM RD.

HALLOWELL RD.

NW 100TH ST.
NW 90TH ST.
NW 80TH ST.
NW 70TH ST.
NW 60TH ST.

Lightning Creek

Stink Branch

Cherry Creek

See Inset

Mined Land Wildlife Area

Deer Trace Canoe Trail Access Point

10

96

36
33
34
35
30
24
31
32
25
27
29
22
23
20
39
40
41
42
43
37
44
18

VERDIGRIS RIVER ABOVE TORONTO LAKE

11.8 miles round-trip, intermediate access available, Class I difficulty
From Moon Bridge Boat Ramp

THE VERDIGRIS WATERSHED

The Verdigris River originates in southern Lyon County in southeastern Kansas and flows south to its confluence with the Arkansas River in southeast Oklahoma. Elevation ranges from about 1,500 feet at the headwaters to about 900 feet at the state line. The Verdigris Basin in Kansas covers approximately 4,440 square miles and encompasses all or part of 11 counties in the southeastern part of the state. Approximately one-third of the entire basin is in Kansas, with the lower two-thirds in Oklahoma. Major population centers include Independence, Coffeyville, Eureka, and Fredonia.

Surface water is abundant; however, river and stream flows are inconsistent, characterized by flooding during storms and low flows in dry weather. These conditions led to construction of four federal reservoirs in Kansas: Toronto, Fall River, Elk City, and Big Hill Lakes. The major tributaries in the basin are the Verdigris, Elk, Fall, Caney, and Little Caney Rivers and Big Hill and Caney Creeks.

Annual precipitation in the basin varies from approximately 34 inches in the west to almost 40 inches in the southeast corner. Land use is primarily grassland, especially in the western part of the basin.

The Verdigris River is at the very northern edge of the Cross-Timber physiographic region. Typical of this region, you will find large outcroppings of sandstone and growths of ancient post and blackjack oak forests in the upland areas and willow, cottonwood, and elm in the bottomlands. The channel is deep and wide near the lake, but becomes shallow where it has been silted over. If the lake is high enough, Cedar Creek and Brazil Creek make interesting detours. The lake and tributaries provide lunker-size crappie, plus good populations of white bass, black bass, largemouth bass, channel and flathead catfish, and walleye.

You can paddle one way with the use of a **shuttle** or, unless the river is high, paddle upstream or down from a launch at either Moon Bridge or the 130th Road Access and then return to your starting point. Alternately, you can paddle all the way to the Toronto Point Boat Ramp, but you will have to buy a park pass for the privilege. A water trail is planned that will start at Toronto Point and tour the many interesting natural features of the area. If you are in the state park, ask about it.

![The Verdigris River looking downstream from the Highway 54 bridge]

The Verdigris River looking downstream from the Highway 54 bridge

To estimate paddling time, figure about 1.5 to 2 miles per hour, unless the Verdigris has a significant discharge. At near conservation pool, the river is floatable all year unless frozen over. There are no **gauging stations** upstream on the river, but you can check the lake level at www.swt-wc.usace.army.mil/toro.lakepage.html. The average gradient between the Moon Bridge and the lake is about 2 feet per mile, but it is considerably steeper upstream.

Campsites are available around the lake (see map.) You can rent **canoes** and **kayaks** at Funk's Boats & Canoe Rental, 416 East River Street, in Eureka, (620) 583-6481 (days) or (620) 583-6345 (evenings).

To get to the Moon Bridge Boat Ramp from the U.S. Highway 54 bridge just east of State Highway 105 near Toronto, go west to GG Road and then south on the first road to the left, where County Road 33 joins from the right. Take that road to the river.

Put in and **take out** at the **Moon Bridge Boat Ramp**. Paddling upstream, it is 2.6 miles to the end of the public use area. After passing under Highway 54, the river will soon begin to narrow. The hills and banks rise slightly. Downstream from the Moon Bridge Ramp, it is 3.3 miles to the 130th Road Access and the Main Street Access, 4.7 miles to the Carlisle Road Access, and 5.7 miles to the Toronto Point Boat Ramp. See the map for driving directions. If the lake is a little low, the river will be too shallow for motorized boats.

Other cool stuff: Walnut Creek, on the northwest arm of the lake, is very beautiful. (This trip is described in the next section.) You can use the Carlisle Access on that creek to paddle either stream. In fact, when paddling the Verdigris River, the Carlisle Access is one mile shorter and far less windy than crossing the lake to Toronto Point.

Local Contacts: U.S. Army Corps of Engineers, (620) 658-4445; Toronto Wildlife Area, (620) 583-6783; State Park Office, (620) 637-2213.

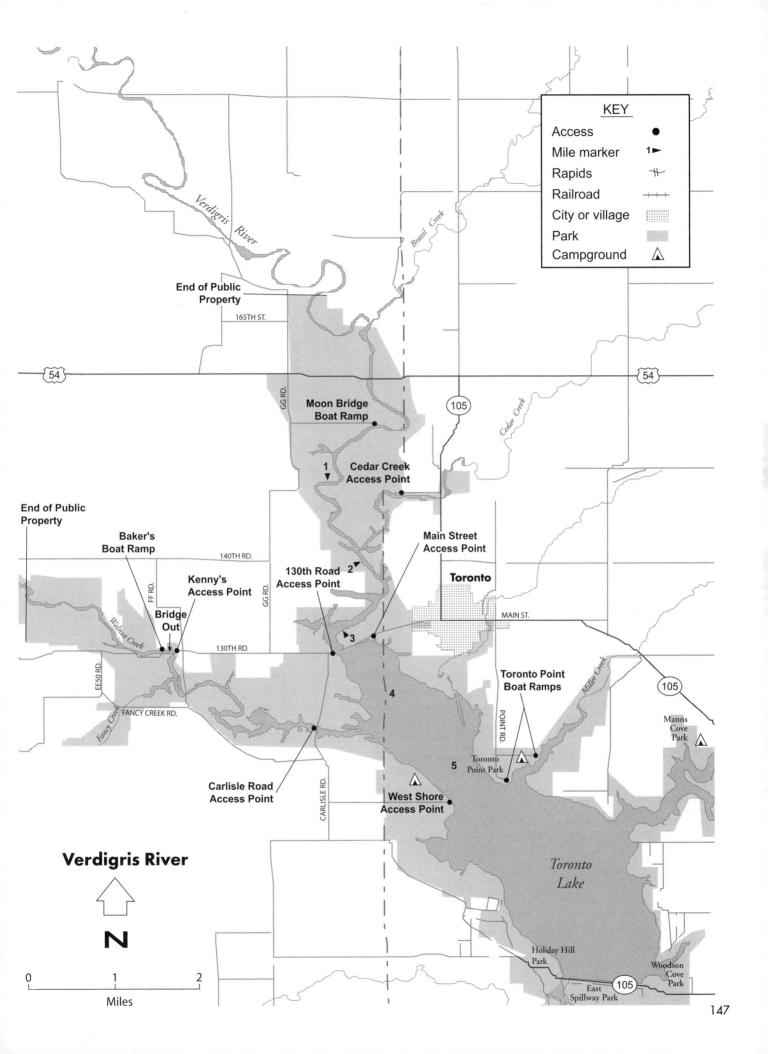

KEY

Access ●

Mile marker 1▶

Rapids ⌗

Railroad ┼┼┼

City or village ▒

Park ▒

Campground ⛺

Verdigris River

Brazil Creek

Cedar Creek

End of Public Property

165TH ST.

54

GG RD.

Moon Bridge Boat Ramp

1▼

Cedar Creek Access Point

105

Main Street Access Point

Toronto

End of Public Property

Baker's Boat Ramp

Kenny's Access Point

140TH RD.

130th Road Access Point

2▶

GG RD.

FF RD.

Bridge Out

Walnut Creek

130TH RD.

3▶

MAIN ST.

EE50 RD.

FANCY CREEK RD.

Fancy Creek

4

Toronto Point Boat Ramps

Miller Creek

POINT RD.

105

Manns Cove Park

Carlisle Road Access Point

CARLISLE RD.

5

Toronto Point Park ⛺

⛺

West Shore Access Point ⛺

Toronto Lake

Verdigris River

⬆

N

0   1   2

Miles

Holiday Hill Park

Woodson Cove Park

East Spillway Park

105

147

WALNUT CREEK ABOVE TORONTO LAKE

**10.6 miles round-trip, intermediate access points available, Class I difficulty
From Carlisle Road Access**

The Cross-Timber Physiographic Region

The lake and surrounding area are at the northernmost tip of the Cross-Timber physiographic region. The post oak and blackjack oaks in this area grow so slow in the infertile sandstone soil that a 20 to 50 feet tall tree may be 400 years old. These ancient trees were already old in the days of George Washington. Unlike other old growth forests in nearby areas, the upland oaks were spared from cutting because they grew neither straight nor tall and because traveling by wagon through this rocky, brush cover area was too difficult to attract many settlers.

Walnut Creek is the best part of the Toronto Lake area from a river-lovers perspective. Vistas of beautiful hills, interesting rock formations, unique hardwood forests, and a variety of paddling experiences set the stage for a beautiful day on the water. The lake and tributaries provide lunker-size crappie, plus good populations of white bass, black bass, largemouth bass, walleye, channel and flathead catfish, freshwater drum, bluegill, and other sunfish.

There are several good ways to enjoy this beautiful stream. You can launch at the Carslisle Road Access and paddle 5.6 miles upstream to the end of the public use area and back (11.2 miles round-trip). You can also start from the Baker Boat Ramp or Kenny's Access and paddle 4.6 round-trip miles upstream to the end of the public use area and back and then downstream to the Carlisle Road Access and back (6.6 miles round-trip). Some touring paddlers enjoy launching at Toronto Point Boat Ramp on the east side of the Toronto Lake and then paddling two miles across open water to start their trip.

Your float on the creek is typically all on backwater from the lake unless the creek is running high. There are no **gauging stations** on the creek, but you can check the **lake level** at www.swt-wc.usace.army.mil/toro.lake page.html. The average **gradient** between the upper reach of the public use area and the Carlisle Road Access is 4 feet per mile, but most of this is flatwater unless the lake is low.

Camping is not allowed along the river, but good campsites are available

Jim Johnson on Walnut Creek near Kenny's Access. In the background, sandstone outcroppings and old growths of post oak and blackjack oak line the shore.

around the lake. (See map.) You can **rent or buy** new or used canoes and kayaks or arrange for guided canoe and backpack trips at Funk's Boats & Canoe Rental, 416 East River Street, in Eureka, at (620) 583-6481 (days) or (620) 583-6345 (evenings).

Unless you are planning a one-way trip, running a **shuttle** is not necessary. Road navigation on the often unmarked back roads of this area will require the use of my map. Please note that Fancy Creek Road and EE50 Road had not been named at this writing, so I took the liberty of naming them myself for the purpose of this book. If the road names in this section do not match the road signs (if any), you will know why.

The **put-in** of choice is at the **Carlisle Road Access**. To get there from U. S. Highway 54, go south on FF75 Road (County Road 33). This joins GG Road. Continue on GG Road (County Road 33) to 130th Road. Go west on 130th to FF Road. Go south on FF and follow it around the wide curve to Carlisle Road. Take the small dirt road north to the creek. East of the old bridge pilings is an unmaintained concrete slab; it is not a boat ramp but it may serve as a ramp during dry conditions. If you are launching a heavy boat on a trailer, check the "ramp" before using it. The area in the bottoms is too muddy for use during wet weather. In that case, use Kenny's Access (see details below).

Put in and **take out** at the **Carlisle Road Access**. From here it is 5.3 miles upstream to the end of the public use area. Moving upstream, the river closes in very slowly as it becomes increasingly scenic. The creek is wide and deep enough for power boats for the first 2.5-3 miles up the creek. This is hog heaven during the white bass run. Once upstream of the Baker Boat Ramp and Kenny's Access, the river narrows quickly and becomes woodsy enough for small creek lovers. The sandstone bluffs of small tributaries like Fancy Creek and the rocky upper reaches of the public use area, combined with the open vistas of the rolling hills on the wider sections, make for a photogenic day on the water.

Kenny's Access is located on the east side of the river and west of the intersection of 130th and FF Roads, where the old Baker Bridge once stood. By stream it is 2 miles downstream to the Carlisle Access and 2.5 miles upstream to the end of the public use area. This is a good access and is easier to get to than the Baker Boat Ramp, which is on the other side of the creek. The Baker Boat Ramp is a good access, but not worth the drive, unless you need a boat ramp or are already on that side of the river.

Other cool stuff: A few miles upstream of the Baker Boat Ramp is a beautiful river crossing called Rocky Ford. Sandstone creates both a low dam and a very long shelf that has been a historic crossing for many years. To get there, go west on 130th Road and then north on CC Road to the ford.

The Carlisle Access (above) also provides good access to the Verdigris River. See the section on the Verdigris River for more details.

Local Contacts: U.S. Army Corps of Engineers (Toronto Lake), (620) 658-4445; Toronto Wildlife Area, (620) 583-6783; State Park Office, (620) 637-2213.

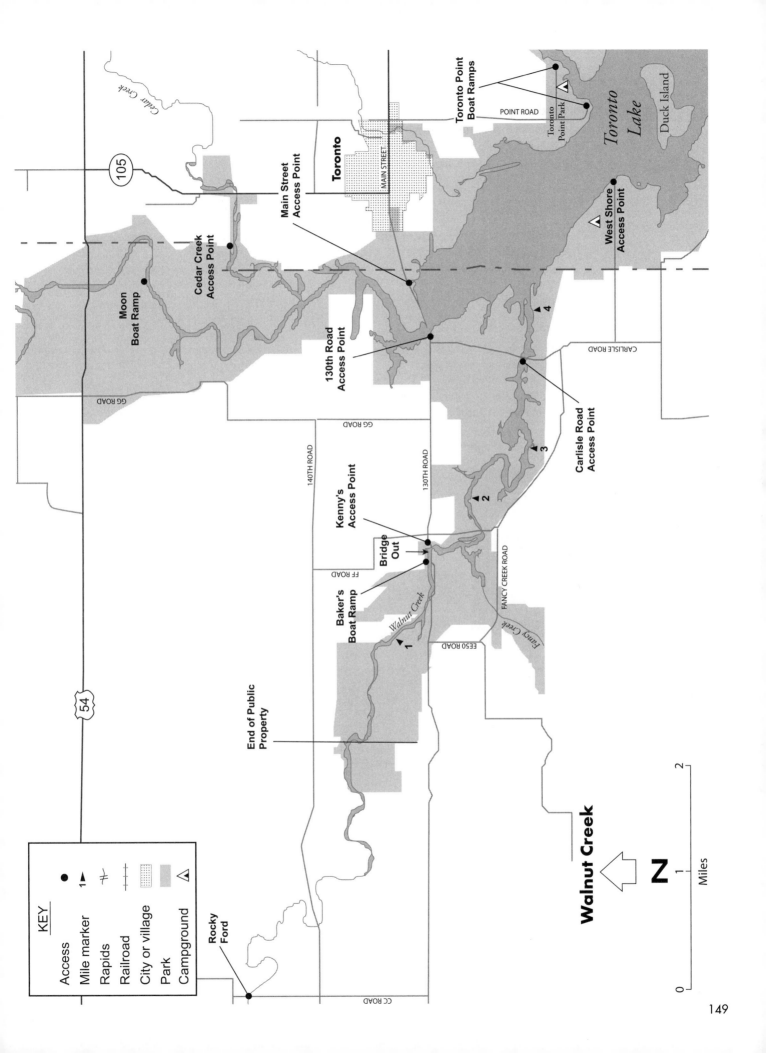

KEY

● Access
▲1 Mile marker
⼯ Rapids
╫ Railroad
▦ City or village
▨ Park
△ Campground

Walnut Creek

N

Miles
0   1   2

Rocky Ford

End of Public Property

Baker's Boat Ramp

Kenny's Access Point

Bridge Out

Moon Boat Ramp

Cedar Creek Access Point

Main Street Access Point

130th Road Access Point

Carlisle Road Access Point

West Shore Access Point

Toronto Point Boat Ramps

Toronto

Toronto Lake

Duck Island

Toronto Point Park

Cedar Creek

54

105

GG ROAD

GG ROAD

140TH ROAD

130TH ROAD

FF ROAD

EE50 ROAD

CC ROAD

FANCY CREEK ROAD

CARLISLE ROAD

POINT ROAD

MAIN STREET

Walnut Creek

Fancy Creek

1

2

3

4

FALL RIVER ABOVE FALL RIVER LAKE
10 miles, intermediate access points available, Class I-II+ difficulty
Hughes Crossing to Climax Boat Ramp

The Fall River is a paradox. For touring paddlers who enjoy long, serene pools, the Fall is blessed with one of the longest and most beautiful natural pools in the state. For whitewater enthusiasts, it has two of the most beautiful, publicly accessible and runnable rapids in the state. For wildlife enthusiasts, the whole river is set within a wildlife management area and crosses through a waterfowl refuge. Although the river is open for recreation all year, some parts of the waterfowl refuge are closed from October 1 to March 1. White bass, crappie, largemouth bass, and flathead catfish are all seasonal favorites for anglers.

The Fall River is Class I-II difficulty. Downed trees can block the channel and strainers are not uncommon. It takes about 3.5 to 6 hours to paddle from Hughes Crossing to the Ladd Bridge Boat Ramp. Alternate accesses along the way and farther downstream provide unlimited possibilities. **Minimum recommended flows** depend on what you want out of your trip. It takes at least **150 CFS** to clear the first half mile of small riffles. If you don't mind dragging your boat over those few riffles, you can paddle the 5-plus-mile-long pool to Mossy Ford, regardless of flow. If you want to have a clean run at Mossy Ford and Twin Falls (aka "Rock Ledge"), you will want **200-400 CFS**.

The Fall River near Hughes Crossing at low flow. At this level, it will be necessary to portage several gravel bars near the put-in, but the long pools below will reward your efforts.

There are **no gauging stations** upstream. To roughly calculate flows, use the Fall River Lake outflow gauge and the lake's precipitation gauge. If the inflow looks healthy and the area has had enough rain, go for it. You should also check the USGS gauging station on Otter Creek at Climax to get an idea of what local creeks are doing. If Otter Creek is running above 150-200 feet, chances are very good that the Fall River is up as well. The **average gradient** between Hughes Crossing and Mossy Ford is a respectable 6 feet per mile.

Camping is not allowed along the river, but good campsites are available at designated sites around the lake. (See map.) You can **rent boats** at Funk's Boats & Canoe Rental, 416 East River Street, Eureka, at (620) 583-6481 (days) or (620) 583-6345 (evenings), open April through October.

To get to the **put-in** at the **Hughes Crossing Access**, from the intersection of State Highways 400 and 99, go north about 11 miles (past Climax) to 130th Road, then east one mile to T Road, then two miles south to the access. Under wet conditions, park on the gravel and carry your gear 200 yards to the river. The 28-mile **round-trip shuttle** goes back to State Highway 99, then south to 70th Road, and then east about 5 miles to the southwest edge of the Ladd Bridge. (Climax Boat Ramp).

Put in at **Hughes Crossing**. There is a short riffle just downstream of the access. The half mile will be a mix of riffles, pools, and ledges. Once past these, a natural pool extends all the way to Mossy Ford, more than 5 miles downstream. Near the 3-mile mark, the river crosses under Rice Bridge. There is an access on river right immediately upstream and one about one-quarter mile downstream of the bridge. The upstream access is best suited for wet conditions.

At **Mossy Ford** the river changes character in an instant. The river suddenly accelerates, broadens, and divides across a monolithic washboard of steeply slanted rock shelves. This is no place for a canoe loaded with fishing gear and coolers. Even with empty boats, novice paddlers are advised to take out on river right, above the first drop to scout this run. Choose your poison: right, left, and middle look entirely different at low, medium, and high water levels. This is the first of two Class II-II+ rapids. The next, **Twin Falls**, is less than a mile farther downstream. Here the river splits around a tall island. The left route might be a little less scratchy at low flows.

Downstream of the bottom rock ledge, the river meets the pool of Fall River Lake. Less than a half mile downstream, Otter Creek enters on river right. After passing Otter Creek, watch for the **Lower Otter Creek Bridge Access.**; it is at the large rocky ledge and gravel bar on river right. Use of this access can shorten a float by almost 3 miles. From here to Ladd Bridge, the pool deepens and gravel bars are buried in water or the muddy deposits from the lake. The **take-out** is at **The Climax Boat Ramp**, on river right, just downstream of the Ladd bridge.

If you have the time, there is still another 5 miles of river and lake between the Ladd Bridge and Fall River State Park. Alternately, you can paddle up Otter Creek until you come to its first riffle.

Local Contacts: U.S. Army Corps of Engineers, (316) 658-4445.

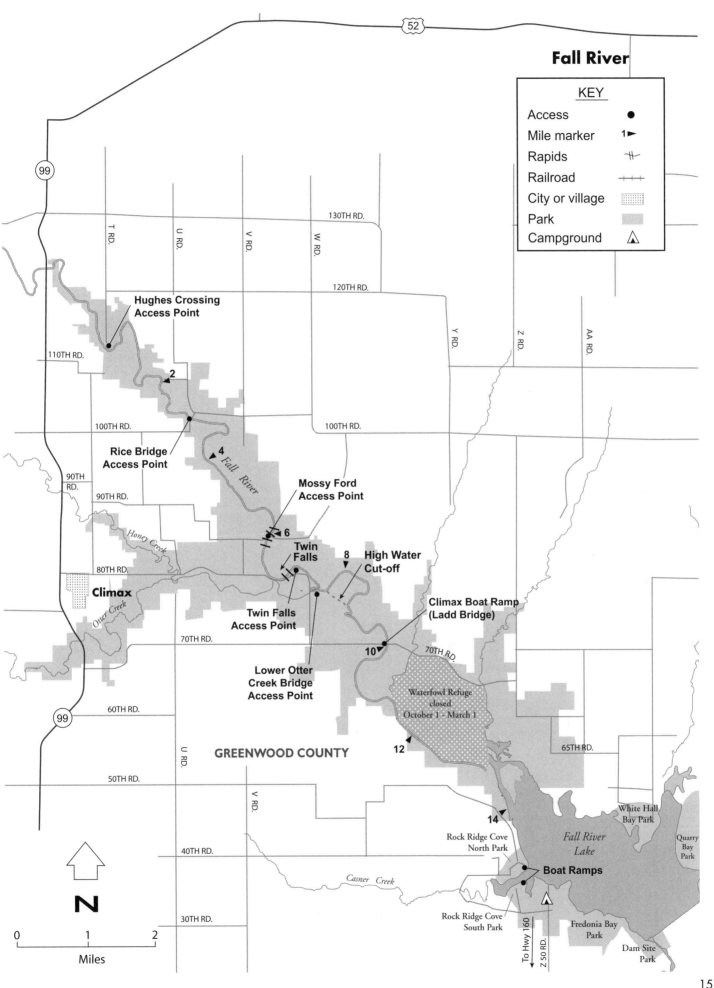

Fall River

KEY

Access	●
Mile marker	1►
Rapids	⌗
Railroad	┼┼┼
City or village	⣿
Park	▒
Campground	⛺

Hughes Crossing
Access Point

2

Rice Bridge
Access Point

4 *Fall River*

Mossy Ford
Access Point

6

Twin
Falls

8

High Water
Cut-off

Climax Boat Ramp
(Ladd Bridge)

Honey Creek

Climax

Otter Creek

Twin Falls
Access Point

10

Lower Otter
Creek Bridge
Access Point

GREENWOOD COUNTY

Waterfowl Refuge
closed
October 1 - March 1

12

14

White Hall
Bay Park

*Fall River
Lake*

Quarry
Bay
Park

Rock Ridge Cove
North Park

Casner Creek

N

Boat Ramps

Rock Ridge Cove
South Park

To Hwy 160

Z 50 RD.

*Fredonia Bay
Park*

Dam Site
Park

0   1   2

Miles

OTTER CREEK ABOVE FALL RIVER LAKE
6 miles, intermediate access points available, Class I-II+ difficulty
Upper Access to Lower Otter Creek Bridge Access

If you can catch Otter Creek with enough water in it, you'll be on one of the most enjoyable creek runs in the area. With a narrow channel, riffles, gravel bars, and rocky ledges, this creek can be both a challenge and a joy. Novice paddlers are advised not to attempt this run except at low flows due to the danger posed by river-wide strainers.

Minimum recommended flows of 50-80 CFS may still be a little scratchy, but will get you from the Upper Access to the Lower Otter Creek Bridge Access in one to two hours. The average **gradient** on Otter Creek is a pleasant 7 feet per mile. With that much gradient, the creek can get very pushy as the flow increases. And it can increase very quickly—the flow can go from 0 to 2,000 CFS in a flash. The USGS **gauging station** on Otter Creek at Climax will give you a good reading, but this little creek goes up and comes back down very quickly. If you are at the put-in and have enough water to make it past the first gravel bar without scratching bottom and if you don't hear thunder, you'll probably be fine.

Camping is not allowed along the river, but good campsites are available at designated sites around the Fall River Lake. Fredonia Bay is a good choice and not far from your boating on Otter Creek and Fall River. You can rent boats at Funk's Boats & Canoe Rental, 416 East River Street, Eureka, at (620) 583-6481 (days) or (620) 583-6345 (evenings), open April through October.

The **put-in** is at the **Upper Access**, located on the first small farm road south and west of the State Highway

99 bridge over Otter Creek (not 70th Road). The road is not suitable for wet conditions; use the Mile 2 Access instead. (See map.) The 11-mile **round-trip shuttle** route, from the Upper Access to the take-out, goes back to Highway 99, then north to 80th Road, and then east, following 80th Road past the land bridge between Otter Creek and the Fall River. After the land bridge, the road curves south and crosses over Otter Creek. Immediately after the Otter Creek Bridge, turn left (east) and follow the access road down to the Lower Otter Creek Bridge Access (on the Fall River).

At the **put-in** at the Upper Access, a nice gravel bar and a small riffle make a good launch pad. The creek is narrow and the channel is lined with gravel and rock. Trees often arch over the creek, making it seem like a tunnel of green foliage, rock, and water. When these trees fall, they can block the channel, creating dangerous strainers at moderate and high flows. At other times, the channel is wide and deep, but you are never far from the next riffle. Near the half-mile point, the river crosses under Highway 99. At about mile 1, pilings from an abandoned bridge and a fair-weather road come down from 70th Road on river right. At mile 1.2, another all-weather access comes down on river right, also from 70th Road. The creek has far more tight turns and small meanders than the map can show; your actual mileage will be slightly more than the map indicates, but between about mile 2.5 and mile 3, Otter Creek roughly parallels 80th Road, just on the other side of the trees. Where Honey Creek enters, a fair-weather road approaches on river left, downstream of the confluence. Near mile 5, Otter Creek divides as it crosses a giant rock shelf. At minimum flows, the right channel seems to be slightly less scratchy. At moderate to high flows, it is a long, fast slide any way you go. Road signs become visible at the approach of a land bridge that separates Otter Creek from the Fall River, near mile 5.2. At normal conservation pool, Fall River Lake typically backs up to this land bridge. Another few bends and a half mile of paddling reveal the Otter Creek Bridge. A few hundred yards beyond the bridge is the confluence with the Fall River.

Take out at the **Lower Otter Creek Bridge Access** on the large rock ledge and gravel bar, on river right downstream of the confluence with the Fall River. Alternately, the Ladd Bridge is only another 2.7 more miles downstream, and Fredonia Bay and Rock Ridge Cove are only another 5 miles beyond that. That trip is worth a day of paddling on its own merits.

Other cool stuff: Paddle the Fall River while you're here.

Local Contacts: U.S. Army Corps of Engineers, (316) 658-4445.

Otter Creek showing off its narrow, rock-strewn channel at bare minimum flow.

Otter Creek

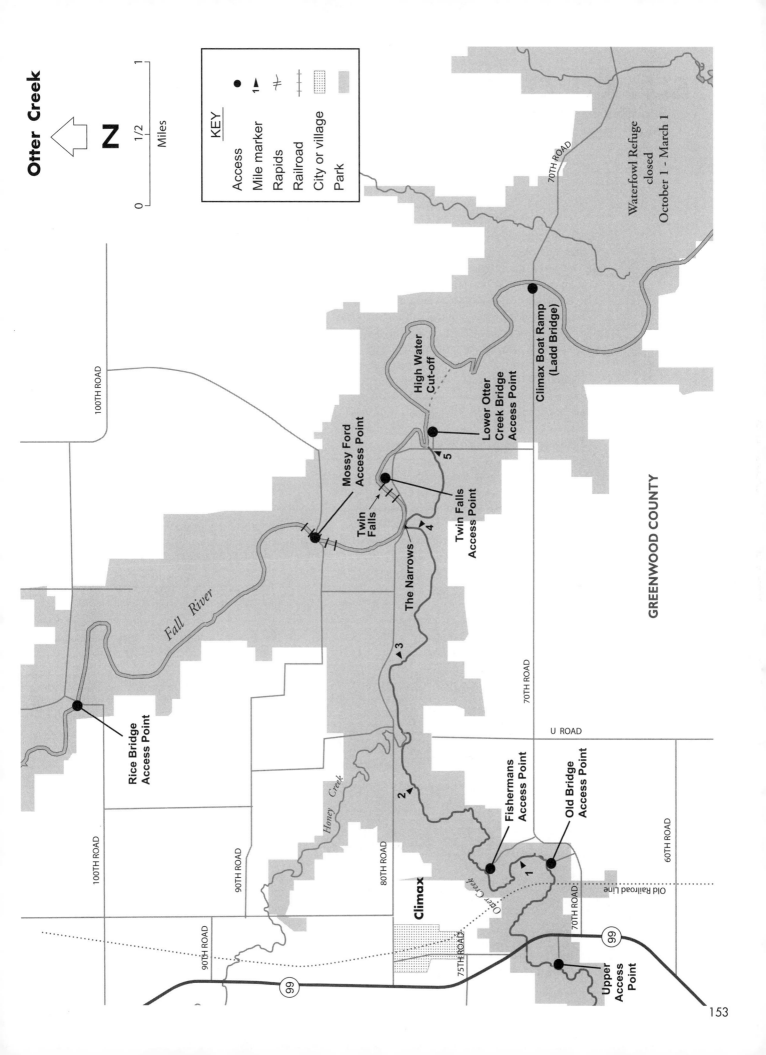

N

Miles
0   1/2   1

KEY

- ● Access
- ▲ Mile marker
- ⊣⊢ Rapids
- ╫ Railroad
- ▨ City or village
- ▨ Park

Rice Bridge Access Point

Fall River

Honey Creek

Mossy Ford Access Point

Twin Falls

The Narrows

Twin Falls Access Point

High Water Cut-off

Lower Otter Creek Bridge Access Point

Climax Boat Ramp (Ladd Bridge)

Waterfowl Refuge closed October 1 - March 1

GREENWOOD COUNTY

Climax

Otter Creek

Fishermans Access Point

Old Bridge Access Point

Upper Access Point

Old Railroad Line

100TH ROAD

90TH ROAD

80TH ROAD

75TH ROAD

70TH ROAD

70TH ROAD

70TH ROAD

60TH ROAD

U ROAD

70TH ROAD

99

99

ELK RIVER ABOVE ELK CITY LAKE

9.2 miles, intermediate access points available, Class I-II difficulty
Elk City Boat Ramp to Card Creek Boat Ramp

This wonderful, rocky-bottom river flows over small ledges and gravel bars within the boundaries of the Elk City Wildlife Area. Sand-and gravel bars are common and the riffles are nicely spaced throughout the first four miles. Thereafter, the river is a long, peaceful arm of Elk City Lake. The channel can become narrow through some of the riffles. Downed trees and strainers often block these narrow slots. Anglers say the white bass, crappie, cats, largemouth, pan fish, and walleye are fair downstream of Iron Bridge.

From top to bottom, it takes only three to five hours to paddle from Elk City to Card Creek, depending on flow and dawdling time. The **minimum recommended flow** for a lightly loaded canoe is about **100 CFS**, but you can get by with less if you don't mind dragging bottom occasionally. The **gauging station** is a fair distance upstream at Elk Falls, so you can usually expect to see more water than the gauge indicates. The **average gradient** is an enjoyable 3.2 feet per mile. **Camping** is not allowed along the river, but the state park at Card Creek has good campsites, group shelters, a boat ramp, and pit toilets. (See the Elk City Lake map.)

The **put-in** is at the **Elk City Boat Ramp** west of the intersection of U.S. Highway 160 and 5250 Road (aka Hickory Street). To get there from the intersection, go west of Elk City on 5250 Road (Hickory) across the bridge, then take the first right turn to the ramp. Your 28-mile **round-trip shuttle** route from the Elk City Boat Ramp to the Card Creek Boat Ramp and back takes you back east to Highway 160, then south, following the highway first south, then east. Turn north on 2500 Road (not marked) and follow the "Card Creek" signs north and then west to the Card Creek Ramp.

Put in at the **Elk City Boat Ramp**. The riffles start soon after you cross under the Hickory Street bridge. Depending on flows, there are a dozen or so riffles in the first four miles. The second drop, less than a half mile down-stream of the bridge, is a small ledge that can be surfed at low to moderate flows. The Riffle Access near river mile 1.2 is served by a fair-weather road. Just below this access is the first significant rapid. Here the river divides into at least three channels. The left channel sports surfing ledges at the top and bottom but is partially blocked by timber. The middle route is an easy, straightforward run. The right route is usually too shallow. Near the bottom of the next riffle, watch for a large eddy on river right. The eddy is called **Simmons Round Hole** and is served by a fair-weather access road.

From there, **Newkirk's Ford Fishing Access** is only another half mile downstream on river left. Then it is only another half mile to Salt Creek and the **Iron Bridge Access**. The old iron bridge was replaced by a new concrete structure, but the name stuck. Fishermen frequently use the gravel bar just upstream of the bridge. The access is just downstream of the bridge on river right.

At normal pool, the water from Elk City Lake backs up to the riffle at Iron Bridge. From there to Card Creek, 6.5 miles downstream, there are no riffles or public access points. The fast shallow water becomes a long, deep pool that is favored by fishermen, novice paddlers, and tour boats.

Card Creek enters from river right near river mile 9. The mouth of the creek is wide and deep and makes a great diversion. The Card Creek Area is just around the next bend. **Take out** at the **Card Creek Boat Ramp** on river right.

Other cool stuff: From the Card Creek Boat Ramp you can paddle 2.5 miles up Card Creek (5 miles round-trip) or you can launch at the Barren Bottoms Access. (See map.) This clear little stream meanders among hills and then opens up on the west side to a wide floodplain. Card Creek is a worthy destination at any flow when the lake is near conservation pool. The flood control pool reaches all the way to U.S. Highway 160, so if the lake is very high, there is the potential for a lot of exploration. For hikers and back-packers, the Elk River Hiking Trail parallels the north side of the river and lake; it is said to be one of the best hiking trails in the state. The west trailhead is north of the river at the Highway 160 bridge and the east trailhead is at the project office, just northwest of the Elk City Lake Dam. The trail can also be accessed off 2100 Road and in the Oak Ridge Area along the river.

Local Contacts: U.S. Army Corps of Engineers, (620) 336-2741; State Park Office, (620) 331-6295; Kansas Department of Wildlife and Parks, Elk City Wildlife Area, (620) 331-6820.

The Elk River's rocky riverbed creates pleasant riffles.

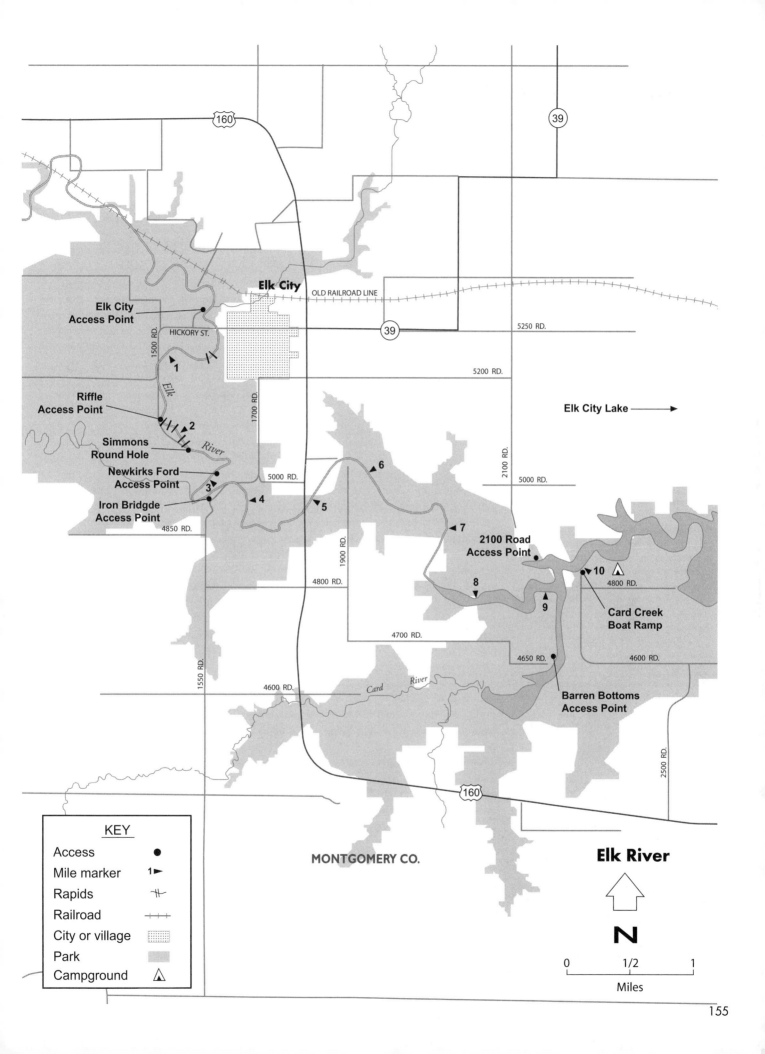

Elk City

Elk City Access Point

HICKORY ST.

1500 RD.

1

Elk

Riffle Access Point

2

Simmons Round Hole

River

Newkirks Ford Access Point

3

Iron Bridgde Access Point

4850 RD.

4

5

6

1700 RD.

5000 RD.

1900 RD.

4800 RD.

4700 RD.

4600 RD.

1550 RD.

Card

River

MONTGOMERY CO.

OLD RAILROAD LINE

39

5250 RD.

5200 RD.

Elk City Lake →

2100 RD.

5000 RD.

7

2100 Road Access Point

8

9

10

4800 RD.

Card Creek Boat Ramp

4650 RD.

4600 RD.

Barren Bottoms Access Point

2500 RD.

160

39

160

KEY

Access	●
Mile marker	1▶
Rapids	ǂ
Railroad	┼┼┼
City or village	▦
Park	▨
Campground	⛺

Elk River

N

0   1/2   1

Miles

LITTLE CANEY RIVER ABOVE COPAN LAKE

2 miles (limited by logjams), Class I difficulty, plus a very dangerous dam
From Caney Waterworks Access

COPAN LAKE is just west and south of Caney, across the Oklahoma border. To get to the project office, drive south on U.S. Highway 75 to State Highway 10, then west about two miles to the dam. The project office is just to the right (north) before the dam. The lake has a number of campgrounds along the south shore and services and supplies are available at convenient locations on access roads leading to the lake. You can reserve a campsite at (877) 444-6777 (National Recreation Reservation Service). The lake has large uncleared areas and artificial fish shelters that were constructed prior to impoundment. The excellent habitats support good populations of largemouth bass, white crappie, channel and flathead catfish, and various species of sunfish. The lake has also received an experimental stocking of the hybrid cross between the white bass and the striped bass, more commonly called the wiper.

PICNICKING AND SWIMMING: Copan Point has been set up as the lake's day use area. This park offers a designated beach area, beautiful picnic sites overlooking the water, and a nicely constructed boat-launching ramp. (See the Copan Lake map in the Appendix.)

The Little Caney River above Copan Lake is a Class I difficulty float that takes you through part of the 2,360-acre Copan Wildlife Area. The beautifully diverse habitat includes riparian woodlands, native grasslands, croplands, and waterfowl marshes. There is plenty of wildlife for hunting, fishing, or just watching.

There are two distinct sections covered here, the backwater of Copan Lake and the pond above the Caney Waterworks Dam. Both segments attract anglers from far and wide. White bass and crappie travel upstream from Copan Lake in Oklahoma to spawn. These and other species provide excellent fishing. Upstream of the Caney Waterworks Dam, channel and flathead catfish and largemouth and spotted bass are found in the deep holes and along undercut banks. Big bass hang out beneath overhanging trees and around old tree stumps.

At high flows, the hydraulic at the bottom of the Caney Waterworks Dam is deadly. **Do not approach the dam** from above or below when significant water is flowing over it. To an inexperienced boater, the danger may not be obvious. For a disabled boat or an unintentional swimmer, the consequences may be unavoidable. At high flows, the hydraulic at the bottom recirculates anything and everything that comes within its giant grasp. On shore, one slip on the severely sloped concrete slab next to the dam during high-water conditions could send you into the water to certain death by drowning. Until the responsible parties change the hydraulics at the bottom of this dam, provide a safety lip at the top of the slab, change the slope of the surrounding slab, put up warning signs (on land and on the water), and close the area to the public during periods of high flow, this whole thing is a deadly drowning machine of the worst kind. You have been warned!

Below the Caney Waterworks Dam, the Little Caney is in the backwater of Copan Lake. Above the Caney Waterworks Dam the river is in the backwater above that dam with an average **gradient** of less than .5 feet per mile. Other than at high flows or when it is frozen over, both sections are floatable all year. Check the USGS **gauging station** at Caney River near Elgin. **Camping** is not allowed along the river, but is available at designated campgrounds around Copan Lake. (Go south on Hwy. 75 into Oklahoma.)

The **put-in and take-out** are at the **Caney Waterworks Access**. The waterworks is northwest of the town of Caney. From U.S. Highway 75 and 1600 Road, go about three-quarters of a mile west on 1600 Road and then north on 1300 Road. Continue north about a quarter mile to the first gravel road west. Take this down to the Caney Waterworks Dam. The road and parking area are muddy when wet. You'll find a place to slide a canoe into the river, about 100 yards below the dam and another access about 50 yards above the dam. You can paddle upstream or downstream as far as the logjams will let you pass. Do not approach the dam from above or below if significant water is going over it.

The public use area extends roughly 1.5 miles upstream of the waterworks dam. Below the dam it is 2 miles to the **Wolf Creek Access**, but logjams typically blockade the channel, so most paddlers put in or take out at the same spot.

To get to the Wolf Creek Access from the town of Caney, go west on 6th Avenue, which becomes County Road 1400 (aka Bronco Road, aka County Road 89). Turn north on Road 24 (aka Road 32), then go east on Cowboy Road, and turn south on 1100 Road. Follow 1100 Road to the access. This access is not suitable for wet conditions or heavy boats. The banks can be very muddy and are steep. Put in and take out at the same spot, since logjams will prevent long-range passage both upstream and downstream. Wolf Creek enters just upstream of the access. If the logjams clear out, your next access is 7 miles downstream at the Cottonwood Creek Access in Oklahoma.

Other cool stuff: The river is surrounded by natural wetlands. The town of Caney got its name from the river and from the canebrakes that were growing in the natural wetlands near the town site in 1871. The town claims to have been the site of the first glass manufacturer in Kansas, beginning in 1902.

Local Contacts: Kansas Department of Wildlife and Parks, (620) 331-6820.

The Little Caney above Copan Lake

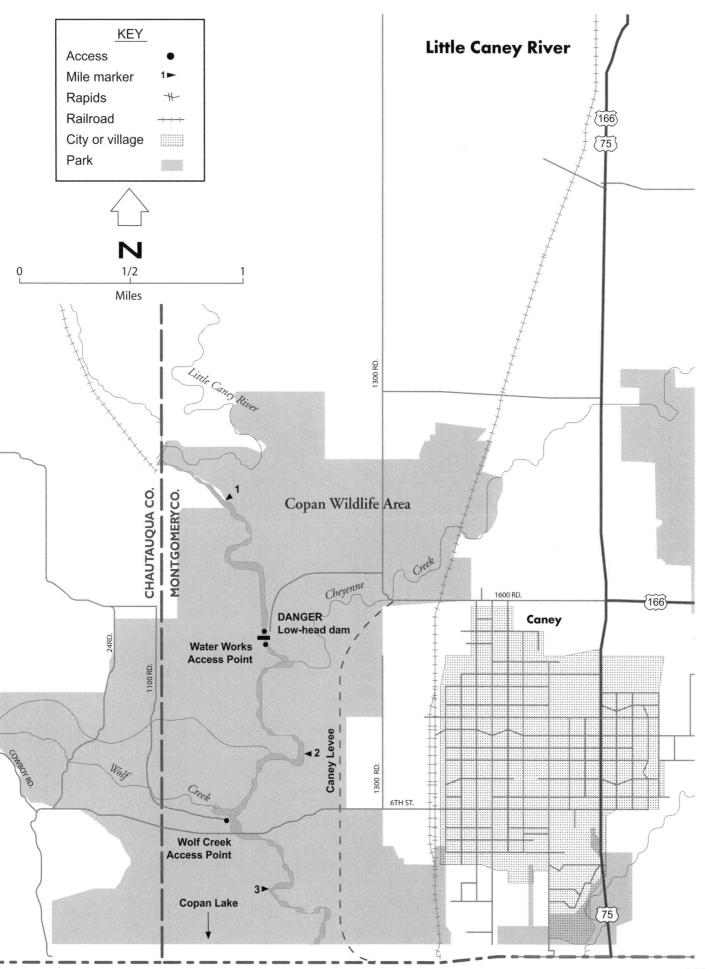

Little Caney River

KEY

Access	●
Mile marker	1▶
Rapids	╫
Railroad	┼┼┼
City or village	▦
Park	▨

N

0   1/2   1

Miles

166
75

1300 RD.

Little Caney River

1▶

Copan Wildlife Area

Creek

Cheyenne

1600 RD.

166

Caney

DANGER
Low-head dam

**Water Works
Access Point**

CHAUTAUQUA CO.
MONTGOMERY CO.

24 RD.

1100 RD.

Caney Levee

1300 RD.

6TH ST.

COWBOY RD.

Wolf

Creek

▶2

**Wolf Creek
Access Point**

3▶

Copan Lake

75

APPENDIX 1

Trip Distances, Difficulties, and Scenic Values

Mileages in this chart are rounded to the nearest mile. The Scenic Value Ratings, which range from A (best) to D, are entirely subjective, based on the author's preference for:

- Free-flowing rivers and streams
- Uninterrupted native scenery
- River-and stream-banks that are undamaged by excessive erosion
- Natural streambeds that are not silted over by agricultural soils
- Waters that are not otherwise visibly, physically, biologically, or chemically impaired
- Habitat that supports a natural diversity of native fish and other wildlife
- An absence of noise pollution

RIVER AND SEGMENT	MILES	CLASS	SCENIC RATING
Missouri River	121	II	C
White Cloud	26	II	C
Nodaway Island	10	II	C
St. Joseph	29	II	C
Atchison	25	II	C
Leavenworth	31	II	C
Kansas River	170	I	B-D
Junction City	7	I	B
Ogden	14	I	B
Manhattan	12	I	B
St. George	10	I	B
Wamego	12	I	B
Belvue	9	I	B
Maple Hill	29	I	B
Topeka	10	I	B-D
Perry	12	I	B
Lawrence	12	I	B
Eudora	11	I	B
DeSoto	15	I	B
Wilder Road	17	I	D
Republican River	13	I	B
Above Milford Lake	5	I	B
Below Milford Lake	8	I	B
Saline River above Wilson Lake	5	I	A
Smoky Hill River	20	I	A
Avenue M near Kanopolis	8	I	A
White Bass Flats at Kanopolis Lake	12	I	A
Big Blue River	19	I-III	B-C
Blue Rapids	11	I	B
Black Vermillion	8	I	B
Rocky Ford	0	I-III	C
Delaware River	15	I	C
Wakarusa River	15	I-VI	B
Wakarusa River at Clinton Lake	15	I	B
Waka Wave below Clinton Dam	0	III-VI	A
Rock Creek above Clinton Lake	7	I-II+	A
Mill Creek near Shawnee Mission Park	5	I-II+	A
Dragoon Creek above Pomona Lake	6	I-II	A
Marais des Cygnes River	25	1-II	A-B
Above Melvern Lake	6	I	B
Above U.S. Highway 69	5	I	B
Below U.S. Highway 69	9	II	A

Arkansas River	415	I	A-C
Coolidge	52	I	B
Lakin	58	I	B
Cimarron	42	I	B
Bucklin Road Access	51	I	B
Larned	46	I	B
Raymond	35	I	A
Hutchison	33	I	B
Bentley	16	I	A
Wichita	17	I	C
Derby	26	I	B
Oxford	23	I	B
Arkansas City	19	I	B
Little Arkansas River	8	I	A
Walnut River above El Dorado Reservoir	6	I	B
Grouse Creek below Silverdale	13	I	A
Neosho River	25	I	C
Above Council Grove Lake	8	I	C
Above John Redmond Reservoir	17	I	C
Munkers Creek near Council Grove Lake	5	I	B
Cottonwood River near Marion Lake	3	I	B
Verdigris River above Toronto Lake	12	I	C
Walnut Creek above Toronto Lake	11	I	B
Deer Trace Canoe Trail	4	I	B
Fall River above Fall River Lake	11	I	A
Otter Creek above Fall River Lake	6	I-II	A
Elk River above Elk City Lake	10	I-II	A
Little Caney River above Copan Lake	2	I	C

APPENDIX 2

Other River and Stream Accesses in Kansas

The Kansas Department of Wildlife and Parks has a number of public fishing access points around the state. This is a list of those access points that are not otherwise covered in this book, either because river mileage open to the public is too limited or because water in the river or stream segment is too scarce.

Saline River, low-water dam at Lincoln
Smoky Hill River at Salina
Solomon River at Beloit
Solomon River, North Fork, Glen Elder Reservoir Wildlife Area
Solomon River, South Fork, Glen Elder Reservoir Wildlife Area
Solomon River, low-water dam at Minneapolis
Solomon River, South Fork, Webster Wildlife Area
Big Creek at Hays
Chikaskia River, Drury Dam, 5.5 miles west of South Haven
Cottonwood River at Cottonwood Falls
Walnut River at Winfield
Caney River, federal land above Hula Reservoir
Cottonwood River, Peter Pan Park in Emporia
Cottonwood River, Soden Park in Emporia
Fall River, low-water dam at Fredonia

Marmaton River, low-water dam at Fort Scott
Neosho River, low-water dam at Burlington
Neosho River, low-water dam at Chanute
Neosho River, low-water dam at Chetopa
Neosho River, low-water dam at Iola
Neosho River, low-water dam at Neosho Falls
Neosho River, low-water dam at Oswego
110 Mile Creek above Pomona Reservoir
Shoal Creek at Galena
Spring River, low-water dam at Baxter Springs
Spring River, southeast of Riverton below Empire Lake
Spring River, off K-96 near Kansas-Missouri state line
Verdigris River, low-water dams at Coffeyville
Verdigris River, low-water dams at Independence
Verdigris River, low-water dams at Neodesha
Verdigris River, off U.S. Highway 54, west of Batesville (undeveloped)

Bibliography

Buchanan, Rex C., and McCauley, James R. *Roadside Kansas: A Traveler's Guide to Its Geology and Landmarks.* Lawrence, KS: University Press of Kansas, 1987.

Kansas Atlas & Gazetteer. Yarmouth, ME: DeLorme, 1997.

Kansas Department of Health and Environment, Bureau of Environmental Field Services. *1998 Kansas Water-Quality Limited Segments (303(D) List).* Topeka, KS: Kansas Department of Health and Environment, 2000.

Kansas Department of Health and Environment, Bureau of Environmental Field Services. *2000 Kansas Water Quality Assessment 305(B) Report.* Topeka, KS: Kansas Department of Health and Environment, 2000.

Kansas Department of Wildlife and Parks. *Fishing Guide to Kansas,* 2005.

Kansas Department of Wildlife and Parks. *Kansas State Parks,* 2005.

McCoy, Sondra Van Meter, and Hults, Jan. *1001 Kansas Place Names.* Lawrence, KS: University Press of Kansas, 1989.

APPENDIX 3

Alphabetic Information and Contact Listing

American Rivers	www.amrivers.org
Arkansas Watershed Advisory Group	www.awag.org
Author, Dave Murphy	kansasriversandstreams@yahoo.com
Clean Water Network	www.cwn.org
Corps campgrounds reservation	www.recreation.gov
Corps, Kansas City District, lake and recreation information	www.nwk.usace.army.mil
Corps, Little Rock District, lake and recreation information	www.swl.usace.army.mil
Corps, Tulsa District, lake and recreation information	www.swt.usace.army.mil
Environmental Protection Agency, Water	www.epa.gov/watrhome
Friends of the Kaw	www.kansasriver.com
Great Plains Nature Center (Wichita)	www.gpnc.org
Groundwater Management District 4 (Northwest Kansas)	www.gmd4.org
eNature (National Wildlife Federation)	www.enature.com
Kansas Canoe and Kayak Association	www.kansascanoe.org
Kansas City District, Army Corps of Engineers	www.nwk.usace.army.mil
Kansas City Whitewater Club	www.kcwc.org

Kansas Department of Health and Environment	www.kdheks.gov
Kansas Department of Wildlife and Parks	www.kdwp.state.ks.us
Kansas Lake Maps	corpslakes.usace.army.mil/visitors/states.cfm?state=KS
Kansas Legislative Officials	www.accesskansas.org/government
Kansas Natural Resource Council	www.knrc.ws
Kansas Paddler	www.kansas.net/~tjhittle
Kansas Chapter, Sierra Club	www.kansas.sierraclub.org
Kansas State Park information, maps, reservations	www.kdwp.state.ks.us
Kansas Water Office	www.kwo.org
Kansas Alliance for Wetlands and Streams (KAWS)	www.kaws.org
Kansas Whitewater Association	www.kansaswhitewater.org
Kansas Real-Time Water Quality (U.S. Geological Survey)	ks.water.usgs.gov/Kansas/rtqw
Little Rock District, Army Corps of Engineers	www.swl.usace.army.mil
National Library for the Environment, National Council for Science and the Environment	www.ncseonline.org/NLE/
National Weather Service, National Oceanic and Atmospheric Administration	www.nws.noaa.gov
Natural Resources Defense Council	www.nrdc.org
Northern Flint Hills Audubon Society	www.k-state.edu/audubon/falcon.html
River Network	www.rivernetwork.org
Southwind Group, Sierra Club	www.kansas.sierraclub.org/leaders.htm#Southwind
Tulsa District, Army Corps of Engineers	www.swt.usace.army.mil
U.S. Environmental Protection Agency, National Pollutant Discharge Elimination System permit requirements	cfpub.epa.gov/npdes
U.S. Environmental Protection Agency, Region 7	www.epa.gov/rgytgrnj/
U.S. Fish and Wildlife Service	www.fws.gov
U.S. Geological Survey, Water Resources of the U.S.	water.usgs.gov
USGS, National Water Information System, Water Data for the Nation	waterdata.usgs.gov/nwis
Waterkeeper Alliance	www.waterkeeper.org

APPENDIX 4

State Park Contacts

Cedar Bluff
Box 76A
Ellis, KS 67637
(785) 726-3212
CedarBluffSP@wp.state.ks.us

Cheney (& Sand Hills)
16000 NE 50th St.
Cheney, KS 67025-8487
(316) 542-3664
CheneySP@wp.state.ks.us

Clinton
798 N 1415th Rd.
Lawrence, KS 66049
(785) 842-8562
ClintonSP@wp.state.ks.us

Crawford
1 Lake Rd.
Farlington, KS 66734-4045
(620) 362-3671
CrawfordSP@wp.state.ks.us

Cross Timbers
144 Hwy105
Toronto, KS 66777
(620) 637-2213
CrossTimbersSP@wp.state.ks.us

Eisenhower
29810 S Fairlawn Rd.
Osage City, KS 66523-9046
(785) 528-4102
EisenhowerSP@wp.state.ks.us

El Dorado
618 NE Bluestem Rd.
El Dorado, KS 67042-8643
(316) 321-7180
ElDoradoSP@wp.state.ks.us

Elk City
4825 Squaw Creek Rd.
Independence, KS 67301
(620) 331-6295
ElkCitySP@wp.state.ks.us

Fall River
144 Hwy 105
Toronto, KS 66777
(620) 637-2213
CrossTimbersSP@wp.state.ks.us

Glen Elder
RR 1, Box 162A
Glen Elder, KS 67446
(785) 545-3345
GlenElderSP@wp.state.ks.us

Hillsdale
26001 W 255th St.
Paola, KS 66071
(913) 783-4507
HillsdaleSP@wp.state.ks.us

Kanopolis (& Mushroom Rock)
200 Horsethief Rd.
Marquette, KS 67464
(785) 546-2565
KanopolisSP@wp.state.ks.us

Lovewell
RR 1, Box 66A
Webber, KS 66970
(785) 753-4971
LovewellSP@wp.state.ks.us

Meade
13051 V Rd.
Meade, KS 67864
(620) 873-2572
MeadeSP@wp.state.ks.us

Milford
8811 State Park Rd.
Milford, KS 66514
(785) 238-3014
MilfordSP@wp.state.ks.us

Perry
5441 W Lake Rd.
Ozawkie, KS 66070-9802
(785) 246-3449
PerrySP@wp.state.ks.us

Pomona
22900 S Hwy 368
Vassar, KS 66543-9162
(785) 828-4933
PomonaSP@wp.state.ks.us

Prairie Dog
Box 431
Norton, KS 67654
(785) 877-2953
PrairieDogSP@wp.state.ks.us

Prairie Spirit Trail
419 S Oak
Garnett, KS 66032
(785) 448-6767
PrairieSpiritRT@wp.state.ks.us

Scott
520 W Scott Lake Dr.
Scott City, KS 67871-1075
(620) 872-2061
ScottSP@wp.state.ks.us

Tuttle Creek
5800 - A River Pond Rd.
Manhattan, KS 66502
(785) 539-7941
TuttleCreekSP@wp.state.ks.us

Webster
1210 Nine Rd.
Stockton, KS 67669-8834
(785) 425-6775
WebsterSP@wp.state.ks.us

Wilson
RR 1, Box 181
Sylvan Grove, KS 67481
(785) 658-2465
WilsonSP@wp.state.ks.us

APPENDIX 5

Other Useful Contact Numbers and Web Sites

WATER LEVELS

Real-Time River Data for Kansas   waterdata.usgs.gov/ks/nwis/rt
Kansas Lake Levels   corpslakes.usace.army.mil/visitors/states.cfm?state=KS
National Weather Service River Information   www.crh.noaa.gov/ahps2/index.php?wfo=ict

WEATHER CONDITIONS

National Weather Service   www.nws.noaa.gov

PADDLING CLUBS

Arkansas River Coalition (Environment/Paddling/Historic)   www.arkriver.org
Friends of the Kaw (Environmental/Paddling)   www.kansasriver.com
Kansas Canoe and Kayak Association (Paddling/Training)   www.kansas.net/~tjhittle
Kansas City Whitewater Club (Paddling/Training)   www.kcwc.org
Kansas Whitewater Association (Paddling/Training)   www.kansaswhitewater.org

CANOE AND KAYAK RENTAL, GUIDES, AND RETAIL

Northeast Kansas

- A-1 Rentals, 14891 East U.S. Highway 40, Kansas City, MO, (816) 373-0234
- Anderson Rentals, 1312 West 6th Street, Lawrence, KS, (785) 843-2044
- Lawrence KOA and Kansas River Canoe Company, Owners: Ralph & Kim Newell, 1473 U.S. Highway 40, Lawrence, KS, (800) 562-3708 or (785) 842-3877, e-mail: lawrencekoa@sbcglobal.net
- Kansas City Paddler, 21911 Branic Drive, Peculiar, MO, (816) 779-1195, e-mail: shop@kcpaddler.com, Web: www.kcpaddler.com. Sales and service on sea kayaks, whitewater, and recreational kayaks and canoes, trailers, cartop carriers, and camping equipment. Store hours: Tuesday-Saturday, 9:00 A.M. to 5:00 P.M.; closed Sunday and Monday.

North Central Kansas

- Tuttle Creek State Park, Manhattan, KS, located below Tuttle Creek Lake Dam, (785) 539-7941. State Park vehicle permit required in addition to rental fees. March and April, 1:00 P.M. to 5:00 P.M.; May to December, 8:00 P.M. to one hour before sunset.
- Kansas State University, Outdoor Rental Center, Chester E. Peters Recreation Complex, Manhattan, KS, (785) 532-6980 or (785) 532-6894. A KSU student or faculty ID is required. Monday, Thursday, and Friday, 4:00-6:00 P.M.; Saturday. 11:00 A.M.-1:00 P.M. Closed Tuesday, Wednesday, and Sunday.
- Fort Riley Outdoor Recreation Center, Building 9011, Fort Riley, KS, (785) 239-6368 or (785) 239-2364. Military ID is required. Located near the Main Post area. Tuesday-Friday, 8:00 A.M.-4:30 P.M.

South Central and Southeast Kansas

- Funk's Boats & Canoe Rental, 416 East River Street, Eureka, KS 67045, (620) 583-6481 (days), (620) 583-6345 (evenings). Open April-October. Group trips, new and used boat sales. Guided backpack trips in March, April, and October.

APPENDIX 6
LAKE MAPS

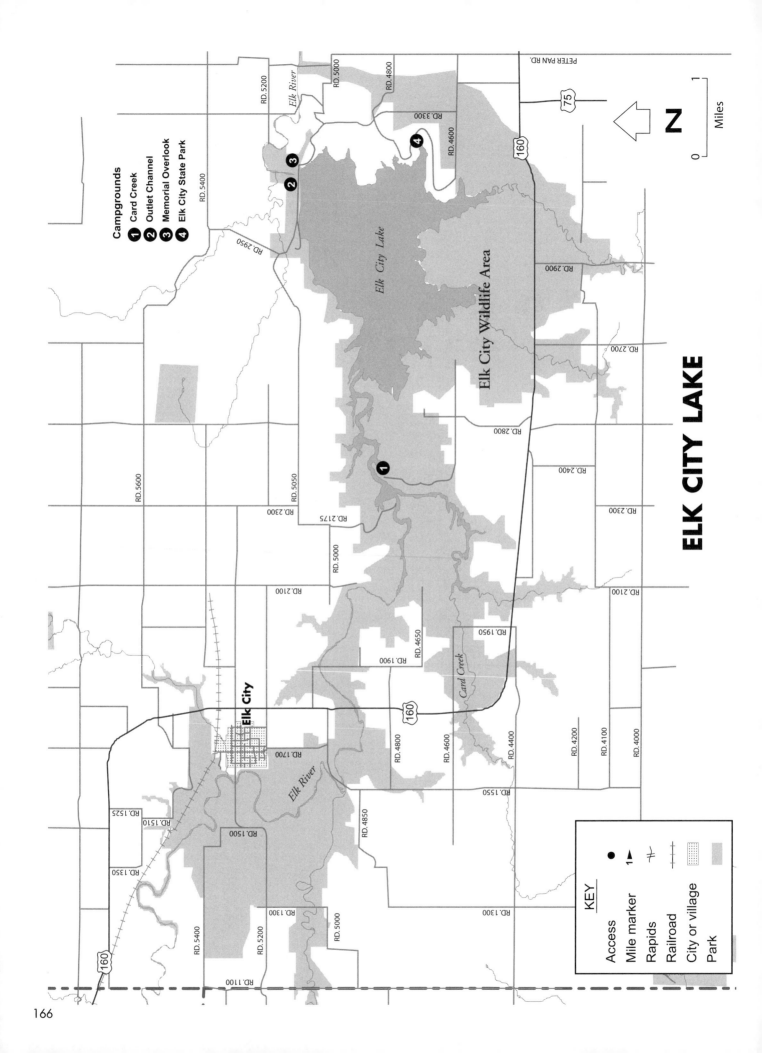

ELK CITY LAKE

Campgrounds
1 Card Creek
2 Outlet Channel
3 Memorial Overlook
4 Elk City State Park

KEY

●	Access
⚑	Mile marker
╪	Rapids
⌗	Railroad
⬚	City or village
▨	Park

JOHN REDMOND RESERVOIR

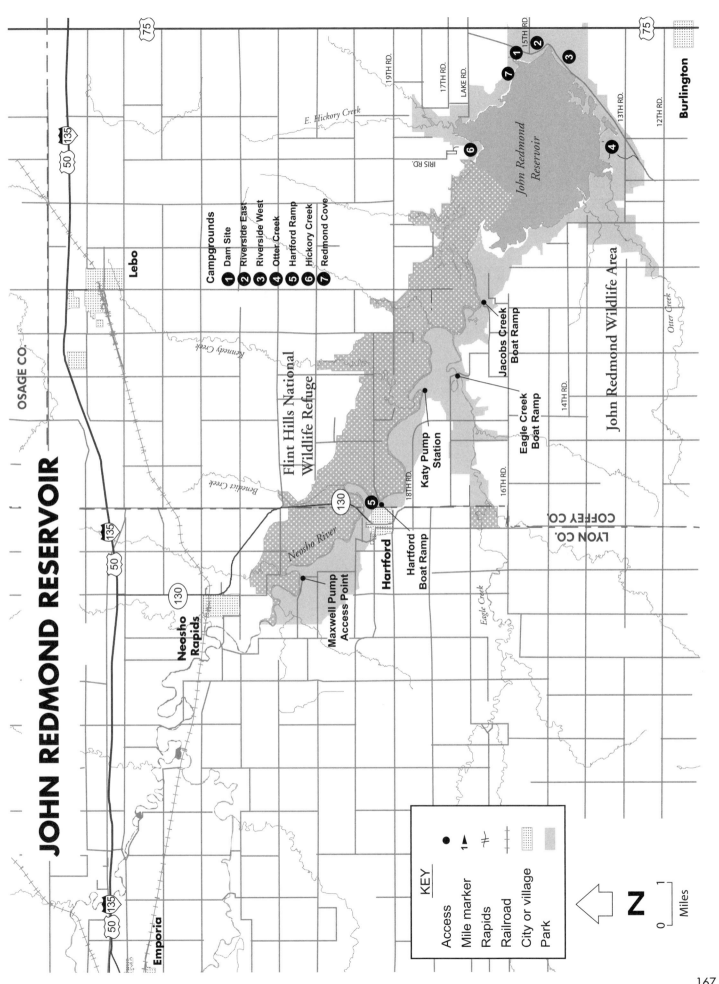

Campgrounds

1 Dam Site
2 Riverside East
3 Riverside West
4 Otter Creek
5 Hartford Ramp
6 Hickory Creek
7 Redmond Cove

OSAGE CO.

Lebo

Emporia

Neosho Rapids

Flint Hills National Wildlife Refuge

Maxwell Pump Access Point

Hartford

Hartford Boat Ramp

Katy Pump Station

Neosho River

Benedict Creek

Kennedy Creek

E. Hickory Creek

John Redmond Reservoir

John Redmond Wildlife Area

LYON CO.
COFFEY CO.

Jacobs Creek Boat Ramp

Eagle Creek Boat Ramp

Eagle Creek

Otter Creek

Burlington

IRIS RD.
18TH RD.
16TH RD.
14TH RD.
19TH RD.
17TH RD.
LAKE RD.
15TH RD.
13TH RD.
12TH RD.

KEY

● Access
⚓ Mile marker
≠ Rapids
╫ Railroad
▦ City or village
▨ Park

N

0 — 1
Miles

MARION LAKE

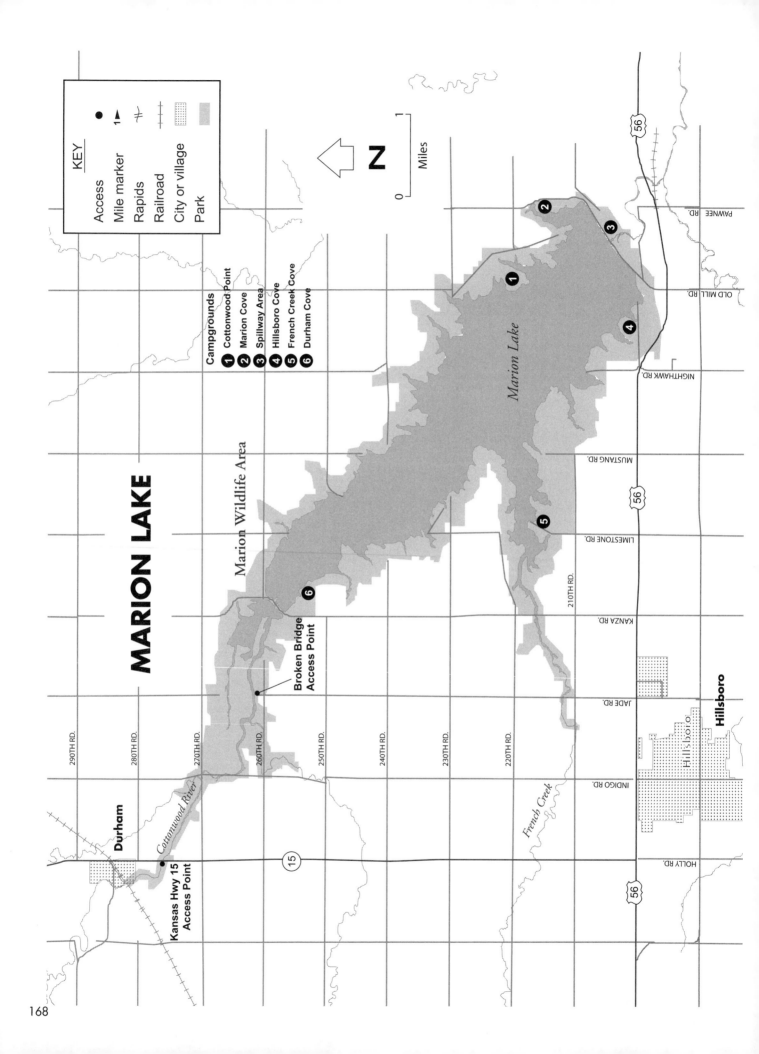

KEY

- Access
- Mile marker
- Rapids
- Railroad
- City or village
- Park

Campgrounds

1. Cottonwood Point
2. Marion Cove
3. Spillway Area
4. Hillsboro Cove
5. French Creek Cove
6. Durham Cove

N

Miles
0 1

Marion Lake

Marion Wildlife Area

Broken Bridge Access Point

Kansas Hwy 15 Access Point

Durham

Cottonwood River

French Creek

Hillsboro

56

15

PAWNEE RD.
OLD MILL RD.
NIGHTHAWK RD.
MUSTANG RD.
LIMESTONE RD.
KANZA RD.
JADE RD.
INDIGO RD.
HOLLY RD.

290TH RD.
280TH RD.
270TH RD.
260TH RD.
250TH RD.
240TH RD.
230TH RD.
220TH RD.
210TH RD.

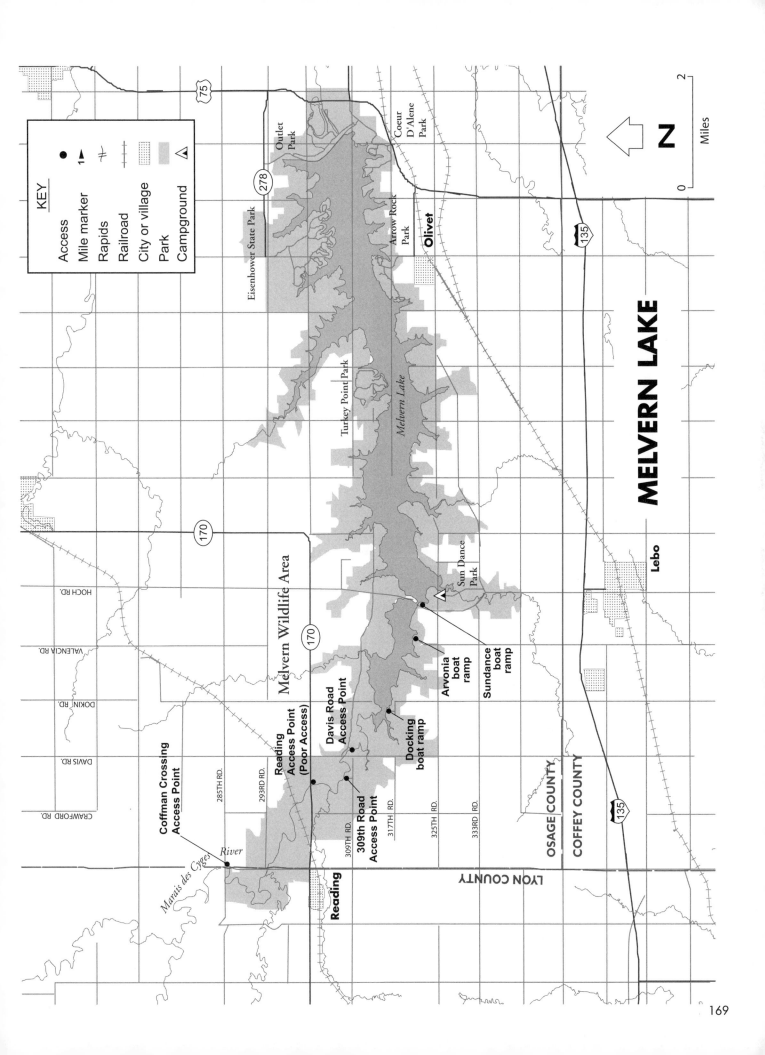

MELVERN LAKE

KEY

Access •
Mile marker ⬥
Rapids ⵜ
Railroad ┼┼┼
City or village ░░
Park ▒▒
Campground ◁

N

0   2

Miles

75

278

Outlet Park

Eisenhower State Park

Coeur D'Alene Park

Arrow Rock Park

Olivet

135

Turkey Point Park

Melvern Lake

170

Melvern Wildlife Area

170

HOCH RD.

VALENCIA RD.

DOKIN RD.

DAVIS RD.

CRAWFORD RD.

Sun Dance Park

◁

Arvonia boat ramp

Sundance boat ramp

Davis Road Access Point

Reading Access Point (Poor Access)

Docking boat ramp

285TH RD.

293RD RD.

309TH RD.

317TH RD.

325TH RD.

333RD RD.

309th Road Access Point

Coffman Crossing Access Point

Marais des Cygnes River

Reading

Lebo

OSAGE COUNTY

COFFEY COUNTY

LYON COUNTY

135

MELVERN LAKE

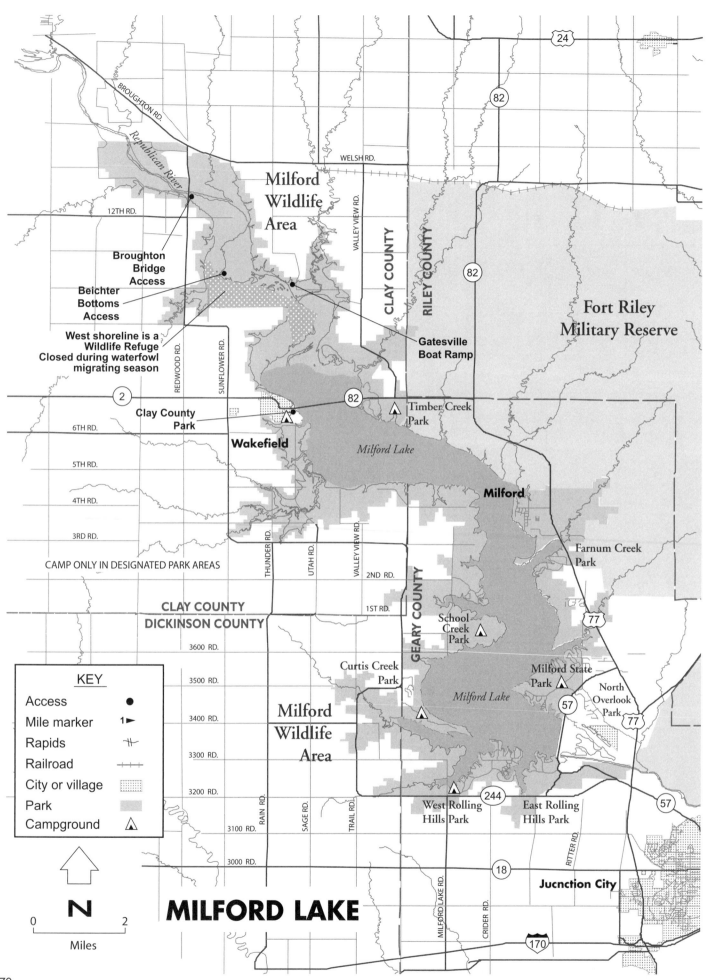

BROUGHTON RD.

Republican River

Milford
Wildlife
Area

WELSH RD.

12TH RD.

24

82

82

CLAY COUNTY

RILEY COUNTY

Fort Riley
Military Reserve

Broughton
Bridge
Access

Beichter
Bottoms
Access

West shoreline is a
Wildlife Refuge
Closed during waterfowl
migrating season

Gatesville
Boat Ramp

VALLEY VIEW RD.

REDWOOD RD.

SUNFLOWER RD.

2

82

Clay County
Park

6TH RD.

Timber Creek
Park

Wakefield

5TH RD.

Milford Lake

4TH RD.

Milford

3RD RD.

CAMP ONLY IN DESIGNATED PARK AREAS

THUNDER RD.

UTAH RD.

VALLEY VIEW RD.

2ND RD.

Farnum Creek
Park

77

CLAY COUNTY
DICKINSON COUNTY

1ST RD.

GEARY COUNTY

3600 RD.

School
Creek
Park

3500 RD.

Curtis Creek
Park

Milford State
Park

North
Overlook
Park

Milford
Wildlife
Area

3400 RD.

Milford Lake

57

77

3300 RD.

KEY

Access •

Mile marker 1▶

Rapids

Railroad

City or village

Park

Campground ⛺

RAIN RD.

SAGE RD.

TRAIL RD.

3200 RD.

244

57

3100 RD.

West Rolling
Hills Park

East Rolling
Hills Park

RITTER RD.

N

3000 RD.

18

Jucnction City

0   2
Miles

MILFORD LAKE

MILFORD LAKE RD.

CRIDER RD.

170

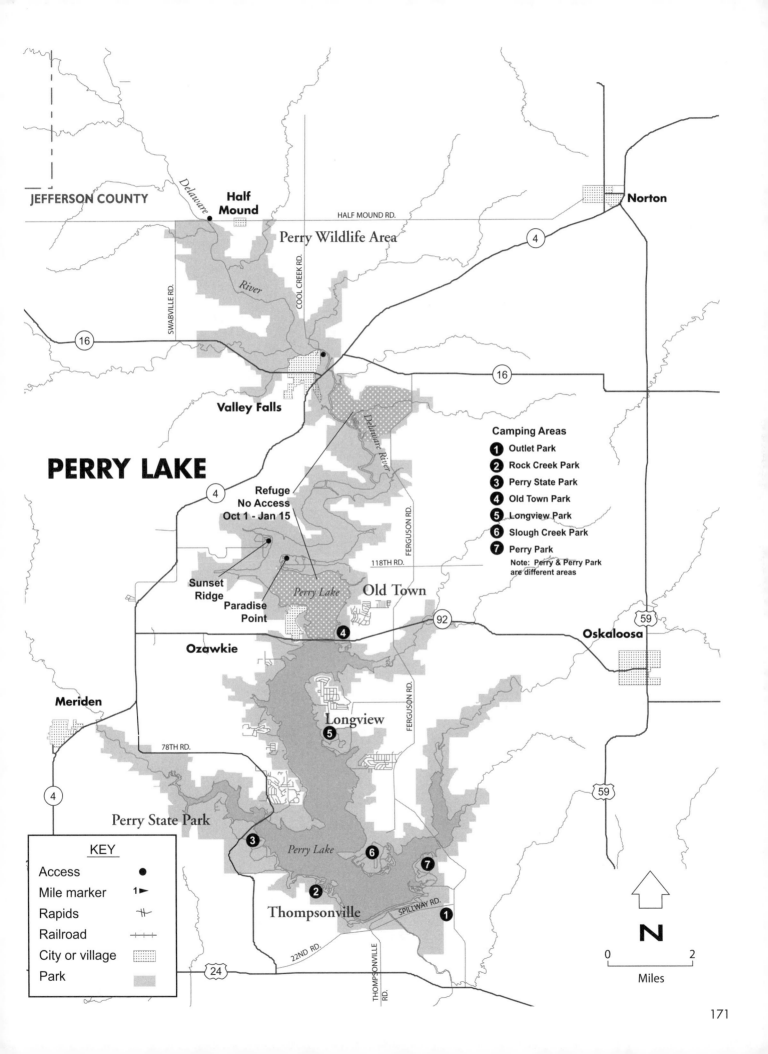

JEFFERSON COUNTY

Delaware

Half Mound

HALF MOUND RD.

Norton

Perry Wildlife Area

④

COOL CREEK RD.

River

SWABVILLE RD.

16

16

Valley Falls

Delaware River

PERRY LAKE

4

Refuge
No Access
Oct 1 - Jan 15

FERGUSON RD.

Camping Areas

❶ Outlet Park
❷ Rock Creek Park
❸ Perry State Park
❹ Old Town Park
❺ Longview Park
❻ Slough Creek Park
❼ Perry Park

Note: Perry & Perry Park
are different areas

118TH RD.

Sunset Ridge

Paradise Point

Perry Lake

Old Town

❹

Ozawkie

92

59

Oskaloosa

Meriden

FERGUSON RD.

Longview
❺

78TH RD.

59

Perry State Park

❸ *Perry Lake*

❻

❼

4

KEY

Access	●
Mile marker	1▶
Rapids	╫
Railroad	┼┼┼
City or village	▦
Park	▬

Thompsonville

SPILLWAY RD.

❷

❶

22ND RD.

THOMPSONVILLE RD.

24

N

0   2
Miles

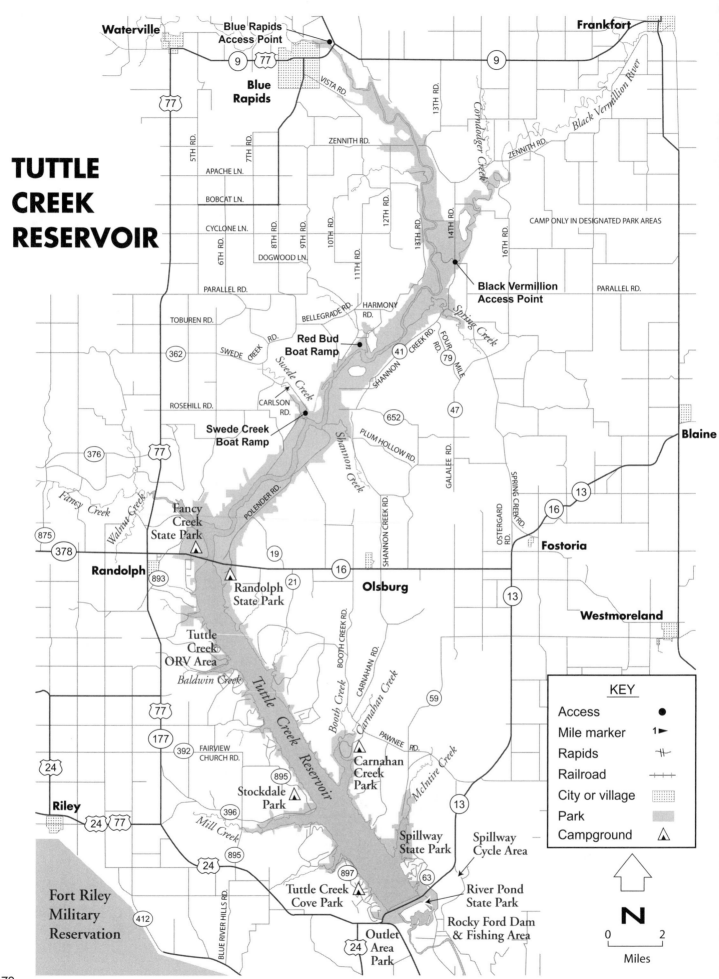

TUTTLE CREEK RESERVOIR

Waterville

Frankfort

Blue Rapids Access Point

Blue Rapids

Black Vermillion River

Corndodger Creek

CAMP ONLY IN DESIGNATED PARK AREAS

Black Vermillion Access Point

Red Bud Boat Ramp

Spring Creek

Swede Creek

Swede Creek Boat Ramp

Blaine

Shannon Creek

Fancy Creek State Park

Randolph

Randolph State Park

Olsburg

Fostoria

Westmoreland

Tuttle Creek ORV Area

Baldwin Creek

Tuttle Creek Reservoir

Booth Creek

Carnahan Creek

McIntire Creek

Riley

Carnahan Creek Park

Stockdale Park

Mill Creek

Spillway State Park

Spillway Cycle Area

Tuttle Creek Cove Park

River Pond State Park

Fort Riley Military Reservation

Outlet Area Park

Rocky Ford Dam & Fishing Area

KEY

Access	●
Mile marker	1►
Rapids	╫
Railroad	┼┼┼
City or village	▦
Park	▒
Campground	⛺

N

0   2
Miles

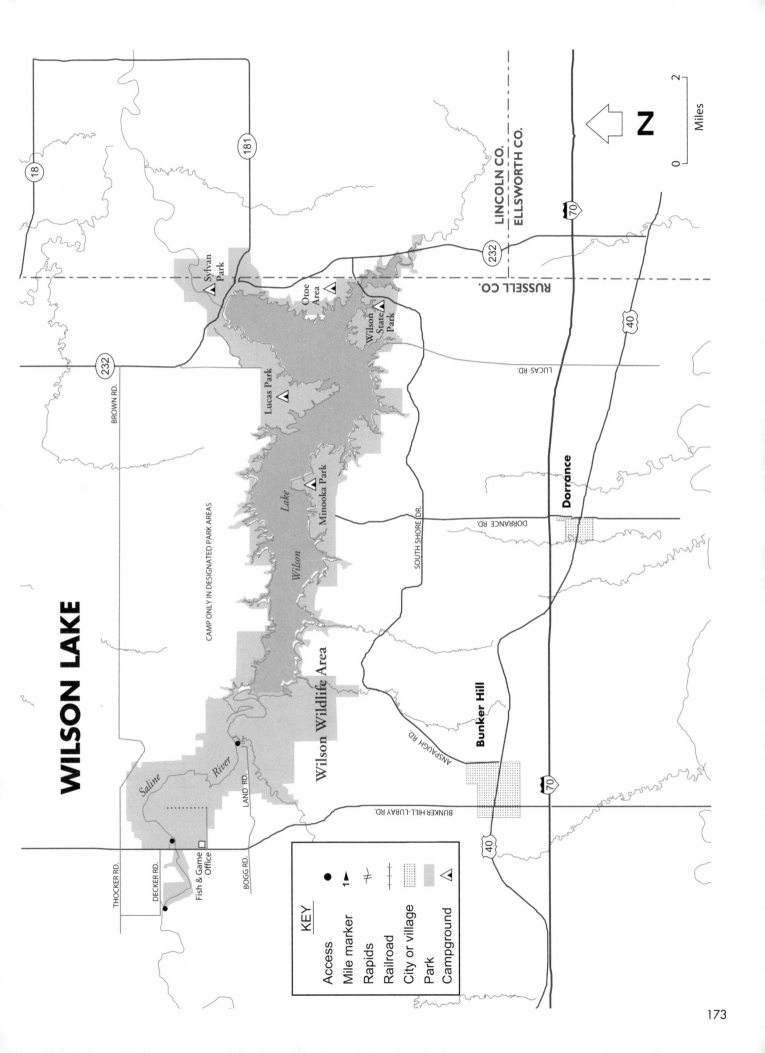

WILSON LAKE

KEY

Access ●

Mile marker ▲

Rapids

Railroad

City or village

Park

Campground ◬

Wilson Wildlife Area

Saline River

CAMP ONLY IN DESIGNATED PARK AREAS

Wilson Lake

Sylvan Park

Otoe Area

Wilson State Park

Lucas Park

Minooka Park

Fish & Game Office

THOCKER RD.

DECKER RD.

LAND RD.

BOGG RD.

BROWN RD.

18

181

232

232

70

40

70

40

SOUTH SHORE DR.

LUCAS RD.

DORRANCE RD.

ANSPAUGH RD.

BUNKER HILL-LURAY RD.

Dorrance

Bunker Hill

LINCOLN CO.
ELLSWORTH CO.

RUSSELL CO.

N

0   2
Miles

KANSAS OUTDOOR TREASURES

Julie Cirlincuina

This comprehensive outdoor guide explores the many natural wonders that America's Heartland has to offer: wooded trails and towering buttes, winding rivers, sterling lakes, breathtaking rock formations, and much more. A native of Kansas, author Julie Cirlincuina describes the best places throughout the state to hike, bike, paddle, fish and hunt, take a scenic drive, or spend the day watching wildlife. You'll also find detailed information on geology, climate, campgrounds and parks, as well as directions and accessibility for each destination. Complete with detailed maps for each region of the state, this guide has everything you need to plan a Kansas adventure.

Paper | 6 x 9 | 248 pages | ISBN 798-1-934552-11-4 | $18.95

For these and other great Trails Books titles, call (800) 258-5830 or visit us online at www.trailsbooks.com